GATEWAY TO THE NEW WORLD

*A History of
Princess Anne County, Virginia
1607–1824*

Florence Kimberly Turner

Copyright 1984
By: Southern Historical Press, Inc.

All rights reserved. No part of this publication may be reproduced, stored in a retrieval system, transmitted in any form, posted on to the web in any form or by any means without the prior written permission of the publisher.

Please direct all correspondence and orders to:

www.southernhistoricalpress.com
or
**SOUTHERN HISTORICAL PRESS, Inc.
PO BOX 1267
Greenville, SC   29601
southernhistoricalpress@gmail.com**

ISBN #0-89308-523-5

Printed in the United States of America

FOREWORD

Having made my home in Virginia Beach for thirty-seven years, I have looked in vain for a history of the early years of this historic area. In these pages the reader will find that history, and those who made it, from the time of the Indians, our first inhabitants, through the colonial years and the upheaval of the Revolution until the lull before the cataclysm of the War Between the States.

More importantly, these people come to life, their courage to challenge the wilderness so successfully, and why they reacted as they did to the internal and external events and changes in the two hundred and fourteen years from the first landing of English settlers on this continent in 1607 at Cape Henry until 1824.

For me, this work has been an absorbing effort. Fortunately, I have had help from many sources.

First on the list is Alice Loyall McCaw, a descendant of one of our earliest families, who has spent a lifetime delving into old records, and whose own fascination with early history here was an inspiration. Her encouragement through trying days has never failed me.

Secondly, Esther Tryba Piskorski's astute criticism and knowledge of structure, as well as her enthusiasm, have sustained me invaluably. Without these two friends, I may well have given up the struggle of searching out the facts and assimilating them into a readable account of the lives and characters of our ancestors.

Professional historians have generously shared their knowledge with me, such as Dr. Peter Stewart of Old Dominion University, Dr. Tommy Bogger of Norfolk State University, and Dr. Stephen Mansfield of Virginia Wesleyan College. Other writers have encouraged me in this endeavor, such as Louisa Venable Kyle, and Elizabeth Wingo.

Floyd Painter's knowledge of the Chesapean tribe, through his study of Indian relics which he has excavated in this area over many years, has kept me spellbound through fascinating hours.

I am further indebted to all those descendants of the early settlers, both black and white, who gave me their time, their memories, and the result of their own research.

Without the gracious kindness of librarians in various library reference departments, and in the Deed Rooms of courthouses, I would still be floundering in the difficult writing and haphazard spelling of the early court clerks.

The City of Virginia Beach has assisted me financially through the Arts and Humanities Commission, and Bob Matthias and Sue Johnston of the City Grants Office have been a great help.

The sponsorship of the Princess Anne County Historical Society, of which I have been a longtime board member, is gratifying. The society has as part of its objective to preserve our historic past, and to disseminate awareness of it to all our citizens.

This volume, by placing the lives of our forebears in the context of national events, will open the door for others to take the exciting journey into our past. The quaint spelling is retained in the quotes to add to the feeling of antiquity. In the bibliography you will find the means for further exploration of all facets of our past and its people.

CONTENTS

Foreword iii
Glossary vii

PART I
THE BEGINNING

Chapter 1	The Chesapeans	3
Chapter 2	The Englishmen	18

PART II
LOWER NORFOLK COUNTY 1625–1691

Chapter 1	First Settlers 1625–1640	27
Chapter 2	The Leaders 1641–1691	41
Chapter 3	The Middle Class	70
Chapter 4	Indentured Servants and Slaves	83

PART III
PRINCESS ANNE COUNTY 1691–1775

Chapter 1	Division of Lower Norfolk County	101
Chapter 2	County Life in "The Golden Age"	117
Chapter 3	The Church and "The Great Awakening"	143
Chapter 4	The Condition of Slavery	151
Chapter 5	Politics—Clouds Gather	160

PART IV
THE REVOLUTION

Chapter 1	War Comes to Princess Anne County	173
Chapter 2	The Loyalists	189
Chapter 3	The Patriots	205
Chapter 4	Yorktown	218

PART V
THE NEW ORDER

Chapter 1	Adjustment	237
Chapter 2	The War of 1812	251
Chapter 3	Settling Down	268
Appendix I		275
Appendix II		278
Index		291

GLOSSARY

Cavaliers—those loyal to the King during the Commonwealth of Oliver Cromwell
Cooper—a barrel or cask maker
Cordwinder—a leather worker, especially of Spanish leather
Corsair—a pirate, or a pirate's ship
Escheat—to revert, or cause to revert to the State or Crown
Escutcheon—a shield or emblem bearing a coat of arms
Ffletcher—one who provides something with feathers, as putting feathers on arrows
Flageolet—a musical instrument resembling a flute, but blown at the end instead of the side
Flux—dysentery
Freeholder—a man holding land without any restrictions or conditions—absolute ownership
Glebe—church land and house for minister
Governor's Council—appointed by the King. Corresponds in modern times to the Senate
House of Burgesses—elected by popular vote of freeholders. Corresponds in modern times to House of Representatives
Headright—right of ownership of 50 acres to anyone entering the colony. These rights could be bought or sold, usually sold by mariners coming in and out who did not intend to settle
Impress—to force into service in the Army or Navy
Patent—a deed of land, registered
Poquoson—a swamp
Proprietors—persons having exclusive title to land, such as Lords Proprietors in North Carolina, who were given large grants of land by the King

Quitrent—an annual rent of one shilling per 50 acres, payable to the King
Sennight—a week
Vidette—a mounted sentinel placed in advance of an outpost
Wellwright—a well digger

Patterns of bricklaying—often called "bonding," in which bricks are laid in an interlocking arrangement to strengthen the walls of a house. This "English bonding" was used before the Great London Fire of 1666 and is useful in determining the date of a house. It was a row of stretchers, then a row of headers, then a row of stretchers.

After the Fire, a great number of bricklayers came to England from the Netherlands, thence to America, using a different pattern called "Flemish bond." This was alternating a stretcher, a header, a stretcher, a header in each row. This was preferred until after 1800. Virginia, or "common bonding" then came into use as easier, and is the usual pattern today. No headers are used, and the stretchers are placed so that the mortar binding two ends is beneath the center of the stretcher above.

Part I
THE BEGINNING

Part I
THE BEGINNING

PART ONE
Chapter 1
THE CHESAPEANS

The dawn of a new world for the white man was already twilight in American Indian history, especially for the Chesapeans. The Chesapeans were a small agricultural tribe whose domain was bounded by the Atlantic Ocean on the east, the Chesapeake Bay and Hampton Roads to the north, the Elizabeth River to the west and Currituck Sound and the Dismal Swamp to the south.

Our history in this area began on April 26, 1607, when English explorers sent by the London Company on the three ships—the *Susan Constant,* the *Godspeed* and the *Discovery*—struggled up the windswept dunes of Cape Henry to mark the first landing of English settlers in North America. Captain John Smith's map of Indian tribes in Virginia, actually drawn in 1608, shows Cape Henry in the left-hand corner. Four hundred years ago, thousands of Indians lived on this land in hundreds of villages, and the present-day city of Virginia Beach was the land of the Chesapeans—a once large tribe whose main village, Chesepioc, was near the mouth of the Lynnhaven River. Although there is not a single Chesapean left here today, hundreds of artifacts proving their existence have been found by archaeologists, treasure hunters and farmers to remind us that they once owned this land and that their history is part of ours.

This band of English adventurers had been instructed to find a more protected spot for a settlement further inland, so they paid scant attention to this land which became Princess Anne County in 1691. They did a little exploring, found no Indians, but saw near the Lynnhaven River a fire going and succulent Lynnhaven oysters roasting. The Indians had fled, evidently surprised by the intrusion, so the Englishmen enjoyed the oysters. Not until they were leaving to go back on board their ships did they see any Indians. George Percy, a member of the company, describes the encounter in his *A Discourse of the Plantation of the Southern Colony in Virginia.*

> "At night when we were going aboard, there came the savages creeping on all fours from the hills, like bears, with their bows in their mouths, charged us very desperately in the faces, hurt Captain Gabriel Archer in both his hands, and a sailor in two places of the body very dangerous. After they had spent their arrows, and felt the sharpness of our shot, they retired into the woods with a great noise and so left us."

The Englishmen left the area after this rather hostile encounter, but they returned about a week later to set up a cross, naming the spot where they had landed Cape Henry. They were kindly treated by other tribes up the James River and on the other side of the Chesapeake Bay, and there is no indication of any further interest in the Chesapeans or their land by the English for the next 20 years. At that time, they could not have known the reason for that unfriendly reception by the Chesapeans, nor did they particularly care, but that reason becomes clear with the recounting of the history of this tribe.

The Chesapeans had once been a large and important tribe, a part of the Algonquin group, which was loosely connected by a similar language and whose member tribes had roamed the forests of the East up into Canada for thousands of years. Gradually, this group separated and became more settled, with each tribe staking out its own land. By the beginning of the 16th century, when English exploration of the Chesapeake Bay area first began, this group had long ago become smaller tribes, and the land of each was clearly defined. Instead of being merely wandering hunters, the tribes formed villages, built houses, farmed and learned to live off the bounty of the land as they found it.

As noted earlier, the main town of the Chesapeans, Chesepioc, was located near the mouth of the Lynnhaven River, near Lynnhaven Inlet on what is now Great Neck Point. This has been established by Floyd Painter, a well-known authority on the Chesapeans. Painter found in that area countless Indian artifacts, including the skeleton of an old man elaborately dressed in a robe, headdress, bracelets and moccasins made of 30,000 small iridescent shell beads which had been laboriously sewn together with a bone needle. Only a king would have been buried clothed in such splendor. Painter believes that this skeleton is very old and may predate another which he found only recently. The latter was clothed in many strings of pearls and copper beads, and was

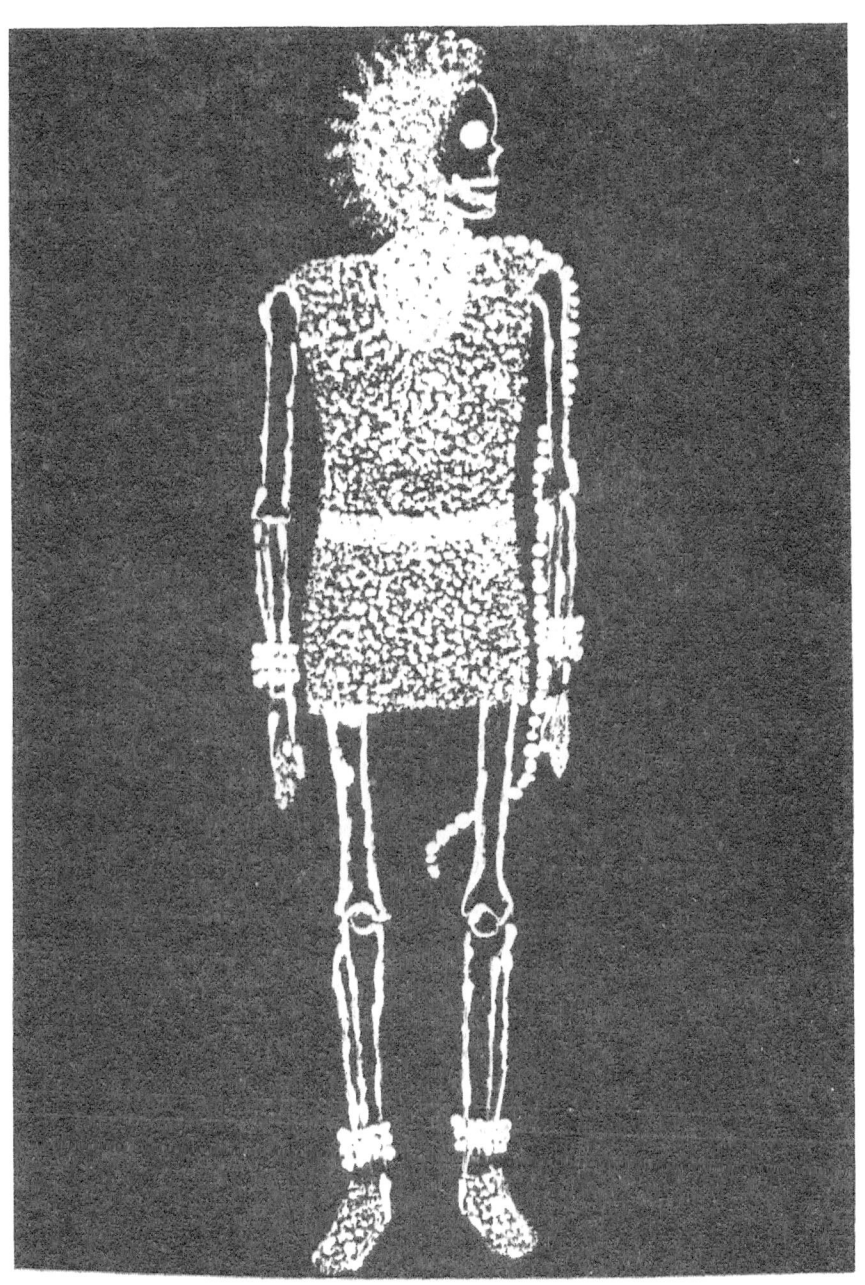

THE GREAT KING OF GREAT NECK
A STATUS BURIAL FROM COASTAL VIRGINIA
FLOYD PAINTER

a king, too, as only a king was allowed to use copper. Copper is not available in this area and had to be traded with Indian tribes further west, near the present city of Roanoke. Many other skeletons have been found in this burial ground, but none equal to these two.

The next largest Chesapean town was Skicoac, located on the Elizabeth River where Norfolk stands today. There were other small villages scattered about the almost 950 square miles of their territory which encompassed the wide sandy beaches and dunes, the rivers, creeks, ponds and marshes and three ridges of high ground running north and south. Indian trails followed these ridges, or criss-crossed from west to east. No Chesapean settlements were near the ocean. They knew about the dangers of storms and hurricanes and wisely preferred to live inland on the more fertile land, always near a creek or river.

The first explorers of this land of the Chesapeans marveled at the "faire meadows" and the forests of great trees, through which one could see almost a mile (Capt. John Smith). The meadows were, of course, the land they had cleared for their crops. The Chesapeans knew the land and how to make the best use of it. As the fields were depleted of nutrients, they cleared more land, leaving meadows. Their habit of burning undergrowth was protection against sudden attack and made hunting easier. This "burning over" enriched the soil, encouraged the growth of tall trees and allowed the many wild flowers to multiply.

The Chesapeans enjoyed a mild climate and a long growing season. Rivers and creeks teemed with fish and there was an abundance of oysters and crabs. The sandy soil was ideal for growing corn, squash and melons, and the forests were home to deer, bear and rabbits, and a variety of wild berries were there for the picking. The trees of the forests yielded walnuts, hickory, hazelnuts and chestnuts. These Indians also had learned the value of herbs and roots for medicine.

Chesapean villages were composed of family groups, with each family having a house. The houses were fashioned of young saplings, bent over at the top and tied with other branches intertwined, and the whole was covered with woven mats. These houses were built close together and were surrounded by cleared fields for crops.

Their canoes were the trunks of trees hollowed out by burning. The Indian method of felling trees for clearing land and for these canoes was to chop around the base of the tree with a stone axe and then set fire to the roots; eventually, the tree toppled over.

Fishing at night was done with a small fire burning in the canoe to attract the fish, which they expertly speared. Daylight fishing was done with traps or nets. They had learned to smoke fish and meat for the winter months and to dry corn for grinding into meal for flat cakes of bread. Prehistoric Indians who roamed the woods following the herds used a large wooden bowl carved out of a tree trunk or stump and a long stone for a pestle for grinding corn, but the Chesapeans used a flat stone with a wooden pestle, which created a depression in the center. Many fragments of clay bowls have been found, decorated on the outside with the typical Indian geometric designs. These clay bowls were used for cooking. Meat was cooked on a spit over the fire. Since there was no iron to use for large pots and since clay could not be put directly into the fire, a hole was dug in the ground the same size as a large clay pot. The pot containing the corn, or anything they wished to boil, was put in the hole and filled with water. Then stones heated red hot in a fire were plunged into the water, and presto, the corn was cooked. Fragments of clay pots survive and have been assembled in museums and private collections.

The Chesapeans used wooden bowls and platters for dishes. These dishes had been brought into shape by charring and scraping. For drinking cups they used shells, such as turtle and conch shells, as well as gourds grown in their fields.

The structure of the Chesapean society was similar to that of other tribes of Eastern Virginia. The chief of each tribe was called a Werowance, and he was a king who had the power of life and death over his subjects. Sons of the Werowance did not inherit power; upon the Werowance's death, the power went to his next oldest brother. After the death of these brothers, the title went to the male or female heirs of the oldest sister. It was rare, but a woman could become a Werowance.

Indian kings had priests as advisors. These priests, always men, had been chosen for their wisdom and their reputed ability to foretell the future. To the agricultural Chesapeans, the priests' revelations concerning the vagaries of the weather were very important, and their advice was always heeded. When to plant and harvest, where to hunt and fish and, particularly, their warnings of impending danger of attack by other tribes or the approach of storms or hurricanes were of utmost importance. Also known to us as "medicine men," their treatment of wounds and disease relied more on their knowledge of the curative powers of herbs and roots than on the mumbo-jumbo usually attributed to them. Their terrifying ritual of exorcising the illness, however, did have a psychological effect.

Laws were strict and punishment harsh. Severe beatings were given for small infractions, and horrible death by fire, by piece-meal amputations or by clubbing constituted the punishment for more serious offenses, such as murder or even stealing. But stealing was rare, partly because of fear of reprisal but mainly because Indians seemed not especially interested in the acquisition of worldly goods. In this, it was a rather socialistic society. In fact, in this seemingly paradisiacal existence, crime was practically nonexistent.

The roles of men and women were clearly defined. Men hunted, fished and made war. They made their own bows and arrows, tomahawks and tools. They felled the trees and made the dugout canoes, cleared and prepared the fields for crops, did the heaviest work of building the houses and made the ceremonial objects.

Women gathered wood, made the fire and prepared the food. They made the pots, mats and baskets; planted, tended and gathered the corn; and did the finishing of the dwelling and kept it in repair. They dressed the skins for clothing, which necessitated hours and hours of chewing to soften the hides. Men and children sometimes helped with this chore, and most of the skulls dug up by Floyd Painter show extremely worn teeth, indicating much chewing.

The Indians grew tobacco and smoked it, but only on ceremonial occasions when the pipe was passed from hand to hand for a brief puff. By all accounts, their tobacco was very bitter, and one puff was enough. Alcohol was unknown, and having no cattle, the Indian drink was water. A fruit drink was made from wild strawberries and grapes, but it was unfermented and used only in ceremonies.

What we consider promiscuity was taken for granted in the Indian society. Courtship was usually initiated by a young girl. She chose the man she liked, and if he was willing and her parents approved of him, the marriage was arranged. The groom gave presents to the bride's parents and arranged suitable payment for his wife. After marriage, the wife was completely subservient to her husband, and infidelity was punishable by death—that is, with one exception. A husband might "lend" his wife for a night to a friend as a gesture of great friendship or in gratitude for some favor, such as saving his life, but these cases were rare.

Polygamy was practiced only by those who could afford it, possibly a Werowance. More often, a Werowance had but one child by a wife. Then he gave her gifts which would ensure her comfort and well-being for the future and took another wife. The first wife was then free to marry again.

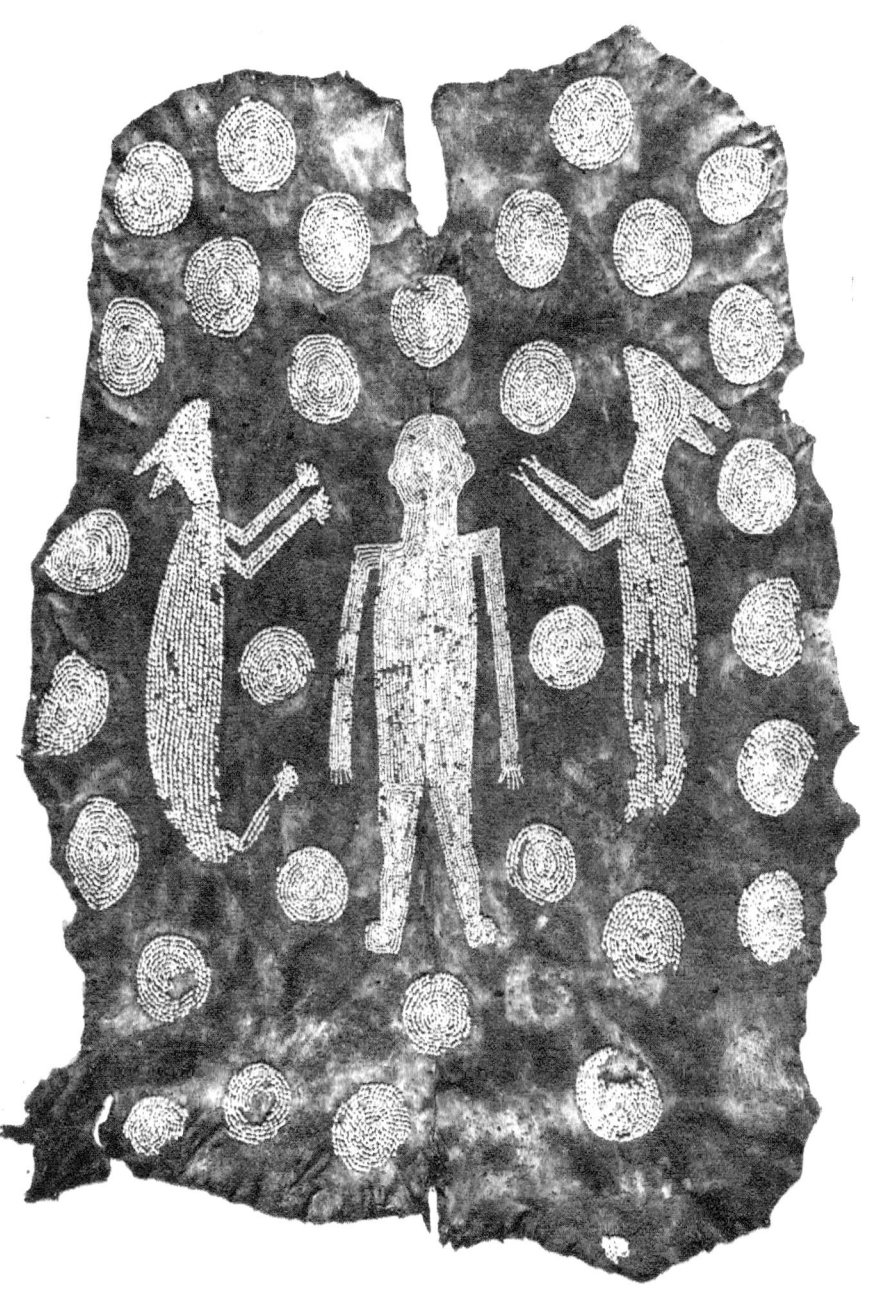

A deerskin robe from Virginia. *Courtesy the Ashmolean Museum, Oxford, England.*

John White, a member of the ill-fated Roanoke Colony in 1585, did watercolors of the Roanoke Indians, the nearest neighbors to the Chesapeans and the tribe with whom they had the most contact. The Roanokes were also Algonquins, and they were so similar in appearance, dress and habits that these pictures describe the Chesapeans as well. John White and other writers of that day—Robert Beverly, John Smith, George Percy and William Strachey—all tell of the Indians as being tall and well-formed and the women very beautiful. The usual clothing for both men and women was just a softened animal skin draped around the waist, the men often with an animal's tail hanging behind. In winter, they added another skin around their shoulders and moccasins on their feet. With so much exposure to the sun, their naturally cream-colored skin became darker, and it took on a reddish hue with the addition of bear grease. They smeared this bear grease on their bodies as a protection against the mosquitoes, flies and gnats.

Both men and women were fond of painting their bodies with colored dyes from roots, berries and earth in fanciful designs. Men painted their faces in preparation for games, ceremonies or war; hence, the English term for the Indian became "red men" and the paint on their faces was "war paint." For war, this face paint was designed not only to terrify but also to identify members of their own tribe, as each tribe followed a different pattern in their facial design. William Strachey says in *The Historie of Travaille into Virginia*, Britannica

> "The women have arms, breasts, thighs, shoulders, and faces cunningly embroidered with divers works, for pouncing (punching) or searing their skins with a kind of instrument heated in the fire. They figure there in flowers and fruits of sundry lively kinds, as also snakes, serpents, beasts, etc., and this they do by dropping upon the seared flesh sundry colors, which rubbed into the stampe, will never be taken away again, because it will not only be dried into the flesh, but grown therein."

This tattooing was widespread, but the custom had evidently died out by the beginning of the 18th century. Ben C. McCary, in *Indians in Seventeenth Century Virginia*, says that priests painted their bodies half black and half red.

The Chesapeans' eyes were black or very dark brown, and their hair was coarse, black, straight, abundant and shining. The men shaved their heads on the right side so that their hair would not become entangled with the bow string, and according to individual taste, either cut it short on the left side, allowed it to hang loose or tied it up in a knot decorated with shells, feathers or even the dried hand of an enemy! Gruesome as this sounds, hands were trophies of war and were displayed proudly. The top hair was short, like a longish crew cut, and greased to stand up like a coxcomb. Priests shaved all the hair off their heads with the exception of this coxcomb, and the Werowance, according to Robert Beverly, "may preserve a long lock behind for distinction." The women were the barbers for both sexes. They "grated away" the hair on the head with sharp shells and used tweezers of mussel shells for plucking hair from the body. Body and facial hair was considered very unseemly, and it was removed in this fashion, which took a great deal of time and must have been very painful. The hair of unmarried women was shaved on both sides of the head, with the top and back hair allowed to grow long and worn in a braid. Married women allowed all their hair to grow long and also braided it, knotted it or allowed it to hang loose according to their fancy. Both men and women often wore headbands or stuck feathers in their hair, and the Werowance wore a crownette of shells, copper beads or dyed deer hair. Earrings made of bone or shells were born by both men and women.

Ralph Lane, the governor of the Roanoke Colony from August 1585 to June 1586, wrote a lengthy report to Sir Walter Raleigh of his nearby explorations and the Indians he encountered. This is the first mention of the Chesapeans on record.

> "To the Northwest our furthest discovery was to the Chesipians, distant from Roanoke [Island] about 130 miles, the passage to it was very shallow and most dangerous by reason of the bredth of the Sound little succour. . . . in case of a storm was there to be had.
> But the Territorie and soyle of the Chesepians (being distant fifteene miles from the shoares) was for pleasantness of seate, for temperature of Climate, for fertilitie of soyle, and for the commoditie of the Sea, besides multitude of Beares (being an excellent good victual) with good woods of Sassafras and Wallnut trees, is not to be excelled by any other whatsoever."

It may seem that both men and women were pretty busy all the time, but actually in this simple life there was ample leisure time for dancing, singing or playing their musical instruments. These instruments were mostly drums and rattles made from gourds, and the flageolet, a flute made from a thick reed. Percy, on a visit to the Rappahannock tribe, says:

> "The Wereoance of Rapahanna came down to the water side with all his train, as goodly men as any I have seen of savages or Christians; the weroance coming before them playing on a flute made of a reed."

Contests of strength or skill such as wrestling and markmanship were very popular, and there were many kinds of ball games. One, a "stickball" game, was the ancestor of our modern La Crosse, and was played by all tribes of the Algonquin group. Each player had a stick 2–3 feet long with a loop at the end. The ball was made of animal hair encased in skin, and the object was to get it through the goal posts of the opposing team. There were no rules and it was absolute mayhem. The women, though not allowed to play this rough game, took advantage of members of the opposing team by grabbing the long hair of the nearest "enemy," and stamping all over one unlucky enough to fall. The name "LaCrosse" is credited to a Frenchman watching one of these Indian contests in the north. (Encyclopedia Britannica)

Women and young boys played a sort of "kick ball." The men had games somewhat like bowling, racing and throwing contests, and all played sedentary games. One, somewhat like poker, was played with rushes instead of cards, using a simple form of arithmetic. Another game was played with the short bones of deer, which were grooved on one side. Holding these bones in both hands, they tossed them into the air, attempting to have the grooved side up when they fell, like throwing dice. A great deal of betting went on in these games, as the Indians were inveterate gamblers.

No burial mounds have been found here as in the western part of the state of North Carolina. We are left to conclude, therefore, that the Chesapeans were buried in the ground. The burial ground which Floyd Painter found near the original site of Chesepioc has yielded up many fragments of clay pots, indicating that the dead went to their graves with a few provisions for the trip to the "Happy Hunting Ground."

Religious ceremonies were frequent, as their gods of nature were numerous and the sun god supreme. Gods were thanked for a bountiful harvest, for rain when needed, for a successful hunting season and for protection from enemies. Also, the ever-present bad god had to be appeased. It is said that sometimes a child was sacrificed to this evil god, but we would prefer to think that this custom was not practiced by the Chesapeans. They did not keep any particular holy days, gathering instead for religious ceremonies in times of distress, want, fear or triumph. There were feasts in gratitude for the coming of wildfowl, for the return of the hunting season and for the ripening of certain fruits.

There is a charming little legend concerning the strawberry. The Indians believed that the "Small People" (plant spirits) were sent to earth to assist in the growth and cultivation of plants for man's use. Some were assigned to the care of the strawberry plants. They awaited the breath of the warm sun-wind, then by the light of a Planter's Moon, they helped to loosen the soil to let the refreshing water of the spring rains soak into the ground. At the first emergence of the plants above ground, the spirits carefully arranged each tricluster of leaves above and around the delicate white strawberry flowers. In the early May twilight, they assisted the timid fruit buds to mature and the roots to reach out to form new runners. After the "Small People" had worked their wonders, there was brought forth a perfect fruit, a ruby-red berry, sweet and fragrant, without briar or blemish. This was a time for rejoicing and feasting as they gathered the sun-sweetened berries and made a sacrificial wine. During the strawberry celebration, the wine bowl was passed from one to another, and each dipped his cup into the wine and gave thanks, all the while chanting.

We may not believe in the "Small People," but we worship the strawberry in our own way by going into the strawberry fields to "pick our own." Spring is surely a feasting time for us, just as it was for the Indians. They also enjoyed the delicious shad, another of our spring treats, trapping them in nets on their run up the Bay; the prized shad roe; and asparagus, which grew wild. Strangely, the Indians only ate the fernlike foliage of asparagus.

On the Chesapeans' great hunts for deer and bear, usually in the Dismal Swamp, some of the women went along to build temporary shelters and to carry home the game. There sometimes were disputes over hunting rights here with the Nansemond tribe to the west, and there also was rivalry between the two tribes. Apparently, this never came to open warfare. There still are black bear and deer in the Swamp. Now most of the northern portion which is in Virginia is a Wildlife Refuge under the control of the government.

The Swamp, still a strange and wild place, is actually a huge peat bog. In the center is Lake Drummond, a shallow bowl with the greatest depth only 11 feet in spots, and it is higher than the surrounding land. Creeks flow out of this lake, not into it, and the water, stained to the color of strong tea by the tannin in the bark of the great bald cypress trees, is pure and fresh. Legends abound from Indian days, and hunters can be hopelessly lost in the depths of this primeval forest. Thomas Moore wrote a famous poem about the legend of the Indian maid who was not allowed to marry her lover because they were of rival tribes. One probably was a Chesapean and the other a Nansemond. She died of heartbreak, but her lover believed that she had escaped into the Swamp, and he followed her there. Those who knew the story have "seen" the lovers paddling their white canoe in the lake at night.

Night is strange in the Swamp. In the eerie silence broken only by night creatures calling to each other, flickering lights appear as gases arise from the peat bog to stir the imagination. There is a resident population of 37 different species of insects, many snakes including the poisonous rattler and copperhead, possums, foxes, beavers and a variety of birds including the great horned owl. Gone are the wolves and panthers. Ecologically, this swamp is unique, for here all northern and southern plants grow side by side in happy profusion.

The Chesapeans had dogs for pets, and they also used them for hunting. Unlike the Indians in the western part of the continent, they had no horses. A letter, supposedly from a Virginia Indian chief to a Frenchman, states that once his people had seen these large, strange creatures come up from the sea and, not knowing if they were gods or devils, drove them back again. If true, these horses may have been survivors of an early Spanish ship wrecked in the bay.

The Chesapeans did not know about the wheel, and they laboriously dragged their belongings behind them, tied on two long poles. They did, however, have fire, which they easily set by the method of twirling a stick in dry twigs and leaves until the friction produced a flame. And their mode of swimming was superior to that of the Europeans who, up to this time, swam a side-stroke. The Indians used the crawl for speed and the old-fashioned breast stroke for silence in the water.

In their simple life, the Chesapeans seemed to have avoided most of the results of ambition and lust for power which affected other Indian tribes north of the James River. The early Spanish and English explorers had passed them by in the 16th century, thinking neither they nor their land to be of any consequence. But one of the Chesapeans' own race, the Great Chief Powhatan, was their undoing.

This Powhatan was a conqueror. Highly intelligent and ambitious for power, he had subdued most of the tribes from the James to the Potomac, forming "The Powhatan Confederacy," and he was anxious to spread his rule even farther. He had endeavored to persuade the Chesapeans to join the confederacy several times, but they had demurred, not wishing to fight his wars across the water or to pay the tribute demanded of his member tribes. Irritated by their aversion to join him peaceably, Powhatan found an excuse for more stringent measures.

Powhatan's advisors, the priests, predicted that he would be overcome by "a great people from the east." Indians had destroyed a Spanish mission near Gloucester in 1571, probably at his instigation, and the Spaniards showed no signs of returning. So he concluded that the "people from the east" must be the Chesapeans. Under the guise of a friendly visit, he sent a delegation of his best warriers to confer with them. Honored by the prospect of a "friendly visit," the Chesapeans gathered at Chesepioc to greet and entertain the visitors at a great feast. But Powhatan's instructions to his delegates were other than friendly. The welcoming celebration over, these warriors murdered all the Chesapean men as they slept, sparing only the women, children and the royal family, decimating this once large and happy tribe. This slaughter occurred in approximately 1595.

It is no wonder that the little boys who were left grew up in fear and fled from the approach of the strange white men in shining armor in 1607, with only a belated attempt to drive them off as they were leaving. After this, the tribe dwindled to a small and insignificant group, scratching along as best they could.

Defeated in mind and body and very few in number, these poor Indians were easily won over when the Englishmen came to settle. These Englishmen had been living on the northern side of the James, and had learned through experience how best to deal with any Indians—through friendly advances.

There is no record of any major difficulty with the Indians here as the English settlers established themselves. It is recorded that one woman was killed by Indians in the area of Norfolk, and later a man was reported murdered by Indians. Both of these occurred in the 17th century, and since the Nansemonds continued to be troublesome for some time, it is thought that these people were their victims. As for the Chesapeans, there are only vague tales of child-like curiosity and rather pitiful attempts to scare people at night by peering into their windows.

Those first settlers must have been diplomatic and also clever, for they introduced the Chesapeans not only to their ways, but in turn, learned from them the best uses of the land and waters. Thus, the remaining Chesapeans were gradually absorbed into the plantations.

The Indians were avid for metal, and the English traded with them fairly. Floyd Painter has found arrowheads made of English flint and, in trash pits, fragments of Indian pottery mixed in with English glass and porcelain.

We know that the English used the Indians as guides and, probably, almost as servants, although the Indians were unaware of this classification. Unfortunately, their introduction to rum and the white man's diseases further reduced their number.

There is no record of a marriage between a white man and a Chesapean woman, although sometimes appearances of descendants of early settlers belie this assumption. With the coming of the blacks, however, the Chesapeans, indifferent to color distinctions, frequently mixed with them. Tall, handsome blacks of a light color are proud of their Indian blood. There are many of these who are part Chesapean, but there is not one full-blooded Chesapean—none. They had a pleasant history but a sad ending.

Since no Indians kept records, we have no way of knowing the actual size of the Chesapean tribe. But the fact that they are located on John Smith's earliest maps indicates that they were once large and important. They were visited by Ralph Lane, the leader of the Roanoke Colony, in 1585, and the Great Powhatan so feared them that he ordered the slaughter of their men. McCary's estimate of their population in 1607 was 375, a very small number in this large area, but this was after Powhatan's massacre. Powhatan ruled 27 tribes by 1607, of which six were much larger than the Chesapeans. The Pamunkeys, the last to be subdued by the English, in 1646, had 1,100 in their main town alone.

Although the Chesapeans have disappeared, they and others have left us a legacy of Indian words which are now a familiar part of our language. Few place names survive here except for Pungo and Croatan, but names of native animals are only slightly changed from Indian pronunciation, such as raccoon, opossum, skunk and chipmunk. Fish names such as porgy and menhaden remain, as do the names of many native trees, among them hickory, pecan, paw-paw, chinkapin and persimmon. Pumpkin and squash are Indian words, and pone, hominy and succotash were foods unknown to the English. Barbeque is an Indian word, used as both a noun and verb.

A more subtle legacy left by the Chesapeans was their love of the land and contentment with it. They might have put off their annihilation a little longer if they had joined the "Confederacy," but their interest did not extend beyond their own borders. Their geographic isolation contributed toward their indifference to the world outside, and both love of their own land and reluctance to be part of a larger team effort carried over to the English settlers all through the colonial era, the Revolution and even today. Beneath the gracious friendliness and hospitality of descendants of those early settlers, there still is a wariness of strangers and an aversion to change.

The work of archaeologists who dig up artifacts of the past and that of historians who study ancient records sometimes leads to different interpretations of their findings. The search goes on for the truth in the dim past, and what seems to be a correct assumption today may be erroneous tomorrow. Either way, uncovering mysteries locked in ancient records and in the ground is a fascinating procedure as we learn more and more of our history and its beginnings.

PART ONE
Chapter 2
THE COMING OF THE ENGLISH

After Christopher Columbus made his first voyage to the New World in 1492, there was a great surge of interest in the possibilities here. The Spanish conquest of the West Indies, Mexico and Peru and the fabulous plunder which they brought back was the envy of all Europe. The English at this time were more concerned with finding the so-called "Northwest Passage" to India. John Cabot, it is believed, had explored the coast of North America as far south as the Chesapeake Bay in 1498, and the Spanish had made an attempt to found a Jesuit mission somewhere in the Bay area near Gloucester in 1570, although the actual site of this mission has never been discovered. The mission was a failure, as it was destroyed and the Jesuits killed by Indians in 1571, and the Spanish did not try again in the Chesapeake area.

In 1583, Sir Humphrey Gilbert obtained a patent from Queen Elizabeth for discovery and colonization in North America, but he only reached Newfoundland and all five of his ships and 260 men were lost in a storm at sea. Sir Walter Raleigh, however, had been spurred on by the Spanish successes in the South, so he, along with Sir Francis Drake, received a renewal of the Gilbert patent. With the help of Drake and the elder and younger Hakluyt, Raleigh formed an expedition to explore the North American mainland, and entering Albemarle Sound, they landed at Roanoke Island. Raleigh named his discovery Virginia, and the party returned to England.

The following year, 1585, Raleigh dispatched a colonizing expedition under the same commanders, Sir Richard Grenville and Ralph Lane.

A fourth expedition, in 1587, to bring supplies and additional colonists unfortunately found no survivors. This expedition was under the command of John White, who made the graphic watercolors of the Roanoke Indians. He left 15 colonists, including his week-old

The Englishmen

grandchild, Virginia Dare, the first English child born on the North American continent. Unable to return until 1590, he found no trace of the colonists except the cryptic letters "CRO" carved on a tree and the word "CROATAN" carved on a doorpost.

After this disaster, no further attempts at colonizing were made until 1605, when Captain John Smith returned to London from his travels and adventures in the East. He urged further action, and two Virginia Companies were then formed: the Plymouth (or North Virginia) and the London (or South Virginia). In December 1606, the London Company sent three vessels to Virginia—the *Susan Constant*, the *Discovery* and the *Godspeed*—under the command of Captain Christopher Newport.

With the arrival of these three ships at Cape Henry four months later on April 26, 1607, a balmy Good Friday, the history of our nation really began, for this was the first landing of a permanent English settlement in North America. It had been a long and arduous voyage, fraught with dissension, discomfort and boredom. The 144 men crowded into the three small ships could not have been a worse choice to found a colony. As 20 of them went ashore and climbed up the dunes, all they could think about were the orders in the sealed box which would tell them which ones were to be on the governing council and further directions as to the site of settlement. These men were rightly named adventurers for, excited by dreams of instant wealth and glory as the Spanish had found in the South, they were not the sort of men to colonize.

Captain Newport opened the sealed box and there were the orders.

> "When it shall please God to send you to the coast of Virginia, you shall do your best endeavor to find out a safe port in the entrance of some navigable river, making choice of such a one as runneth farthest into the land, and if you happen to discover divers potable rivers, and amongst them any one that hath two main branches, make choice of that which bendeth most toward the sea. . . ."

Back home the English were still dreaming of a Northwest Passage to India. Captain Newport's command was to end once he had determined on the site for the colony. Next was the naming of the council.

> "Captain Christopher Newport
> Captain Bartholomew Gosnold
> Captain John Smith
> Captain Edward Maria Wingfield
> Captain John Martin

Captain John Ratcliffe
Captain Gabriel Archer
Captain George Kendall."

No president was named, so they took a vote—the first democratic election in America—and Captain Wingfield was elected. Old and sick, he was the least controversial of the group. Captain Gosnold, a veteran mariner, was disinterested in settlement, and he died in that first dreadful summer. Captain Newport sailed back to England with his ships as soon as they were unloaded.

Captain Ratcliffe was hardly a notable figure. He allowed himself to be trapped by Powhatan when he went to bargain for supplies. He and the 50 men under him were tortured until they died.

Captain George Kendall, suspected of being a Spanish spy, was convicted of being involved in a plot against the Colony and shot. Captain John Martin and Captain Gabriel Archer were a troublesome pair, both enemies of Captain John Smith, and each determined to gain control. They returned to England with Captain Newport on his next supply trip.

Captain John Smith had not been present at the landing at Cape Henry. He was chained below decks, the victim of a story cooked up by Archer and Martin that he planned to take over the expedition. A military man and certainly an adventurer, John Smith was nevertheless the most able leader among them. Short, stocky and no aristocrat, he had so irritated the others on the voyage with his constant bragging about his adventures and accomplishments that they were ready to cut him out in any way they could. But even though John Smith was obnoxious to the other egomaniacs of the expedition, he believed in a hard line with the Indians, and if his dictum of "he who doth not work, doth not eat" had been obeyed by the other colonists, many of the troubles of those first two years may have been avoided. The date of 1606 on his map is in error, for his famous exploration of both sides of the Chesapeake Bay was in 1608. Disgusted by the way things were going, he returned to England in 1612.

John Rolfe, another member of the company, was the gentleman who married Pocahontas in 1614, thereby securing peace with the Indians until the death of her father, Powhatan. Rolfe had introduced a strain of tobacco from the West Indies in 1613 which was milder and caught the fancy of the Europeans. With the prospect of grand profits from "the obnoxious weed," so termed by King James, the London Company was able to send more and more shiploads of supplies and immigrants until finally the colony was firmly established. Tobacco quickly became the economic mainstay of this Colony all through the colonial period.

The Reverend Robert Hunt was the third exception to this group of adventurers. He truly believed that the Indians would welcome the opportunity to discard their old gods who had served them well and accept Christianity if just given the chance. He tried. Tireless in his ministrations to the sick in the miserable first summer, he unfortunately killed more than he cured. This poor, idealistic man was a carrier of the fever which finally killed him.

Of the rest of the 144, 30 were gentlemen with titles, or connected thereto, who had brought their footmen with them. There also was a tailor, a perfumer, a barber, a goldsmith, a few inexperienced boys and even some felons England wished to be rid of. Not one of these 144 was accustomed to the manual labor needed to survive, and they were unwilling to demean themselves by starting. The choice of Jamestown Island proved to be a mistake as it was surrounded by swamps. By the end of that summer, all but 38 of the entire company had died of fever or starvation.

In defense of these first colonists, we must agree with Dr. Carville Earle, who, in his essay *Environment, Disease and Mortality in Early Virginia* proposes that this tragic mortality in the first year and succeeding years until 1624, was due to diseases incurred by drinking the water of the James River.

In that first year only John Smith noted with concern that in June the Indians had abandoned the estuaries and moved to higher ground inland. He attempted to disperse the colonists in the same way but unsuccessfully because of opposition.

Dr. Earle explains that the actual causes of death to so many were typhoid, dysentery, malaria and salt poisoning. In winter and spring the river water was fresh, pouring downstream from the mountains, and pushing the salt water back to the bay. But by early June this runoff had greatly diminished and the salt water pushed upstream filling Jamestown's marshes with still water already being polluted by Jamestown's wastes.

The first symptoms of these diseases were lassitude, laziness and irritability, which helps to explain the constant infighting among the colonists. But soon the diseases struck with deadly rapidity. On July 6th the first man died, of the "bloodie Flixe," according to George Percy, and the others quickly followed. When the first supply ship arrived in January, these 38 remaining were also ill.

The virulent nature of these diseases is that they did not go away, and no immunity is built up. Of those who survived, many were "carriers," as was the Reverend Hunt.

This disastrous destruction of lives was repeated summer after summer while the Company claimed that these deaths were due to "starvation"—hardly reasonable as the forests were filled with game and the river with fish. Still the immigrants came, and 50% of them died in their first summer. Finally, in 1611, Governor Dale, heeding the advice of John Smith, dispersed the colony and began construction of the town of Henrico further up the James at the Falls.

It is a miracle that any survived. Since they would not plant crops themselves, they were told to get food from the Indians by trade, if possible. But if trade was not possible, they were told to use force. In retrospect, their methods present an amazing paradox, for the punishment ordered for the Indians who would not supply them with corn was to burn their fields. Even the Indians thought this was ridiculous, as one told John Smith, "We can plant anywhere, and we know you cannot live if you lack our harvest." We probably never will know why the Indians, who did not want the English there in the first place, did not remove themselves elsewhere and let the colonists starve, or just die of disease.

Here, we will draw a compassionate veil over the horrors of those first two years but quote one passage from John Smith's "Travels and Works."

> "So great was our famine, that a Salvage we slew and buried, the poorer sort took him up again and eat him and so did divers one another boyled and stewed with roots and herbs. And one amongst the rest did kill his wife, powdered (salted) her, and had eaten part of her before it was known; for which he was executed, as he well deserved; now whether she was better roasted, boyled or carbonade'd [*grilled*] I know not; but of such a dish as powdered wife I never heard of."

In spite of tales such as this, the London Company continued to send boatloads of immigrants but never enough provisions. Once here, these immigrants continued to die at an alarming rate, but more came to take their places. In "Colonial Papers" of the Public Records Office in London, it is recorded in 1618 that:

> "Patent granted this year to the Society of Southhampton Hundred, Capts. Bargrave and Ward, who have undertaken to transport to

Virginia great multitudes of people with store of cattle. Said 1,261 persons being arrived from England in Virginia, 500 cattle, with some horses and goats, and infinite number of swine broken out into the woods."

This number of people came in 12 ships and included "650 persons for public use as tenants for Governor's Company and Minister's Glebe land, 90 young maids for wives and servants, 100 boys as apprentices to tenants, 50 servants for public use and 150 to set up iron works." All along there had been some good, sturdy men, and their number increased.

Order was finally brought out of chaos by Sr. Thomas Dale, governor from 1611–1614, who discarded the system of community property as unworkable in favor of land grants. In 1619, Governor Sir George Yeardley called the first meeting of the House of Burgesses, whose members were elected from each of the eight shires: Accomac (Northampton), Warrosquyoake (Isle of Wight), Charles City, Henrico, Warwick River (later dropped), York, James City and Elizabeth City. This was the first representative assembly in America, and Virginia was the only Colony in the world which had one.

A few months later, the first Negroes were brought to Virginia in a Dutch ship which had put in at Jamestown for provisions. Virginius Dabney, in *Virginia, The New Dominion*, says that this vessel, with a Dutch captain, was in reality owned by the Earl of Warwick. This would indicate that the Earl was already in the slave trade.

Meanwhile, the London Company was in trouble. After several unprofitable years and conflict within by two warring groups that drove it into receivership, the Charter of 1612 was revoked in 1624. Virginia became a Crown Colony at that time, with the King and Privy Council in control. Nothing much changed, although the colonists did feel more secure under the King than under a private company.

Desirable land in Elizabeth City Shire was rapidly being taken up on the north side of Hampton Roads. Hampton and "Kiccoughtan" had become ports of entry for shipping and immigrants, both being more convenient than Jamestown. It was not until after 1620, however, that much attention was paid to the southside of Hampton Roads. Little exploring had been done there even though this, too, was part of Elizabeth City Shire, stretching down to about the 36th parallel. But land meant riches, and the quest for virgin land on navigable waterways aroused the interest of ambitious men who wished to acquire more land than they had on the north side.

In 1616, John Rolfe had estimated the population of the entire Virginia Colony as being 351, including 65 women and children. He also stated that, "In that year there were 144 cattle, 6 horses, 216 goats, hogs wild and tame not to be numbered and poultry a great plenty." In 1624, when the shires became counties, Elizabeth City had a population of 859, even in spite of the high death rate from disease and Indians and the exodus back to England of those who could not or would not take the rough life. And since the desirable land on rivers and creeks had already been taken up and more land was harder to come by, land hungry men began finally to look to the south side of Hampton Roads as a better opportunity for larger land grants and more agreeable homesites.

PART II
LOWER NORFOLK COUNTY
1625-1640

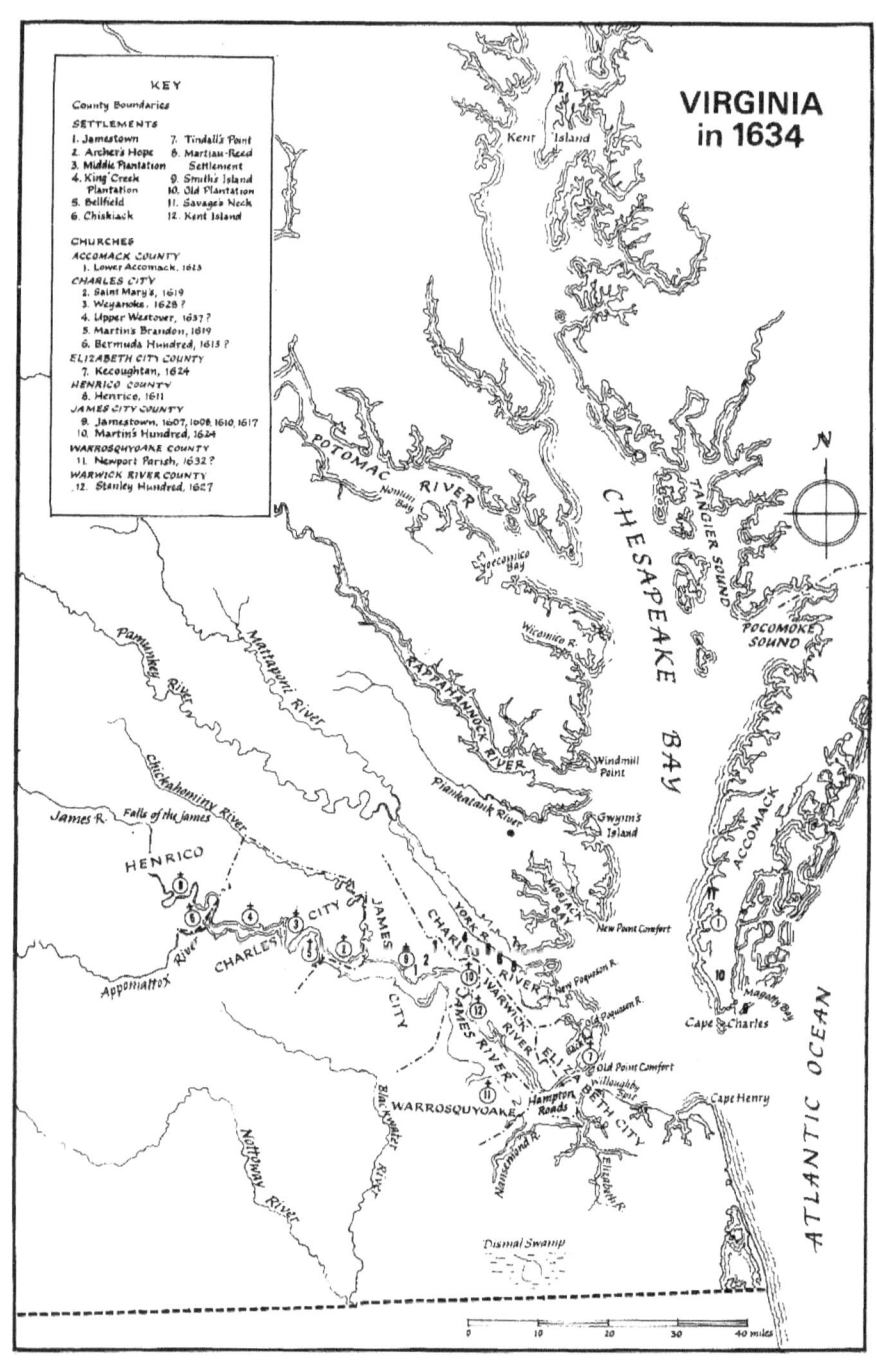

Virginia in 1634. From *The Old Dominion in the Seventeenth Century*, Warren C. Billings. *Courtesy of the North Carolina University Press.*

PART TWO
Chapter 1
FIRST SETTLERS, 1625-1640

In the years from 1607 to 1625, while the colony of Jamestown was struggling to survive, the English paid little attention to the 950 square miles south of Hampton Roads. This area was part of Elizabeth City Shire, extending from the Atlantic Ocean on the east to beyond the Nansemond River, and south to the proprietory grant of North Carolina. After the Indian Massacre of 1622, however, some of these Englishmen started to look further afield for safer ground and better opportunity. The northern part of Elizabeth City Shire was filling up as more and more boatloads of immigrants came in eager for land. Some of the more enterprising, who saw the chances for adding to the land they already had and who were imbued with the same pioneer spirit which had brought them to this continent in the first place, began to explore the unknown wilderness across the water to the south.

In absence of exact records, we can surmise that the first four men to stay permanently in the southern area were Adam Thorowgood, William Julian, Francis Mason and Thomas Willoughby, although which one actually settled here first remains an intriguing riddle. All four had been living in the northern part of Elizabeth City Shire, and all four were established leaders there. But they were looking for a more advantageous place to settle permanently in order to make the best life for themselves and their families. Exporing this southern side of Hampton Roads, they saw a wilderness with all its difficulties, but they also saw a virgin land with a network of creeks and rivers for easy navigation, forests of great trees for building and, apparently, little or no trouble with the remnants of the Chesapean Indians. So they claimed the land they wanted, from the Lynnhaven to the Elizabeth River and along the shore of Hampton Roads, and began their move.

As always, the name of the game was "follow the leader." As these men went back and forth across the water, tending to their businesses on the north side and building their houses on the south side, word got around and others came in rapid succession. So many came that in 1629, Elizabeth City Shire was divided into two parishes, the Upper and the Lower Parish. The southside of Hampton Roads was the Lower Parish with three elected representatives in the House of Burgesses.

Despite the appalling death rate and the danger from the Indians, immigrants continued to pour into the whole Colony. The former eight shires were made counties in 1634, and the Lower Parish of Elizabeth City County was made a separate county in 1636 and named New Norfolk. Even this was not adequate for the accelerating immigration here, and in 1637, New Norfolk was divided into Upper and Lower Norfolk Counties. Upper Norfolk County ran from a line between the Elizabeth and Nansemond Rivers, west to Isle of Wight County. All the rest to the east was Lower Norfolk County. This whole area remained Lower Norfolk County until 1691, when the western two-thirds became Norfolk County and the eastern one-third became Princess Anne County, now the City of Virginia Beach.

When the colony was only eight shires, each parish in a shire was required by law to have a court and a church. With formation of the counties, each county required the same, with the records to be kept and copies sent on to Jamestown. But these were rough times. The earliest records are dated in 1637 and are in the Norfolk County Clerk's office in Portsmouth. (Book A)

"Court January 10, 1637
Christopher Burrough of Linnehaven planter fined 500 weight of tobacco . . . bargaining with two Indians without a license. . . ."

Eight depositions were taken at that court, reason unknown:

"Richard West,   aged 24 years, or thereabouts
Thomas Chesly   "   40   "   ,   "   "
Thomas Keeling   "   24   "   ,   "   "
ffrancis Mason   "   42   "   ,   "   "
Robert Hayes   "   44   "   ,   "   "
Daniel Tanner   "   56   "   ,   "   "
Jarvis Mason   "   26   "   ,   "   "
Henry Thomason   "   26   "   ,   "   "   "

Then, in March of that year, the following:

"At a Court holden in the Lower county of New Norfolk the 15th of March 1637: Present:

	Capt. Adam Thorowgood, Esq.
Capt. John Sibsey	Mr. ffrancis Mason
Mr. Edw. Windam	Mr. Robert Camm (Cane)
Mr. Willm. Julian	..........(illegible)

These records show additional names of those living here in that year. In the above record, the placement of Capt. Thorowgood's name means that he was "Commander" of the court, that is, Chief Justice. The next existing record shows that a church had been ordered, and also provides us with an additional name of one who also became a leader.

"Court: Nove. 21, 1638
Whereas there has been an order of Court granted by the Governor and Counsell . . . the Building and erecting of a Church in Upper part of this County with a reference to the Commander and Commissioners of the sd. County for the operating of a place fitting and Convenient for the situation and building thereof, the sd. order being in part not accomplished, but standing now in erection to be voide and the work be fall into ruins. So now the sd. Commissioners taking into consideration doe appoint Capt. John Sibsey and Mr. Henry Seawell to provide workmen for the finishing of the same and what they shall agree for with the sd. workmen to be levied to us, the Commissioners (Justices)."

This became the Elizabeth River Parish Church, the first in Lower Norfolk County. Henry Seawell had already given some of his land for the church, and his will requested that both he and his wife be buried beneath the floor of the chancel. The first minister was the Reverend William Wilkinson, who was already residing in the county. Wilkinson's grant of 700 acres was recorded in 1635 when the first grants here were recorded, and his land was adjacent to the land of Thomas Keeling and Adam Thorowgood.

All of these men lived in what became Lower Norfolk County in 1637, and of these 17, the land of Adam Thorowgood and that of Thomas Keeling were in the part which became Princess Anne County. Some of their descendants are still living here. Of the others, Francis Mason's land was in the future Norfolk County, and he and particularly his son Lemuel were prominent members of the leading class in Lower Norfolk County. Due to the heavy death toll, especially of children, the families of the others have either died out or only had daughters living whose maiden surnames were never mentioned in the wills of those days so are impossible to trace.

Henry Seawell had only one son, and he chose to stay in England after his father had sent him there to be educated. John Sibsey had only one living child, a daughter, and William Julian had no children. These three men were leaders in their time, but they were in their forties when they first came to the Colony, and the hardships of the wilderness were not conducive to long life. It was too bad, for these men who were younger sons of well-to-do families in England had some education and at least a meager knowledge of the law. This education was not available to their children here, only whatever their fathers had time to teach them at home, and while they were taming the wilderness, there was not much time for education.

Henry Seawell's name survives as "Sewell's Point" in the City of Norfolk, now the location of the U.S. Naval Station, and "Sewell's Point Road," running through his original grant. Those who named these dropped the "a" from "Seawell." "Mason's Creek," just north of the Naval Station, establishes the location of Francis Mason's land.

Life as pioneers was not easy. With no maps and no roads, the search for springs with potable water, the learning to grow crops to sustain their families and adapting to the dangers of the many swamps would seem enough of a struggle. Unlike New England, where the settlers built their homes close together in little communities for protection from the Indians, with their fields on the outskirts, these men, in their overpowering drive to own the best and the most land they could acquire, chose land far apart from each other and built their houses on high land near a creek or river, their only means of communication. True, the danger from the Indians here was minimal, but love of land was of prime importance then, a trait in common with the Indians. Wolves were numerous and a menace to cattle and man alike, but did not deter these men from building their houses in isolated spots. The greatest danger was really from the mosquitoes, unknown in England, and the "fevers" they carried. By 1640, there were several doctors here, called "chirosurgeons," but their knowledge of treatment for anything consisted mostly of "bleeding" (letting blood) and "physics" (an extremely strong cathartic). With all these difficulties, however, a surprising number survived, and it was up to the leaders to enforce law and order in this then wild place. This they managed to do very well.

There are no records concerning the relationships of these first settlers with the Chesapeans until the statute of the House of Burgesses in 1662 (Hening's Statutes, vol. II).

> "Concerning the great use and benefit the country may enjoy from the Chesokoiack (Chesapeans) being very kindly used by us, and being sensible that with the few guns they have amongst them, they cannot prejudice us, being a small inconsiderable nation. It is therefore ordered by the present Grand Assembly to shew other Indians how kind wee are to such as are obident to our laws, and that the said Cheskoiack Indians quietly hold and enjoy the land they re now eated upon and have the free use of the guns they now have, any act or order of assembly to the contrary notwithstanding."

We can be sure that these men had created a friendly relationship with the Indians by a bit of trading, by allowing time to watch while they worked on the houses, and by letting them see the uses of their tools. Indians had been employed as guides all over the Colony, and their knowledge of the lay of the land was extremely important to the English. Knowing only vaguely the location of the Lynnhaven River and the Elizabeth River and not much else, the settlers could not have selected such ideal spots for their claims without the help of the Chesapeans, who knew all the rivers and creeks, the location and size of the swamps, the high ground and their own trails. Sugar always catches more flies than vinegar, and these men were smart enough to play on the Indians' intense curiosity about anything mechanical and their avid desire for metal. Even a small knife was a treasure.

There still were lingering fears of what lay ahead as the actual move across Hampton Roads began. For the women especially, as their boats approached this sandy shore with the dark forests looming behind, the unknown was a terrifying prospect. Fortunately, children have a great way of breaking the ice, and soon after landing, they were playing with the Indian children, each learning the other's games and languages. The men were learning where to hunt and fish, and the women were learning the Indian ways with cooking and gaining knowledge of the wild berries and herbs. The English had servants of various degrees of ability (William Julian is listed as having 30), and some of them were perhaps already skilled carpenters and brickmakers.

None of the original houses of the four first settlers of this area remain, unfortunately, because these houses were of frame and deteriorated faster than they would have had they been of brick. But time of building was important then, so only the foundations were of brick. According to Mrs. Kellam's *Old Houses in Princess Anne*, a brick mason hired to build the Rolfe-Warren House in Surry County was taken to court as late as 1654 for poor workmanship. His defense was, ". . . that a brick house of that size (not as large as the Thorowgood one) could not be so well built when the short time of five years was allowed for the building." (*Old Houses in Princess Anne*, Sadie Scott Kellam and V. Hope Kellam). Some houses were built before Governor Wyatt was instructed in 1637 to require every owner of 100 acres or more to build a brick dwelling 24 × 16 feet with a cellar.

Of these first four challengers of the wilderness, William Julian was 43 when he first came to the Colony in 1609 and at least 49 when he settled on the Elizabeth River. He soon died, leaving no children. Francis Mason lasted a little longer—he was 40 when he first came to the Colony and 56 when he settled here, also on the Elizabeth River. Mason's son Lemuel married the daughter of Henry Seawell, and their descendants are still in the area. Thomas Willoughby and Adam Thorowgood were much younger. They not only survived and had living children, but they quickly became the most powerful men in Lower Norfolk County.

Thomas Willoughby came to the Colony in 1610. By 1623, he was termed "Ensign" on his recorded grant of that year and was a member of the House of Burgess in 1628. He was one of the first justices of Lower Norfolk County in 1637, and in 1640, he was appointed a member of the Governor's Council. Besides acquiring 3,600 acres west of Little Creek on the south shore of Hampton Roads, he had large mercantile interests and made frequent, lengthy trips to England. He was a man of power in the Colony and one of the wealthier at that time. He was the progenitor of a large family, his sons continuing to live on this land until after the Revolution.

The Willoughbys were staunch Royalists, either by birth or pretension, and the head of the family in 1775 was John Willoughby, so important in the later Norfolk County that he was named chairman of the Norfolk Committee of Safety. John was unable to bring himself to take the oath of allegiance to the Rebel Cause, however, and was shunned by friends and neighbors as a Tory. He finally boarded Lord Dunmore's ship in the Elizabeth River with one of his sons and returned to England. Other Willoughby men felt differently and fought with distinction in the Virginia Army of the Revolution. There are numerous descendants of Thomas Willoughby living here in Norfolk today.

Unlike Thomas Willoughby, who had come with obvious financial backing, Adam Thorowgood had first come to the Colony as an indentured servant to Col. Edward Waters of Kiccoughtan in Elizabeth City Shire. When his term was up, he returned to England, singing the praises of the new land. He married Sarah Offley, daughter of a well-to-do London merchant, and brought her back to the Colony with him. He first bought 200 acres near the land of Col. Waters, but he soon looked across Hampton Roads to the south side as a better opportunity.

On March 20, 1628, Adam Thorowgood was commissioned by Gov. Francis West to hold court in his house. This may have been his house on the northern side of Hampton Roads, but some records indicate and we believe that he had already built a house on land he had claimed on the south side by that time and had moved over. In 1629, when he was a member of the House of Burgesses for Elizabeth City, Thorowgood was instrumental in the separation of Elizabeth City Shire into the two parishes, the Upper and Lower, with a court to be held in each.

As those in England who had fallen under the spell of his enthusiasm began to arrive, Thorowgood foresaw the prospect of a large land grant coming to him. With this expectation, he surveyed the land he wanted and applied for the largest grant ever recorded in what became Lower Norfolk County two years later. It gives a good description of the location, and you will see that some of these persons for whom he claimed headrights had arrived as early as 1628. In the seeming duplication of names, everyone who left the Colony received 50 additional acres for coming back!

(*Cavaliers and Pioneers*, Abstracts of Virginia Land Patents and Grants, 1623–66. Nell Marion Nugent.)

> "CAPT.. ADAM THOROWGOOD, 5350 acs. lying Nly upon Cheopean bay, to begin at the first Cr. of that river, running to a broad cr. that shooteth behind a long point of land Wly. into the maine land, Ely. up the Riv. to a little island shooting into Chesopean Riv., E. upon the same, this land lying upon the west side & if in case these bounds or neck of land doe not include the sd. 5350 acs, then he shall measure upon the first sd. Cr. soe farr as the remainder of his sd. acs. shall extend. Sd. land granted at the especiall recommendation of him from their Lordshipps and others his Majesties most Honble. privie Counsell to the Govr. & Counsell of State of Va. 24th of June 1635. Also due as followeth: 50 acs. for his personal avd. 50 acs for per adv. of his wife Sarah Thorowgood & 5350 acs. for trans. of 105 persons. Trans. of himselfe, wife Sarah, and Thomas Thorowgood, Francis Newton, James Leading,

Stephen Bernard, Joh. Newarke, Edward Pitts, Rich. Jenerie, Wm. Edwards, Dennis Russell, John Bernards, Jon. Waters, Jos. Leake, Thomas Brooks, Jon. Moise, Jon. Penton, Edward Parish, Thomas Melton, Augustine Warner, Tho. Chandler, Andrew Chant, John Persie, Edmund Wallis, Thomas Boulton, Robert Heasell, Richard Johnson, Margaret Bilbie, Jane Prosser, Jane Westerfield, Ann Spark, Susan Colson, in the *Hopewell* in 1628, John Harris, John Lock, Andrew Boyer, Thomas Boyer in the True Love in 1628, Thomas Keeling, Rachel Lane in the *Hopewell* in 1628 William Hines, Edward Reynolds, Wm. Hookes, Edward Palmer, Edward Jones, John Dyer in the french ship in 1629, Victo Fraford, Casander Underwood, Merciful Halley, Ann Long, Dorothy Wheeler, Ann Allerson, in the Africa, Eliz. Gosmore in the Christopher & Mary, Francis Bramly in the Ark, John Writt, Wm. Fawne, Wm. Was, George Mee, Gilbert Gye, John Enies, James Wilson, Daniel Hutton, Wm. Gastrock Wm. Speed, Jon. Reynolds in the *Hopewell* in 1633, Jon. Wakefield, James Belly, Patrick Blacock, Stephen Swaine, John Cowes, Ann Boulton, in the *Bona Adventure* in 1634, Wm. Fletcher in Mr. Middleton in 1634, Robert Westwell in the *Merchants Hope* in 1634, Robert Spring in the *Jon. & Dorothy*, Adam Thorowgood, Edward Windham, Cob. Howell, Tho. Creaser, Henry Hill, Roger Ward, Jon. Withers, Wm. Holton, Wm. Kempe Humphrey Heyward, Jon. Alporte, Symond Stanfield, Robt. Gainie, Thomas Smith, George Whitehead, Henry Fanklin, Jon. Hill, Joseph Sedgewick, Arthur Eggleston, Richard Poole, Jon. Holton, Stephen Withers, Christ. Newgent, Jon. Brewton, Thomas Atmore, Mary Hill, Henry Wood in the *Jon. & Dorothy* in 1634, Wm. Burroughs, Ann Burroughs, Ann Whitthorne, Eliza. Creaser, Eliza Curtisse, Mary Hill, Jr. Wm. Atkins.

Included in the list are four friends of Adam Thorowgood: Thomas Keeling, Gilbert Gye, Edward Windham and Richard Poole. The repetition of Adam's name several times may indicate that he had his own ship by this time in which he returned at times to England and probably brought some of the others back with him.

The following court case speaks for Adam's exacting nature. It further indicates that his house, later called "The Mansion," was already built and that his finances had improved considerably. (Lower Norfolk County Records, Book A, part 1, f. 3, para. 8) Dated 10 Jan. 1637.

> "Whereas Daniel Tanner of Elizabeth City, carpenter . . . for the performance of certain buildings due to Capt. Adam Thorowgood, but the sd. building not being finished to . . . laity specifications?; whereby the foresd. Capt. Adam Thorowgood was Constrained to hire men to finish the same. . . ."

These buildings would have been outbuildings.

The site of Thorowgood's original house was found in 1955 by archaeologist Floyd Painter, in the modern development of Baylake Pines. It was of frame construction and contained six rooms, a passage, and a milk room in the cellar. Only the foundation was brick, although the remains of a kiln were found nearby. Actually, the site was found by accident. This was private property, and the owner in excavating for his cellar found enough suspicious looking objects to call in an expert. Construction was held up for a while, and many interesting artifacts were recovered. These have been identified by Painter and the Virginia Center for Archaeology in Yorktown filling three shelves and ten boxes. The most interesting of them are a thimble and an "apostle spoon," both of brass, a pike head and the sword hilt of a once handsome dress sword. Among the fragments of Dutch and English pottery and glass of the early 16th and 17th centuries were found pieces of Indian pottery and a quantity of almost intact glass bottles which once held Holland gin. These are the earliest historic relics that have been found here, except for those of the Chesapeans.

Adam Thorowgood was a busy man. In addition to his responsibilities in court—as a member of the House of Burgesses and later as a member of the Governor's Council—and his large estate to which he had added 800 acres, he started a ferry from the eastern shore of the Elizabeth River to the western shore in 1636 as a private enterprise.

We have no picture of Adam Thorowgood or his wife Sarah, but it is said that he was handsome and fun-loving, and he must have been fond of gin. He was not so fun-loving, however, that he overlooked any personal offense. (Lower Norfolk County Order Book, 1637–1640.)

> "The deposition of Gilbert Gye, age 28 years or thereabouts Sworn and Examined, Sayeth that being at the house of William Fowler, discoursing with him concerning certain casks found by the Servant of Capt. Adam Thorowgood by the Seaside but afterward being seized and fetched away by the aforesaid William Fowler, the aforesaid deponent told him to have the said casks taken away from him. Thereupon the wife of the said William Fowler asked him who would take them from him? The said deponent answered he Capt, upon which she, the said Ann Fowler answered "Let Capt. Thorowgood kiss my arse." William Tanner age 36 years or thereabouts, Sworn and Examined, sayeth that being in company with Gilbert Gye at the house of William Fowler he, the said Fowler said that it would vex him to have the casks which he had fetched home taken from him. Whereupon the said wife of the said Fowler asked

who would take them from him. The said Gilbert ansered "Capt. Thorowgood," upon which she, the said Ann answered "Let Capt. Thorowgood kiss my arse." Whereas it doth appear to this court by the oaths of several witnesses that Ann Fowler, the wife of William Fowler of Linhaven, planter, did in a shameful, uncomely, and irreverent manner, bid Capt. Thorowgood Kiss her arse, with the assignation of many unusual terms. It is therefore ordered that the said Ann Fowler shall, for her offense, receive 20 stripes upon the bare shoulders and ask foregiveness of the said Capt. Thorowgood here now in Court and also the ensuing Sunday at Linhaven."

Two generations later, Adam's grandson, Argall Thorowgood, married Pembroke Fowler, the granddaughter of William and Ann Fowler!

To Adam Thorowgood, right was right, and he would not tolerate slander born of jealousy. Nor was he any respecter of the upper class if he felt that one of them had wronged him. In October 1637, he had taken Francis Land to court for violating an agreement with him. Francis Land had come to the County shortly before with a land grant adjoining Adam Thorowgood's. For some unknown reason, Land had made an agreement with Adam Thorowgood not to make any bargain with Cob Howell. Adam took him to court in the matter, and judgment was given in favor of Adam Thorowgood. Not satisfied with the lower court's decision, Francis Land appealed to the Quarter Court at Jamestown—to his sorrow. This was the result.

"18th October 1637
This is to certify that ye Commissioners of the Lower Norfolk Court have found by diverse witnesses that Francis Land could make no bargaine whatsoever with Cobb Howell without the consent of Adam Thorowgood. . . . Whereas it doth appear to this Court that Francis Land hath most falsely scandalized Capt. Adam Thorowgood as by sufficient witnesses apeareth. It is therefore ordered that the aforesd. Francis Land shall for the sd. offense ask the sd. Capt. Thorowgood's forgiveness now in Court and on Sunday come sennight at the pish. church at Linhaven."

Although these cases only concern Adam Thorowgood, he set an example for democracy in the court. Everyone could bring a case to court, and everyone was treated fairly. It may seem that the wealthier, if guilty, got off with a fine and an order to apologize in court and sometimes in church, while the poor often were subjected to corporal punishment, such as whippings or time in the stocks. In reality, the court badly needed funds for its many responsibilities, so for those who could pay, minor infractions such as drunkenness or swearing were punished with a heavy fine. And for those who could not pay, time in the stocks was a means of sobering up. In the case of one skilled carpenter, he was ordered to build a new set of stocks or give time for some other public work.

Slander was a different story. For those able to pay, there was the added humiliation of an apology in court and in church. For those unable to pay, the punishment definitely was lashes if they were found guilty.

Adam Thorowgood set another good example by his interest in the church. He was born in 1603, the seventh son of the Vicar of St. Boltolph's Parish Church, Grinston, Norfolk, England; therefore, a deep religious feeling was instilled in him at an early age. The Vicar of a country parish received only a small stipend, so his sons had an education but no future financing. Coming to the New World was an opportunity for this enterprising boy, but he never forgot his early religious training. He gave land for a new church on the Lynnhaven River, and he was surveying the bounds for the Lynnhaven Parish when he died at the early age of 36 in Jamestown. While attending a session of the House of Burgesses there, he and his servants were taken suddenly with some sort of fever. The following was recorded in Jamestown the next year.

> "At a Quarter Court holden at James City on the 8th of April 1641 Whereas it appeareth to the Court that the estate of Adam Thorowgood, deceased, stands indebted to the estate of George Calvert, physician, in the sum of 20:16.6 sterling for physics administered to the sd. Capt. Adam Thorowgood and his servants in the time of their sickness . . ."

His will had been probated there on April 27, 1640, at a Quarter Court, and the church must have been built, or at least started, and the graveyard laid out.

The boundaries for the Lynnhaven Parish that Adam Thorowgood had been laying out at the time he died are a memorial to him since they became the boundaries of Princess Anne County and, later, almost the exact boundaries of Virginia Beach.

Will of Adam Thorowgood:

> "I bequeath my soul into the hands of my Creator and Redeemer and my body to the earth from which it was taken, to be buried in the Parish Churchyard near my children, and I desire that all such as are owing by me either in England or Virginia, discharged and paid. I then give to the Parish Church of Lynnhaven one thousand

pounds of tobacco in leaf, to be disbursed for some necessary and decent ornament; to my well beloved brother, Mr. Edward Windham, one cow-calf of this year's fall, and one breeding goat; to my brother, Robert Hayes one breeding goat, and to each of Robert Hayes three sonns a breeding goat; to my godson, Adam Keeling, one breeding goat; to Jane Wheeler, one breeding goat, and one sow-shoat of half a year old; to William Stephens one breeding goat and one shoat of half a year old; and to my wife one mare and one foal, she to take her choice of wich she pleaseth, and one of the best sows and calves in the pen with half a dozen breeding goats and four breeding sows, together will all the houses and the orchard with the plantation at Lynnhaven, so as it extendeth, to wit: from the pond to the further side that parts it, and the ground called by name of the Quarter during her lifetime.

Item: do give and bequeath unto my son Adam all the rest of my houses and lands here in Virginia and elsewhere, when he shall come to the age of twenty-one years, for him and his heirs forever, and after the decease of my wife, then my son Adam is to enjoy and possess all that land, houses and orchard which I have given unto her during her life.

Item: For my cow, goats, hogs, servants and crop, and the rest of my estate, my will and desire is that they be divided amongst my wife and children, namely, Mrs. Sarah Thorowgood, my loving wife, my son, Adam Thorowgood, and my daughters, Ann, Sarah, and Elizabeth, with my mares and horses, excepting that mare and foal that I have given unto my wife particularly.

Item: In this, my last will and testament, I do make my dearly beloved wife, Mrs. Sarah Thorowgood, my sole executrix, and my wish is that she shall have the guardianship of all of my children, and their estates, until my daughters come to the age of sixteen years, and my son Adam to the age of one and twenty, and if in case any of my children die before they come of age above specified, that then it go to the rest of the children living. And for my wife's care and pains in bringing up the children in good virtue and training, and likewise for the handling and looking after their stocks of cattle, my will and desire is that she shall have all the male increase during the time of their guardianship.

Item: My will and desire is that my well beloved friends, Captain Thomas Willoughby and Mr. Henry Seawell, here in Virginia, and my dearly beloved brother, Sir John Thorowgood of Kensington, near London, and Mr. Alexander Harris, my wife's brother, living on Tower Hill, shall be my overseers of this my last will and testament.

Item: I do bequeath unto each of my overseers one gold ring apiece of twenty shillings price, as a pledge of my love."

Adam Thorowgood's untimely death was a blow to the county, but he already had set a pattern for others to adhere to, so his influence continued. His was a hard act to follow as more and more immigrants of all sorts and conditions poured into the Colony. But the older leaders' ranks were augmented by newcomers of background and ability. They included William Moseley, Henry Woodhouse and Simon Cornick, whose sons married into the established upper class, cementing the perpetuation of the old order.

This order was the rule of the Church of England and the law as laid down by the Governor, as the agent of the King, with the tacit approval of the House of Burgesses. The very first requirement of all immigrants was the oath of allegiance to King and Church, with obedience to both.

Since the power of the Church was as supreme as that of the King, positions on the vestry were eagerly sought in spite of their many responsibilities. It was the vestry who looked after the sick, the poor and orphans, as well as the morals of the congregation. The churchwardens had the more onerous task of ferreting out sinners and presenting them to the court. But election to the vestry was the cradle of a political career and a decided move upward in the social scale.

The justices of the court usually were or had been vestrymen. The only one who ever turned down an appointment to the court was Thomas Willoughby, who did so only because he expected to be out of the country for the following six months.

There was no courthouse built in Adam Thorowgood's lifetime. Until one could be built, the court met in a private house in different parts of the county. The docket was always full, what with the busy churchwardens and the sheriff (who presented transgressors of minor secular laws), and every court day, the third Wednesday of every month, was well attended. Everyone who could get there came, except women who were barred unless they had a case. It was not only the entertainment of the court proceedings which drew them, but it was a time to hear the news, to discuss candidates for elective offices, to do business, to socialize and to indulge in heavy drinking. Games of skill, strength and chance went on all day, and an occasional duel settled a case out of court. The host of the day was paid for the use of his house and for liquid refreshment for the justices. If he could obtain a license to operate a tavern at the same time, it was a lucrative opportunity in spite of any damage resulting.

Among the reasons for the court's constant need of funds was its responsibility for the collection of all taxes. These taxes included not only tithes for the maintenance of the church and salary of the rector, but also taxes imposed on every county for the salary and upkeep of the governor and his family, his servants and his contingent of soldiers. The court was also responsible for all salaries of justices, jurymen and sheriff and all expenses of burgesses for travel to Jamestown for the sessions, their expenses there and the recording of the proceedings.

Extra levies were imposed from time to time by the higher court for expenses of Indian wars and locally for unforeseen occurrences in the community, such as the Great Storm of January 1638. That storm not only did a huge amount of damage to the houses and cattle, but also wrecked and destroyed a ship of Swiss immigrants that had come into the Lynnhaven River. Some 300 of these immigrants were found either drowned or frozen to death.

Still another regular duty of the court was to approve all land grants already recorded in London and approved in Jamestown. This was more than routine because it was up to the justices to determine that there was no duplication in grants and no overlapping. Once a year, the court appointed inspectors to redefine all boundaries in order to avoid disputes over ownership. In this area which covered 950 square miles, this was no small chore.

All these duties were quite a burden, but these positions on the court were important to ambitious men. They meant prestige and, through that prestige, a rise in the social hierarchy.

So the church and the law worked hand in hand to keep the peace and maintain moral standards; that is, they did the best they could. The isolation of this county from the seat of government in Jamestown as well as its isolation from even another county by the three large bodies of water that surrounded it often led to an interpretation of the law as was most expedient at the time. There was little traveling about, except when the burgesses went to Jamestown or the wealthier crossed to England on business, so the colonists knew each other pretty well. The first estimate of the population was 305 in 1645. This number included the combined congregation of the Elizabeth River Parish and the Lynnhaven Parish, but it did not include women, children under 16, or servants.

Now that the rush of immigrants, which had begun in 1637, was increasing, so was trade with the outside world. The once ignored wilderness was leaping into an era of prosperity which brought its own problems and changes to the county.

PART TWO

Chapter 2

THE LEADERS, 1640–1691

Just a few months after the death of Adam Thorowgood, the first vestry of the Lynnhaven Parish was elected at a court sitting at the house of William Shipp. (Lower Norfolk County, Book A, part 1, f.3.)

"Court Aug. 3, 1640 .... the names of those which are recognized for the vestrie of the aforesd. pshe:

Mr. Edward Windham	Mr. Thos. Bullock
Mr. Henry Woodhouse	Mr. Thos. Danggone
Mr. Bartholomew Hoskins	Mr. Thomas Keeling
Mr. Thomas Todd	Mr. Robt. Hayes
Mr. Christopher Burrowes	Mr. John Lanckfield

Church Wardens: Mr. Thomas Todd and Mr. John Stratton"

While the church services had been held in Adam Thorowgood's house as early as 1637, the parish and its bounds had to be authorized by Jamestown, and the church had to be built. The creation of this parish was the result of the rapidly increasing population along the shores of the Lynnhaven River and farther south in the county. The boundaries of a parish were coterminous with the county boundary lines, and this was the first indication that Lower Norfolk County would eventually be split and Princess Anne County would come into being. When this split occurred in 1691, the parish boundaries became the boundaries of Princess Anne County, and so they remained almost exactly when Princess Anne County became the City of Virginia Beach in 1963.

A third division of the county, Southern Shores Parish, is referred to obliquely in an act of 1644, which confirmed the establishment of Lynnhaven Parish.

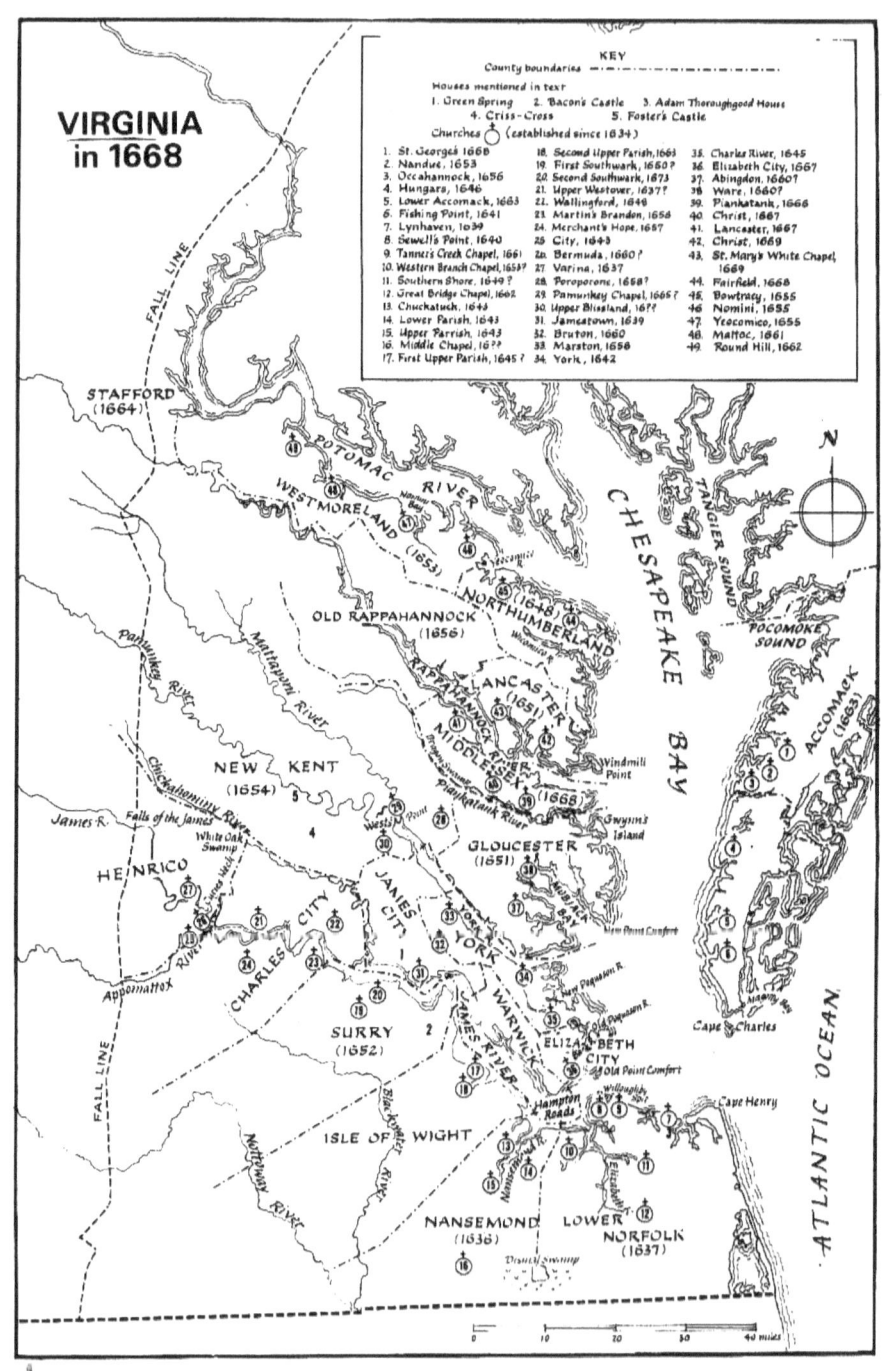

Map showing Tidewater Churches 1668. From *The Old Dominion in the Seventeenth Century*, Warren C. Billings. *Courtesy of the North Carolina University Press.*

"Provided that it be not prejudicial to the parishe of Elizabeth River and Southern Shoare by taking away any part of the said parishes . . ."

Southern Shores Parish is shown on an old map, a copy of which hangs in the office of the Clerk of the Court at Princess Anne. It was soon absorbed into the Lynnhaven Parish, due to the death of its minister, John Wilson, who in his lifetime was unable to collect his tithes of corn from his communicants and was frequently taken to court for his debts. It is important here only to show that there were at that time sufficient people in this lower part of the county, on the eastern side of the Western Branch of the Elizabeth River, to warrant a church at all.

The Established Church was soon in an uproar. With the execution of Charles I in 1649 by Oliver Cromwell, the State Church became Presbyterian until the overthrow of the Commonwealth and the accession of Charles II in 1660. An interesting story told in the town of Gloucester concerns a larger-than-life full-length portrait of Charles II, which hung in the hall of Whitemarsh Plantation. It was said that during the exile of the Crown Prince Charles in Paris after the death of his father, the wealthy leaders of Gloucester County at that time, Carters, Burwells and Warners included, visited the Prince in Paris and invited him to come to Virginia to be King of America! He was said to have politely declined, saying that he expected to be King of England before long, and gave the delegation this portrait for their trouble. Of course, other colonies had been established in America by that time, but since Virginia was the richest and most populous, these men apparently felt that they spoke for Virginia and that was all that was necessary.

In a way, they did speak for this Colony, for Governor Berkeley, immediately upon the death of Charles I, announced loyalty to the House of Stuart and extended a welcome to all refugee Cavaliers, the term "Cavaliers" meant loyal to the crown. It took two warships from England to force the submission of Governor Berkeley and the Council, but the Colony continued to welcome these refugees from the Commonwealth. Lower Norfolk County, in particular, ignored the Commonwealth, for the meteoric rise of aristocratic William Moseley and his family to wealth and prestige went further than mere hospitality.

"At the Court held for Lower Norfolk County Nov. 10, 1649: Upon the peticon of Mr. Wm. Moseley, it is thought fitt & ordered that the Sheriff bee authorized by vertue of this order, on munday next to put the sd. Moseley in possession of the houses & plantation, which he hired of George Heigham, and Mr. Moseley is to enjoy the same according to agreement proved by several testimonies on oath, & sd. Heigham to pay all court charges."

Mr. Moseley was so impressive that his oath to repay Mr. Heigham was sufficient. In 1652, however, he did receive a grant of 540 acres for the transportation of himself, his wife, his two sons and seven others. But it is said that they arrived with no money—only family portraits, jewels and a court calendar! He and Mrs. Moseley exchanged the jewels later for cattle with Francis Yeardley.

William Moseley was first appointed a Justice of the Court on March 16, 1649, even before he owned property, and he continued to serve until April 16, 1655. He was also a vestryman of Lynnhaven Parish in 1651. His will is that of a well-to-do man. It was written in 1652, but he did not die until late in the year of 1655, and his wife, Susannah, died shortly thereafter. His son William was granted probate of the will of his father and the same day qualified as administrator on the estate of his mother, "Mrs. Susan Moseley, Widd."

In 1650, William Moseley, Sr., built "Rolleston," a showplace of the time, and he also bought 800 additional acres from Thomas Todd. The house and all the land were escheated during the Commonwealth, but they were restored to his grandson, Colonel Edward Moseley, after the accession of Charles II. This Colonel Moseley added 1,110 more acres by two grants, in 1684 and 1688. Besides being a colonel in the militia, he held other prominent offices, and the family continued to be prominent through the colonial period. But a later Colonel Moseley, Edward Hack Moseley, Sr., who had been elected Burgess several times, was a friend of the traitor Benedict Arnold, as evidenced by this invitation, issued when the British occupied Portsmouth:

> "Brigadier General Arnold presents his Compliments to Colonel Edward Moseley Senior and requests the favor of his and Mrs. Moseleys Company to dinner and pass the Evening on Wednesday next.
> Portsmouth Feb 22 1781"

The Moseley family continued to live at Rolleston until 1865, when it evidently was escheated again, this time to the Union. It is said that it was used as a center for employment of freed slaves after the Emancipation. Today, not a trace of this fine home remains.

Henry Woodhouse, who was a member of the first vestry of the Lynnhaven Parish, came to Lower Norfolk County in 1637 from Bermuda, where his father had been governor. An educated man, he came from a long line of country gentry in England. His career was not as colorful as that of William Moseley, but he established a long line of respected descendants who continued to hold positions of prominence in the county, some of whom still own part of the original grant on Great Neck Point. Dr. Robert Woodhouse, who died in 1967, was the most beloved man in Virginia Beach. As one patient put it, "When I die, I hope that I will go to Heaven, for I am sure that Dr. Woodhouse will be there."

Henry Woodhouse was a member of the House of Burgesses in 1647 and 1652, and he was a County Commissioner (justice) from 1642 to 1652. He had come to Lower Norfolk County with his second wife, Mary, and his daughter by his first wife. Although he subsequently had seven children by Mary, she let him down in his last illness. (Book C. f.57.)

> "This Court, having heard many complaints concerning the unkinde usage of Mistress Woodhouse toward her husband, Mr. Woodhouse, in the time of his present sickness. It is by this Court thought fitt, that some adjacent Neighbors by appointment and consent of Mr. Woodhouse & the approbation of Coll. Sidney, shall have free liberty to resort to the house of Mr. Woodhouse to see that he have what shall be both sufficient & necessarie for him during his sickness, and according to his quality."

Mary Woodhouse had tired of all those eight children and had obviously run off with Nathaniel Batts. When Mr. Woodhouse died, she married Batts, and he sued for her share of the estate. In that same court, Mary Batts was presented "on suspicions of having familiarity with unclean spirits." She was exonerated, but she was not exactly popular. Nathaniel Batts was a rather unsavory character, as he had been in trouble for illicit trading with the Indians in the southern part of the county. Women were still extremely scarce at this time, and a woman with good prospects for an inheritance was an easy target for a glib-talking man.

In spite of their mother, all eight of Woodhouse's children married into other prominent families in the county, led exemplary lives, and had many children. The men served the county in important positions and were officers in the militia, fighting in the Virginia and Continental armies during the Revolution.

Two Woodhouse houses of different periods remain. The earliest is the charming little brick house on London Bridge Road known for many years as The Princess Anne Hunt Club. It was built by Captain William Woodhouse in 1760, and one brick in an outside wall is incised with the initials, "W W P—1760." His wife's name was Pembroke. Unfortunately, it was gutted by a fire just before Christmas 1981, after the present owner had carefully restored it. It is hoped that it soon will be re-restored.

In the area of Alanton is a house, now called "Old Comfort," that was built by a later Henry Woodhouse, about 1845. It is of frame construction and is on land which is part of the original Henry Woodhouse grant. Woodhouse family gravestones are behind it.

These are only two examples of the upper class immigrants of this period. There were many others who came with the background and ability to replace the ones who had died but we cannot name them all. However, the Cornick, Whitehurst, Lovett and, especially, the Lawson and Walke families were outstanding.

Not all of those who became leaders in the latter half of the 17th century were heroes, or even solid citizens. The growing prosperity had brought in British and Scottish merchants and many mariners, who were here for what they could get. Among them were rather "high flyers," notably Cornelius Lloyd, Charles Egerton and William Daynes.

Cornelius Lloyd was a merchant, a mariner and a land speculator. In 1635, he received a grant for 800 acres in the northern part of Elizabeth City Shire and, in 1636, 100 acres on the Elizabeth River, adjoining the land of Thomas Lambert (where Lambert's Point in Norfolk is now). In that same year, he also received, with his partners, 8,000 acres in Berkeley Hundred, upriver from Jamestown. He spent a good deal of time in this area, for in 1638, he furnished "buff coats" for the 15 men conscripted from Lower Norfolk County to fight the Nanticoak Indians. He expected to be reimbursed for this, but the court refused. The court overruled him again in 1640 when he tried to prevent a marriage and could not, or would not, give sufficient reason (LNC Book A, part 1 f.25. Dated 28 Sept. 1640.)

> "Whereas it appeareth to this court that Cornelius Lloyd hath fforbidinge ye bannes of matrimony between Tho. Tucker and Edy. Hawkins not Showing any cause. . . . Shall Quietly and peaceably agreed in the lawful course of marriage."

The Leaders 1641-1691 47

Also, there had been a previous scandal concerning Lloyd. (Book *A*, part 1, f.5. Court Sept. 10, 1638.)

> "Margaret Larrington servant to Mr. William Julian hath most infamously and maliciously scandalized and defamed her mistress, Mrs. Sarah Julian by reporting that she had often seen Cornelius Lloyd wth. her sd. mistress in ----- --- -----. But not being able to prove or substantiate same it is therefore ordered that she, the sd. Margaret shall receive one hundred stripes upon her bare shoulders and also mke. her sd. Mistress forgiveness heare now in Court."

Cornelius Lloyd was only 33 at the time and rich and glamorous, as well as smart, so these little peccadilloes did not deter the voters from electing him to the House of Burgesses in 1645, 1647, 1651 and 1653. He frequently received an appointment as Justice, also, and was made Lt. Colonel in the Militia in 1652.

Lloyd acquired 650 more acres in 1647 and 1653, but then he decided to move to Maryland. He leased his land near Little Creek, to be turned over to a John Watkins when he came of age, and departed with his wife, Elizabeth. He was dead by 1655, and at the death of his wife, his two sons inherited the rest of his property.

William Daynes did not get away with his philandering so easily. He had been a Burgess, the High Sheriff and a Justice in 1652, but in 1661 he got his comeuppance. (Book D p.303. Court: 15 Aug. 1661.)

> ". . . present: ffran: Morrison esq. Lt. Governor . . . having heard ye Scandalous report abroad of Mr. Wm. Daynes his entertaining & Living with Sarah ye wife of Thomas Watson, keeping her from her sd. husband, doth suspend ye sd Wm. Daynes from setting in Court & officiating the place of a Commander in ye County. . . ."

Charles Egerton's affair with Ann Bennett defies understanding. It seems that her husband had gone off in a huff to somewhere in the bay, but he threatened to come back and kill them both. He must have died along the way though, for when Charles Egerton died in 1688, he left all his land to the four children of Ann Bennett, since she had died, also. The only time Egerton had been taken to court was in 1683. (Order Book 1675 1686. Court: 18 March 1683/4.)

> "Whereas Mr. Thomas Gordon minister of Elizabeth River Parish made Complaint to Capt. Wm. Robinson & Mr. Mala. Thurston two of the members of this Court against Charles Egerton for mutinous words by him spoken . . . bound over to answer . . . att the Court and now nothing thereof appearing It is order that hee . . . bee acquitted from the same."

Philip Felgate never got into trouble with the Court, and there is no record that he had a land grant. But the following items from his inventory, just kept in a shed on land he rented, make an interesting list. (Book B. f.47. 1646.)

> "Philip Felgate, Gent.
> Lining for a short coat of squirrel skins
> 1 old beaver hat, one old gray felt, 1 old
> Montero cap, & a silver hat band
> a gold hatrht (?) sword
> And old crossbow, & an old Cibron (?), a suit of black armor, a head piece of white armor, a plain musket & rest, and a suit of bandeluroes (?)
> 2 fowling pieces & 1 birding piece, and a carbine without a lock.
> His coat of arms, 2 old pictures & escutcheon
> 5 barrels of powder, 5 barrels of shot
> 3 Monmouth caps."

Many of the early leaders died leaving no sons, but Thomas Willoughby, Francis Mason, Thomas Keeling and Adam Thorowgood all had sons who continued to expand their holdings and to maintain their positions of power and prestige through their own ability and their family connections. Two houses built by early leaders remain, beautifully restored as memorials of their owners' success in the 17th century. More importantly, they give us an intimate picture of upper class life in Lower Norfolk County at that time.

One is the house now known as "The Adam Thoroughgood House." Somewhere along the line, even the family changed the spelling of their name. As we have said, the site of the original Adam Thorowgood house, circa 1625-30, was found in 1955. But this house, circa 1640, was built either by Adam II or for him by his mother, Sarah. Adam II was not of age at this time, but he was either married or planned to be. This charming small house is of brick, with two walls laid in English bond and two in Flemish. Built on land of the original grant, it stayed in the Thorowgood family until 1804. It has been carefully restored and furnished, and it is one of the oldest brick houses in America. Now owned by the City of Norfolk, it is open to the public for a small fee.

Adam Thorowgood II had five sons and a daughter, all marrying into prominent families. He followed in his father's footsteps as a member of the vestry of Lynnhaven Parish, a Justice and a member of the Houses of Burgesses, and he became a colonel in the militia. In 1671, he received the following letter from the then justices. (Book E, f.24. Dated 18 April 1671.)

"Major Adam Thorowgood ---
 Sir: wee understand that by God's grace you are bound for England this Present Shipping, and therefore wish you a prosperous voyage & Safe Returne—ee ---- nott butt your sensible that we are Enjoyned by act of assembly to provide Severall Law books for the use of our County Court, and --- Request you bring with you att your return for the County Courts' use these several books. Viz: The Statutes at Large, a Doultan's Justice of Peace, and Office of Sherife and Swinbornes book of Wills and Testaments. . . . oblige . . . mayne your friends: Lemuel Mason, Wm. Moseley, Tho. Fulcher, francis Sayer, Gorge Fowler . . ."

The Act of Assembly ordering these books to be placed in every court had been passed years before, and these men, who had little knowledge of the law, were only now seeking them!

The other house, beautifully and authentically restored, was built in 1680 by Adam Keeling, son of Thomas Keeling. One of Adam Thorowgood's headrights in his "Grand Patent" of 1635 had been Thomas Keeling, and Keeling's grant here, dated 1651, was adjacent to Adam Thorowgood's land. Keeling named his eldest son Adam, after Thorowgood, and also named Thorowgood the boy's godfather. Thomas Keeling was a member of the first Lynnhaven Parish vestry and was a justice in 1656. He also was a lieutenant in the militia. (Order Book C. f.224 1656.)

"Lower Norfolk. Att a Court held the 26th of
 July 1656
Present: Lt. Col: Thomas Lambert
        Mr. John Martin
        Mr. Robert Powis
        Lt. Tho: Keeling—Commander
The Late coming in of ye Indians to Capt. Nathaniel Batteson—being taken into Consideration, It is ordered that Lt. Tho. Keeling shall have ye Command of ye Esterne & Westerne shoare of Lynhaven Untill ye next meeting of the Militia, to raise or Levy forces as occasion shall require & that Capt. Batteson shall Whensoever any Indians Come Unto him, acquainte Lt. Keeling Wth. it—Upon Complaint made Unto ye board It is ordered that W. Basnett nor none other shall Entertaone any Commerce Wth ye Indians at noe time whensover an Indian shall upon Occasion Come Into Capt. Battesons, but that the Inhabitants thereabouts shall assent to Conveye them to ye sd. Capt. Batteson his house."

People were still nervous about the Indians, but we believe that these Indians must have come from across the James River.

Thomas Keeling's will has never been found, but his son Adam's has. Adam Keeling's will was written in 1683. From it we have learned that his mother, Anne, married Robert Bray after Thomas died, and that his wife, also Anne, had been Anne Martin, daughter of John Martin from whom he had bought 1,400 acres. He left those 1,400 acres to his son John, "provided John makes a deed to his brother Adam for 2,000 acres, the plantation known as 'London Bridge' where his mother now lives, after her death." His eldest son, Thomas, was left 400 acres and "the home plantation." The Keelings had the habit of naming the eldest son after his grandfather, so it was Thomas to Adam, Adam to Thomas and Thomas to Adam for generations.

The Keeling house, known as "Ye Dudlies," on Great Neck Point, is a large two-story brick house and has many interesting features. The bricks are laid in the Flemish bond pattern, and there is an unusual design of blue headers in the north wall. There are cupboards on the inside of that wall on each side of the fireplace, and there is a small window in each. To the left of the eight-foot-wide hall there is another large room with a huge fireplace. That was the kitchen, dining hall and general family living room. In the 17th century, there was no outside kitchen building for summer cooking, and food was cooked over an open fire or in a pit. The two bedrooms upstairs seem inadequate for a man of Keeling's means with four children, but people were indifferent in those rough times as to where they slept, and in winter, the choice spot was near the kitchen fire. Children were bedded down three, four or more to a bed.

Two other small houses remain—that of Thomas Allen, a mariner, and a slightly larger one which we believe was built by John Stratton. These houses have been changed much over the years, however. Thomas Allen's one-room house is now the kitchen surrounded by a large house built around it much later. This house is known as Broad Bay Manor.

Forty years had passed between the building of the first Adam Thorowgood house and the Keeling house. The fight to survive in the wilderness was fast fading into an era of prosperity for the upper class. Slavery had become a fact of plantation life. The upper class remained the rulers, but they were hard-pressed to keep up with the demands of Jamestown and the problems of the rapid population growth. In addition, the church was attempting to end the free-wheeling independence of the local courts towards "Dissenters" and minor infractions. Thomas Willoughby and Lemuel Mason were both tried for profanity and fined 200 pounds of tobacco each while they were members of the court! (Order Book 1675–1686.)

The wives of these leaders were busy having babies, watching them die, and becoming pregnant again. Only the strongest of these women survived all of their pregnancies, and it was a toss-up as to which was the worst, the midwives or the doctors. But, then, there was Sarah Thorowgood, the widow of Adam Thorowgood I, a woman so strong that she was the envy of every woman in the Colony and a match for any man. Here is her story.

Beautiful and high-spirited, Sarah Thorowgood managed to bend every man to her will. Although her ambitions were purely selfish, she was an outstanding leader of women as well as men. Born Sarah Offley, the daughter of a well-to-do merchant of London, she was only 15 when she met and married Adam Thorowgood and returned with him to the New World. Like other women, she had several children in rapid succession and watched them die. Then, she had three daughters and a son, all of whom lived and were minors at the time of Adam's early death. She doubtless had helped her husband in his rise, and they probably had used her dowry to buy the first land in Elizabeth City. But she stayed in the background while he was alive.

Once Adam was dead, however, Sarah emerged into the limelight. Even though Adam's bequests to her in his will seem most generous, she was not satisfied and requested the court at the time of the recording of the inventory to reserve the following for her own use.

> "Imprimis: One bed, with blankets, rug and the furniture thereunto belonging; two paire of sheets and pillow cases; one table with carpet, table cloth and napkins, knives and forks; one cupboard and cupboard cloths; six chairs, six stools, six cushions, two coverlets, one linen, one woolen; six pictures hanging in the chamber; one pewter basin and ewer; one pair snuffers, one warming pan, one bed pan, one pair of andirons in the chimney; one pair tongs, one ash shovel; one chair of wicker for a child.
>
> Plate for the cupboard; one salt cellar, one bowl, one tankard, one wine cup, one dozen spoons (which I claim as a gift exprest in the inventory.)."

Captain Thomas Willoughby and Henry Seawell, named in Adam's will as overseers of the estate, knew Sarah well and were reluctant to tangle with her in any administration of the will. (Book A, part 2, f.3.)

> "Dated 15 March 1640.
> Captain Thomas Willoughby hath disclaimed in Court for himself & Mr. Henry Seawell ye Overseeing of ye Last Will & Testament of Captain Adam Thorowgood, desed."

Perhaps she had requested their resignation, but either way, she had gained command.

In her defense, we must report that Sarah firmly established her loyalty to her deceased husband, at least in her own eyes. Fast with a subpoena, she shortly took one Goody Layton to court for saying to her face that "No one could get a bill [payment] out of Capt. Thorowgood." Under oath, Goody Layton admitted that she had, and she turned away with a "Pish!" when asked to produce one who had not. Then, said Madam Thorowgood, "Goody Layton, you must not think to put me off with a pish, for if you have wronged him, you must answer for it. If he is dead, I am here in his behalf to right him." Goody Layton was ordered to ask her pardon by kneeling before the court and again on the next Sunday at the parish church.

Sarah Thorowgood was not a woman to stay unmarried long. Within a year, she married John Gookin, son of Daniel Gookin, a wealthy landowner from Newport News who had imported eight servants for himself in the "Flying Hart" in 1621 and 12 more in 1623 in the "Providence." Daniel Gookin had come from Carringgaline, Near Cork, Ireland, where he had made a fortune exporting oxen, horses and cattle to Virginia. When he decided to remove himself to the Colony, he received a grant of 2,500 acres and, subsequently, 500 more acres on the Rappahannock. Then he moved to Massachusetts where his tombstone was found many years later. His son John received a grant of 500 acres on the Nansemond River in 1636, another 500 acres there in 1638, and in 1641, 640 acres in Lower Norfolk County on Samuel Bennett's Creek and adjoining Adam Thorowgood's land.

John Gookin was immediately popular, becoming a captain in the militia, then a colonel, a vestryman and a justice. After they were married, he moved into Sarah's house, "The Mansion," and the couple had one child, Mary. It was a happy marriage, but a short one. Within two years, John Gookin was dead, leaving Sarah with another child to bring up, Mary Gookin.

Both Sarah and John Gookin knew the law regarding the property of minors; nevertheless, Capt. Gookin wrote the following letter to Governor Berkeley in 1642.

> "To Ye Right Worshipful Sir William Berkeley Knt. . . . behalfe of Capt. Thorowgood's Children . . . . showeth . . . . parcell of land in two dividents ye one Six Hundred Acres belonging to Adam, ye heire of Capt. Adam Thorowgood dec. ye other two hundred Acres belonging to Anne Thorowgood, bequeathed to her by Will of one Robert Camm . . . The land being Orphants' we desire to have Act explained whether or not it may be sould from them.
> John Sibsey   Henry Woodhouse
> Edw. Windham   Henry Seawell"

The answer was:

> "The Answer of ye Governor and Counsell to ye request of ye Commissioners Say that it is ye positive resolution of ye Act that no Orphant's land can be any wayse be lett sett or alienated for longer time than Ye Expiration of their minorities.
> Richard Lee Cler. Court."

The Justices should have known what the answer would be, but Sarah was determined. There had been a long controversy between Sarah vs. John Stratton and Thomas Causon over this land, which was on the east side of the Lynnhaven River. It seems odd that there was any case at all, for in Land Grant Book 1, p. 217, is recorded, "CAPT. ADAM THOROWGOOD . . . 600 acres northerly upon the first or second creek upon the *Eastern* side of the Lynnhaven River & Chesopean River." It dragged on, however, and among the dispositions taken in this case was that of Henry Woodhouse. (Book A, part 2. f. 17.)

> "Henry Woodhouse aged 35 years or thereabouts . . . Sayeth that he neaver heard Capt. Adam Thorowgood make any other Clayme for his 600 acres of land but beginning at ye Second Creeke, and that ye reason he Claymed ye ponds or oyster creeke was to Carrie some times a dish of Oysters to Sir John Harvie and that he thought he might have a little more privilege than others in respect he was Commander . . ."

The case was finally settled, and John Stratton and Thomas Causon relinquished all claims.

Although John Gookin had died and could not help her in her next case, Sarah did not hesitate to defend her daughter's good name. (Order Book 1637–1675.)

> "Court 8 Oct 1644
> Whereas it appeareth to the Court the confession of James Lapham, that he has in a most bestial and uncivil manner by most scandalous and false suggestions defamed Sarah, the daughter of Capt. Adam Thorowgood, dec. to her great disparagement and defamation. It is therefore ordered that the sd. Lampan receive 50 lashes at the mulberry tree well applied to his bare back."

Also:

> "Whereas it appeareth to the Court that John Farnehough hath defamed the daughter of Mrs. Gookin widow of Capt. Adam

Thorowgood to her discredit through most rude and false suggestions. It is therefore ordered that the sd. Farnehough shall publicly in the Parish Church at Lynnhaven in the time of devine service, ask the sd. Mrs. Gookin and her children's forgiveness, put in security for his good behavior and pay unto the sd. Mrs. Gookin 815 lbs. of tobacco for her charges herein expended."

Sarah's daughters married well: Sarah to Simon Oversee, Elizabeth to Capt. John Michael of Northampton County, Anne to Job Chandler of Port Tobacco, Maryland, and Mary Gookin much later to Anthony Lawson.

Since 1640, the court had been attempting to get an accounting from Sarah of the cattle left to his children by Adam Thorowgood. The best they could get was the following, which meant as little to them as it does to us. (Book A, part 3. f.17.)

"Jan. Court 1645
A true and perfect account of the Meat Cattle belonging to the estate of the Children of Capt. Adam Thorowgood, Lynhaven. Geofry Wight Goat Keeper:

```
ffower old Rammes .............................. 004
Three weakers .................................. 003
Eleaven old Ewes................................ 011
Young Ewes ..................................... 033
     Ye total dead.............................. 033
```

This may be an account of those killed by wolves, which had become so numerous at that time that the bounty for killing one had been raised from 50 pounds of tobacco to 200 pounds.

Edmund S. Morgan, in *American Slavery American Freedom*, has an amusing account of the efforts of the court to get a proper accounting.

"The commissioners of Lower Norfolk County, who were obviously afraid of her (Sarah), asked her politely but unsuccessfully on ten different occasions to render an account of the cattle of her children by Adam Thorowgood. Finally they sent the under sheriff, Thomas Ivey, to levy a fine of 500 lbs. of tobacco on her. She replied to the sheriff's hesitant communication with a letter in which she flatly refused to pay a fine or to appear in court, and hinted broadly that the court was going beyond its jurisdiction. It was unheard of, she said, that a mother should be asked to account for the property of her own children. She closed with a characteristic feminine touch—'My respects to yourselfe and wyfe most kindly remembered to whom I have sent a basket of apples per the bearer.' The next sheriff, the following year, like Ivey, lacked the nerve to press the matter further. The court threatened to fine him if he did not proceed. But before anyone else dared to face up to her, Francis Yeardley had married her, and upon his promise that he would render the account, the court, with "undisguised relief repealed it's 500 lb. fine."

Shortly before Sarah's marriage to Francis Yeardley took place, there was a court investigation of the death of Mr. Peregrine Bland, and Francis Yeardley testified as follows. (Book B. p.42.)

"I ffrancis Yeardley, deposed this 12th day of June 1647 before Capt. Edward Windham doe testify as followeth, vizt. That on the eleventh day of this instant month Mr. Peregrine Bland being at the house of Mrs. Sarah Gookin in Linhaven broke his fast, at the table in company with me this deponent and others, and fell hartily and passed away his time healthfully and cheerfully; and after breakfast past some tyme with the company, in divers discourses, drinking in the interim moderately a dramm, and a cupp of Sack: till his occasions calling him to goe with Mr. Eyres and Mr. Hall, Chirosurgeon, to the Eastern Branch, he went to the gate with me the sd. deponent in various discourses, when being at the gate I requested him to goe in againe until the heate of the day was over but could not persuade him, and he tried to sit down at the gate till Mr. Eyres came; but rose suddenly up againe and went on his way, whereupon I returned in to call Mr. Eyres whoe went forth with out after him desiring a man to direct them to Little Creek, myselfe remaining within sent a negro to them. The next tydings I heard was that he was turned aside into the barnefield and fallen asleepe; some three hours after Mr. Windham and Mr. Eyres brought me in the sadd tydings of his death in the barnefield. I went out to see him, and found him lying on his right side, his Arms under his head, dead and also purging at the mouth frothy blood."

This testimony excused Sarah from having to go to court and from being implicated in any way. She then married Francis Yeardley, even though he was only 23 to her 32 or 33. A younger son of Sir George Yeardley, who had been governor of the Colony from 1619–1621 and who made a fortune for himself as governor as well as by acquiring a great deal of land on the Eastern Shore of both Maryland and Virginia, Francis is described by Beverly Fleet as "a pompous ass," taking people to court on the slightest provocation. He received a grant of 590 acres in Lower Norfolk County in 1648, and he was a Justice in 1651 and 1652 and a Burgess in 1653.

The story of Capt. Yeardley's trade with William Moseley in 1652 for the Moseley family jewels is well-known and is in the Lower

Norfolk County records for that year. It is so lengthy, however, and the language is so difficult that we will give the details of that transaction here in simple English. For nine head of meat cattle, two draft oxen, two steers and five cows belonging to Capt. Yeardley—that is, to Sarah—William and Susannah Moseley gave him one gold hatband, one buckle and tipp (?) of gold set with diamonds, one diamond ring, one ruby, one sapphire and one emerald, worth in all 11 lbs. 4 shs. Sending them to Capt. Yeardley, Mrs. Moseley included a letter in which she graciously wished "Mistress Yeardley health and prosperity to weare them in, and I give you both thanks for your kinde token." (*Lower Norfolk County Antiquary*, Edward W. James, vol. 11, p. 121, 122.)

As he saw how much his wife loved jewelry, Colonel Yeardley (he had been promoted) continued his gifts. He died in 1655, and Sarah was a widow for the third time. But she lived only two more years, hardly enough time to contemplate another marriage. A fighter to the end, her last court case was just a few days before she died (Book D. p. 900.)

> "Court 18 Aug 1657
> Whereas certain differences are depending betweene Mistress Sarah Yeardley plaintiff: and Jonathan Taylor defendant, ye plantacon ye sd Taylor lives on for ye planting of an orchard and ground made waste of. It is therefore ordered that Mr. Hoskins and Lancaster Lovett for Mistreee Yeardley and Thomas Allen and Edw. Cooper (made choice of by the court) for ye sd. Taylor are requested to meet on ye first September next at ye sd. Taylors plantation & there to View & take notice of some trees planted pretending it to bee a sufficient Orchard & also of land made waste of by ye sd. Taylor & to give in their report at ye next Court in writing upon oath how they find it & then to bee determined."

Sarah Offley Thorowgood Gookin Yeardley died in August 1657 after a full and adventurous life. Her will left no doubt that of her three husbands, she preferred John Gookin. (Book D. p. 117.)

> "Whereas Mistress Sarah Yardley late deceased did by her last Will & Testament order that her best diamond necklace & Juell should bee sent for England to purchase six diamond rings & two black tombstones, as by ye sd. Will appeareth. I Nicholas Trott Merchant have received of Coll: John Sidney, Exec. of ye sd. Mistress Yardley ... necklace & Jewells ... promise ... to make sale ... to purchase ye above menconed rings and tombstones (ye Dangers of ye Seas only expected) & to send them in to ye Virginia next shipping especially ye two tombstones ... ye first february 1658."

The two black tombstones were for herself and John Gookin, and her order was that she be buried beside him. The six diamond rings may have been for her daughters and daughter-in-law, but they more likely were for friends whom she wished to remember her favorably.

When storms and erosion caused the whole graveyard at the first Lynnhaven Church at Church Point to disappear under the water, the stones of all those buried there were lost. But as late as 1819, one was still barely visible below. We are indebted to the anonymous person who copied the inscription on Sarah's stone, and happily, it is preserved for us.

> "Here lyeth ye body of
> Captain John Gookin
> and also ye body of
> Mrs. Sarah Yeardley
> who was wife to Captain Adam Thorowgood
> first, Captain John Gookin and
> Colonel Francis Yeardley
> who deceased August 1657"

Sarah's death was no doubt a relief to many, including her son, Adam Thorowgood II. He soon came of age, assumed his rightful place as a leader and moved his large family of five sons—Adam, Argall, John, Francis and Robert—and a daughter Rose into his mother's house. In the circle of leaders, he was joined by others, sons of immigrants who quickly surpassed the accomplishments of their fathers, such as William Cornick, son of Simon, Francis Land II and Thomas Willoughby II. New names came into prominence as the older leaders died or stepped aside, such as Lemuel Mason, son of Francis Mason. Anthony Lawson and Thomas Walke strode on the scene with education and family backing, and enterprising members of the middle class began to assert themselves.

One of the problems which beset these leaders was the power of the Church of England, which was shared with the King who was reigning "by the divine right of God." So many statutes were imposed on the colonists concerning their absolute personal purity that not only do they seem ridiculous to us today, but they also seemed ridiculous to the justices then who were striving for common sense in interpretation of the laws. The following scandals in the Elizabeth River Parish Church focused unwelcome attention on ecclesiastical conduct here and made the vestrymen and justices very uncomfortable, as they were representatives of the Church as well as the King. It was the responsibility of the Bishop of London to send ministers to the colonies, but often he sent men who really were not qualified by training and character to assume the guardianship of the souls of the colonists. Some did not wish to come at all, for part of their meager compensation was the food they could produce for themselves on the Glebe, land set aside for this purpose.

Such was Thomas Harrison, minister in 1645, who was accused in court of not reading the books of Common Prayer and not administering the Sacrament of Baptism according to the Canons of the Church. He was ordered to the next Quarter Court at Jamestown and fired. Actually, he was a Puritan, and he departed for New England.

The next minister, Sampson Calvert, in 1649 confessed to adultery. (Book B. f.126.)

> "Court 10 November 1649
> Whereas Mr. Sampson Calvert, Minister of Elizabeth River Parish, hath acknowledged to have Committeed ye grivous Sinne of Adultery with Anne, ye wife of Lawrence Phillips: Now upon ye hearty Contrition of ye sd. Mr. Calvert concerning his sd. foule offense in writing under his own hand, It is therefore ordered that hee doe make ye same confession in both Churches by reading ye sd. Writing to ye people several Sundays, Vixt: Sunday next Come sennight at ye parish Church & ye Sabbath day following at ye Chappell."

Needless to say, he was thereupon out of a job, and in 1650, at a court held 20 March:

> "Upon ye request of Capt. Tho. Willoughby esqr. (by his sonne) an attachment Is granted against as such of ye estate of Sampson Calvert (when he shall find it) as shall make Sattisfaction for Eight hundred pounds of tobacco & Cask, with Court Charges, upon order of the Court."

This, after Mr. Calvert had been so carefully chosen by the vestry and sanctioned by the Bishop on London! Anne Phillips may have seduced him, for she was not only notorious herself, but she had been convicted in court of defaming a dozen others. She eventually married Francis Land.

Then, an act of the House of Burgesses condemning the whole county for not attending church was an open invitation to those of other sects to come in. (Book C. f.113.)

> "Court: 15 Dec. 1654
> We of ye Grand Inquest after due Inquiries made doe present unto

ye Court ye general breach of ye Sabbath throughout the whole County; which we conceive is now chiefly occasioned through want of a godly Minister amongst us in ye county. Wherefore, wee humbly pray and desire that some speedy course may be taken to procure an able minister & Same employed for that purpose, lett ye Charge be what it will. Wee. . . . (and hope all ye rest of ye County) shall bee verry willing and reddy to undergoe."

The Lynnhaven Parish Church was also without a minister at this time, which happened frequently. Many Presbyterians had quietly moved into the county during the period of the Commonwealth, and they even had a church on what is now First Colonial Road. Two of their ministers at different times were borrowed to read services for the Lynnhaven Parish Church. They were the Reverend John Porter and the Reverend Josias Mackie.

The Quakers were a different story, as their religion did not allow them to take the oath of allegiance or take up arms for any reason. They were particularly obnoxious to Governor Berkeley, who wrote the following letter to the High Sheriff, Richard Conquest, the son-in-law of John Sibsey. (Book D. f.264.)

"Mr. Conquest -
I hear with sorrow that you are very remiss in your office, in not stopping the frequent meetings of this most pestilent Sect of ye Quakers. Whether this be so or not, I doe hereby order you, by virtue of ye power ye grand assembly has intrusted mee with, not to suffer any more of their meetings or Conventions & C. . ., if any such shall be refractory, that you send them up prisoners to James City. I expect your obedience to this which I send you without closing, that all may take notice of it.
ffor: Mr. Richard Conquest: sherr
of Lower Norfolk County
Dated: 27 June 1663 Your loving ffiend
William Berkeley"

It is recorded that Mr. Conquest sent his constables out several times to round them up, but there is nothing in the order books to confirm that they were ever sent to Jamestown. Since we hear no more of them, they more than likely went to either North Carolina or Maryland or just kept out of sight. By 1687, one Raymond, a Papist priest, was celebrating mass, claiming the Liberty of Conscience Act of 1665 and a young man about that time was taken to court for not attending church. When he said, "I'm a Catholic," he was excused. The attitude of laissez faire still prevailed.

At any rate, the Established Church recovered from the crisis, and the church wardens continued to present to the court cases of "Incontinence before marriage," profanity and defamation of character. Even so, the Church here was not as strict nor the punishments for refractions so severe as the Puritan Church in New England. There, the Church was "the law" and only members could vote or even own land.

Other troubles concerned the people here more. The Dutch, following the exploration of Long Island and the Hudson River by Hendrick Hudson, chartered the Dutch West Indian Company and founded New Amsterdam after purchasing Manhattan Island for 60 guilders, i.e., $24. This led to a struggle for colonial supremacy between the English and the Dutch (Anglo-Dutch War, 1652–1654). The English took New Amsterdam and renamed it New York, but there were repercussions and hostile acts by the Dutch against the shipping activities in the Chesapeake Bay.

On June 4, 1667, a tobacco fleet of 20 vessels, lying off Hampton and protected only by one British frigate, was attacked by five Dutch men-of-war, and all 20 were captured. Again, in 1673, nine Dutch warships overcame two British frigates and captured nine tobacco ships of a convoy, the rest escaping up the Nansemond and James rivers. These disasters to the tobacco fleets caused great financial losses. After the first one, an act was passed to erect five forts against invasion and depredations of hostile men-of-war, one on each of the "main" rivers—the James, the Nansemond, the York, the Rappahannock and the Potomac; and in 1673, two more forts were authorized— one in Isle of Wight County and one in Lower Norfolk County, on the Elizabeth River where Norfolk stands today, possibly on the site of Fort Wool. This fort was maintained until at least 1679, as an account of fort duties to the county to May 29, 1679, was presented to the court. Colonel Lemuel Mason was commander of the fort at that time.

Bacon's Rebellion of 1676 did not affect Lower Norfolk County, as the hostilities mostly took place elsewhere. Only one resident of this county is recorded as being a member of that rebellion: William Carver, a captain in the militia who had served as a Justice and a Burgess and who was a wealthy landowner. He was hanged and his land escheated to the Crown, but it was later restored to his son, Richard. This land is now part of the City of Portsmouth.

There were also great losses due to storms. The violent storm in January 1637 had caused much damage to livestock and property.

Another terrible storm occurred in 1667, similar to the hurricanes which we still experience occasionally, only worse. Crops were ruined, houses were flattened, and cattle in the marshes drowned as the flood tide, pushed by the wind, rushed up the creeks and rivers. It is reported that hailstones as large as turkey eggs fell with enough force to kill man or beast. This was followed by a particularly frigid winter incurring severe mortality. At the same time, an epidemic struck the cattle, and half of them in the county died. Also, French and Spanish ships were beginning to make periodic raids, and pirates had now begun to roam this exposed coast.

The colonists had thought that once Charles the Second was on the throne, at least some of the strict laws would be relaxed. But along came an "updated" set of laws, with the command that they be strictly observed. (Book D. ff351 & 352.) Jealous of their accustomed power to rule by "common sense," the leaders here were infuriated, to say the least. We have put these laws in modernized English and punctuation for easier reading.

"Recorded 16 Aug. 1662
The names of the Grand Jury sworn on the behalf of the County for six months:
Thomas Fulcher—Foreman

James Thelaball	William Capps
John Gigg	John Workman
John Kelly	George Fowler
James Harris	Thomas Harding
Richard Jones	George Ashall
	Thomas Green

The Charges to the Grand Jury FIRST you are to present such as offend God's law by swearing, blashemy, contempt for His ordinances, profaning the Sabbath, absenting themselves from public worship, frequenting of unlawful assemblies under pretense of religion, fornicators, either open or such as live by color of pretended marriage, or such as refuse to have their children baptized in contempt of the sacrament.

NEXT—such crimes as are directed against the Majesty of the King, as treason, petty treasons, murders, rapes and all other felonies. And then such as shall violate the laws of this, his Majesty's Country, made especially for the welfare of his subjects here.

IF—the County Court shall neglect to set up a pillory, a pair of stocks & a whipping post and a ducking stool within six months, or to build a prison within eight months, or to order the Vestry of each parish to divide their parish into precincts for the neighborhood to enjoy, & to see that the bounds and marks of every man's land renewed between Easter and Whitsuntide next, or to appoint surveyors of highways yearly in October Court, or to provide English weights and measures for standards, whereby to try others by Christmas come twelve months, such neglect of Courts you are to present every March at the General Court to the Governor and Council, or to the Assembly if the sitting.

ALSO—the Vestries or persons not obeying the said orders and all persons transgressing the penal laws following you are to present to the Court at the end of six months, Viz: All persons enclosing or stopping the highways, this being a common offense. Also divulgers of false news that tend to the breach of his Majesty's peace. Those that shall plant or replant after the tenth of July or make seconds or slipps. Those who by December come twelve months shall not have planted their portion of mulberry trees, being ten trees for every hundred acres of land they possess. And those not planting two acres of corn for every tithable person planting tobacco in their family. Those that shall export hides, wool, or iron, or mares, or sheep, or English goods bought in that country, coopers making tobacco casks above the standard guage, or of unseasoned timber, persons proclaiming their drunkeness by shooting at weddings and funerals, persons not providing their portion of arms and ammunition, i.e. a gun, two pounds of powder and eight pounds of shot for everyone in their family able to bear arms, millers taking above six pence for two, or not keeping weights and standards, persons killing hogs in the woods under pretense of wild ones and cutting off their ears, and also the receivers of such hogs. These several things we have charged you with, you shall be careful in making due presentment of according to the oath you have taken, by performance of which you will discharge your duties to God and to the King, and prove yourselves necessary members in promoting the good of the Commonwealth you live in."

In explanation, the banning of planting after the tenth of July means tobacco, as the government was attempting to stabilize the price and the quality of the crop.

As to the mulberry trees "ten to be planted for every 100 acres," Charles II was still trying to establish the manufacture of silk by the silkworms feeding on the leaves. Most sources say that idea, one of the earliest dreams of the London Company, was a failure, but it is said that Charles II's coronation robe was made of silk from this Colony. If so, he had a sentimental desire to see this industry flourish, as well as the practical one of replacing silk from the Orient with the Virginia product. But we believe that the project came to naught, as the imported white mulberry trees, which the silkworms preferred, did not flourish here. Even the native red mulberry is seen only occasionally now, grown solely for ornamental purposes, as the fruit is soft and insipid. Corn has always been the best crop in this sandy soil, grown both for home consumption as well as export,

Exporting hides, wool, horses and sheep from here was strictly forbidden, as that would have meant competition with the Mother Country.

The colonists considered the banning of shooting their muskets at weddings and funerals an affront. The firing of cannon as a salute has been a longtime custom in England, witness the cannonade at the birth of the new prince, the son of the Prince of Wales, and the custom carried over to this country as a salute to visiting dignataries from other governments. Having no cannon, the colonists felt that firing their guns, which they were required by law to carry, was a fitting salute to the dead and, also, to a couple entering the new world of matrimony. Of course, this was a waste of precious gunpowder and, along with the huge consumption of rum at these events, which usually lasted for several days, there also were some accidental murders. But the people felt that one of their inalienable rights as Englishmen had been taken away with this ban, and they were disgruntled. The Lower Norfolk County Court got around this unpopular edict by stating that no gun could be shot off without an officer of the militia present. The penalty was 1,000 pounds of tobacco.

These acts also prohibited import into England of any goods from America, except in ships of which the owner, the master and the major part of the crew were English. They also excluded all foreign ships from the English coastal trade. (Encyclopedia of American History, Richard B. Morris.) There had been heavy trade by Dutch ships, and the Virginia Assembly in 1655 declared that freedom of trade would be maintained. This protest was ignored by Parliament, whose act of 1660 required that articles of colonial growth be shipped only to England, or her colonies, with ships sailing from the colonies required to give bond that they would unload the enumerated commodities only in the Realm. Further, an act of 1663 dictated that all European goods destined for the colonies must be shipped from England on English-built ships. This was followed by required duties at the ports of clearance in 1673; and by 1705, the list included naval stores, which hit this area hard as there had been a brisk trade in Europe, as well as England, of rosin, turpentine, hemp, masts, yards and bowsprits.

All of these restrictions led to a growing disenchantment with Parliament and a common practice of smuggling. In the remaining old houses from the colonial period, there are still evidences of what was once an underground tunnel leading from the cellar to the adjacent waterway. These tunnels were once thought to be a means of escape from the Indians, but that is erroneous. They were well-built and lined with brick to facilitate the moving of goods to and from a ship by night without being seen by the customs officers. These acts were obnoxious to all Virginians, but particularly to the men of this county who had enjoyed the independence of their isolation and the freedom of their connecting waterways leading to the sea.

About this time, the area around Currituck Sound and the North River was attracting many settlers. The following court order relating to the discovery of an inlet "to the southward" was, we believe, the inlet known as "Old Currituck Inlet," which was inside the Virginia line and across from the mouth of the North River. It was filled in by sands in an ocean storm. If so, this was a very handy inlet for ships to come in and out, away from the prying eyes of the customs officers. (Book D, p.85.)

> "James City Court: 1657
> Recorded: the 17th August 1657
> Att a quarter court held in James Citty the:
> 11th June 1657
> The Court taking into Consideracon ye great paines & trouble Wch Mr. Nathaniell Batts hath taken in the discovery of an Inlett to the southward which is likely to bee much advantageous to the inhabitants of this Collony: have therefore ordered that ye sd Batts be hereby protected from all his Creditors Within this Country for one yeare & a day, Without any trouble or Molestacon upon Consideracon that the sd Batts shall always bee ready upon ye Countries service & to peticon to the next Assembly for Confirmacon hereof."

Nathaniel Batts must have been in trouble again after his free year was up, for in 1660, he moved to North Carolina. (Book D, p.293.)

> "Court Jan. 18, 1660
> To all to whom these presentments Come—greeting. These are to certifie that I Kisontaneoch Kinge of Yansakin have Sold & alienated from myselfe my heirs or assigns that Land which Mr. Mason & Mr. Willoughby formerly bought of mee but never paid me for, to Mr. Nath. Batts for a valuable Consideracon in hand receized, viz: all ye Lands on the Southwest side of Pascotanck River, from ye mouth of ye sd. river to ye head of Bogin Creeke, to have & to hold to him & his heirs for Ever, as Witness my hand ye twentieth fowerth of Sep. 1660.
>
> Kisotanecoh
> his mark"

Mr. Willoughby and Mr. Mason did not necessarily renege on their bargain, for it lately has come out that Manhattan Island was sold twice to the Dutch, by two different Indian tribes, and the same land on Long Island was sold several times.

But even before this discovery, settlers had started to move into Currituck. Many of the wealthier planters had patented land for their cattle in the marshes there. William Basnett, who had come to the Colony as a headright for Henry Southell and evidently an indentured servant to him in 1636, received a grant in 1658 for 800 acres "on the seaboard" and had already been living there for some time, as had William Brooke, who owned adjoining land according to the grant. In 1664, Basnett patented 510 additional acres, "Dividing the land of Richard Selby," and in 1675, 1,500 more acres. New names settled on the North River: Thomas Jackson, John White, James Heath, Francis Skipper, Henry Southern and still others. Edmund Moore had land before 1657, for his grant of 200 acres was bounded by Willian Basnett's land. A William Capps received a grant of 500 acres in Currituck on Nonney's Creek in 1684. He was the son of the William Capps who earlier had settled on Stratton's Creek.

Records from New England whaling ships show that they came into this inlet in Back Bay. (Book E. f.175.)

> "Dated 23 March 1673
> ... Mordecay Bouden of Road Island merchant ... unto John Swayne of Elizabeth River in Virginia Ship Carpenter .... my plantation lying on the East side of the North River of Corrotuck."

Mordecay Bouden, mariner, had received the grant for these 600 acres in February 1673 for the importation of himself four times, as well as others he had brought in.

> "Court: 16 May 1684
> Whereas Capt. Jno. Gibbs and Henry Gibbs his brother Some time before this sitting of this Court & afterwards the Court being sett did in the Court house yard draw their swords in a quarrel betweene them & others, whereby much mischief might have Ensued had It noot beene prevented by the standers by, and the Capt. Jno. Gibbs being thereupon Seased by the Sheriff drew a pistole out of his pockett. It is thereupon ordered that the Sheriff. take the sd. Capt. Jno. Gibbs & Henry his brother and them disarme and in safe prison to detain them until they Enter into bond with good Security for their future good behavior."

These were still rough times. In another case, one William Goulston "laid hands on one of the justices" and was put in the stocks for three hours.

The earliest grant mentioning Knott's Island was that of Patrick White: "—323 acs. at N. end of Knot's Island, in Currituck, 20 Apr. 1682." But there were already settlers on this north end of the island, for it was not only visible from the North River and the Inlet, but also so inviting with its great trees on high land.

There had been controversy over the southern boundary line of Virginia for some time. The House of Burgesses had been encouraging people to settle down as far as the Chowan River for protection of Virginia's southern frontier (1653-4—Morris.) North Carolina was then divided into proprietories and did not become a Crown Colony until 1729. This was after William Byrd II's survey of the line in 1728. The line that he laid out was just below Old Currituck Inlet, in a straight line to the west, leaving the north one-third of Knott's Island and half of the Dismal Swamp in Virginia. It took so long for this line to be firmly established that the people were being hounded for levies by both Virginia and North Carolina. (Order Book 1675-1686.)

> "Court 13 November 1679
> Upon the complaint of divers of the Inhabitants of this County Living nigh the branches of Currituck River who have patented their Lands & paid levies divers yeares in the Same that the officers of Carolina doe threaten to distreyne upon their goods for the payment of Levies & Quitt Rents, etc. to that Government. It is ordered that the Clerke of the Court draw up the sd. Complaint to bee by our burgesses presented to the next Assembly to the End that Course may be taken for the Laying out the bounds of Virginia to the Southward."

Further evidence that many people had settled in this southernmost part of the county and that there had been a third damaging storm is in the following. (Order Book 1675-1686.)

> "Court: 16 Aug. 1683
> Whereas by the late Storme, these few roads which were formerly made In the precincts of the black water and branches of Corotuck are soe dammed up with trees fallen acroste them that It is very difficult and dangerous for any of his Majesties Legal people to travel that way about their Lawful occupation. It is therefore fitt and ordered that Capt. Plumer Bray bee hereby appointed head surveyor of the High ways in that precinct & Liberty given him to appoint such surveyors under him as hee shall think fitt who are with all Convenient Speede with the assistance of the neighborhood Required to Cleare these roads, and make bridges where they find occasion Require, and more especially the Road from Mr. William

Cornix to machapongo and soe the most Convenient way where a bridge may be made over bouden's Creek towards Mr. Joseph Chases and that the Inhabitants of Blackwater bee assistant thereto and the bridle ways be made into Roads by the Severall Inhabitants in a neck of Land downe towards dennis dolleyes." (Dennis Dawley)

Mr. William Cornix's plantation, called "Salisbury Plains," was where the extended runways of the United States Navy Oceana Air Station now are located on the present Oceana Boulevard and old road to Kempsville dating from before 1683. A pillar of the community, as his descendants have continued to be, Joel Cornix (changed to Cornick) gave land adjacent to his house for the Third Eastern Shore Chapel of Ease (Eastern Shore Chapel), built in 1754. Oceana Boulevard is one of the oldest roads in the county, joining Princess Anne Road, the oldest, at Nimmo Church and running east, then south through Machapongo (now called Pungo) to Knotts Island, at the mouth of the North River. As we come back up the North River, Blackwater precinct is to the left of this river. Past the wide swamps which surround this river is rich farmland, and there were farms here in the 17th century and enough people in this precinct, as well as that of Currituck, to require a constable for each.

Continuing up the North River, we reach the head of a small branch of the Eastern Branch of the Elizabeth River. Some old maps show that they met here at Kempsville, but a grant to John Porter, Sr., in 1663 of 3,000 acres describes the location as being near the path from the Eastern Branch of the Elizabeth River to the North River. Be that as it may, George Kemp (or Kempe) received a grant of 400 acres in 1652, as "crossing the Eastern Br. of the Eliz. R.," which appears that he owned land on both sides of the river. He was enterprising enough to see the possibilities of profit here, and he built a public landing and warehouses. He was right, for this spot became a busy trading post for ships coming up from Currituck and North Carolina, as well as a shipping point for tobacco to Norfolk and out to sea from the many surrounding farms on this Eastern Branch of the Elizabeth River. There is no trace of a river at all in modern Kempsville, but it was sufficiently important in the 18th century for a town to spring up here, then known as Kemp's Landing. In 1783, it became the town of Kempsville, with a courthouse, jail and church.

About this time, discontent with the rule of the Established Church began to surface, even among the leaders. George Kemp was a vestryman in 1649, but that did not deter him from an interest in another sect and not attending his own church. Unfortunately for him, he was caught. (*Lower Norfolk County Antiquary,* James.)

> "Court 15 Aug 1649
> Whereas George Kemp with seven others presented as Seditious Sectuaries for not repairing to their own parish Church for three months. The fine was 20 b per month and they were ordered to appear at James City the 8th October to answer before the Governor and Council."

That was the end of political power for George Kemp, but he and his sons continued to buy and sell land at a rapid clip and to operate his landing and warehouses. Their descendants continued to live here until at least after the Revolution.

Richard Whitehurst had settled here before George Kemp, as his first grant for 250 acres was in 1648, on Gayther's Creek on the south side of the Eastern Branch of the Elizabeth River. His sons, William and Richard, accumulated 1,150 acres from Kemp's Landing to the Indian River by 1690, and another son, John, owned another 700 acres. This Whitehurst land also extended down to the Dismal Swamp. They were an outstanding family of successful farmers and leaders in the area. The only Whitehurst house still standing is near Princess Anne, on North Landing Road, and was built much later, about 1790.

The only brick colonial house still standing in Kempsville is a beautiful Georgian now known as "Pleasant Hall." It had been believed that it was built by Peter Singleton, for he owned the property in 1779, the date incised in a brick on the south wall. The eminent genealogist Mrs. Elizabeth Wingo, however, has uncovered evidence that it was built by George Logan, the Kempsville Tory, at an earlier date. We shall hear more of him in a later chapter.

We now see that the whole area of Lower Norfolk County was well settled. Lower Norfolk County Records, Book 5, gives the population in 1689 as 1,108 tithables, a tremendous increase over the estimate in 1645 as 305. But that first estimate only included members of the two parishes, Elizabeth River Parish and Lynnhaven Parish. The mortality rate had continued high, but in the last half of the 17th century, there was a great increase in the importation of servants and slaves.

The leading families of the first half of the century continued in power but with additions. As members of the middle class of tradesmen, artisans and men of some education accumulated land and married into this leading class, they profited by the democratic standards of the early settlers. They quickly absorbed the same feelings of isolation from the rest of the Colony, love of their land and a tolerance not entirely acceptable to the laws made in England or by the Church.

PART TWO
Chapter 3
THE MIDDLE CLASS

In 1625, this small group of first settlers in Lower Norfolk County was only upper class and servants. That was soon changed, however, and a middle class arose. Servants completed their terms of from five to seven years and became landowners, either by gift of 50 or 100 acres from their former masters as a reward for good work, or by "squatting" with the expectation of acquiring headrights and a grant. Even if their grant had not been recorded, they were now entitled to vote under Governor Yeardley's establishment of the democratic House of Burgesses in 1619. The vote, plus membership in the parish of the Church of England, made them equal to any large landowner in feeling, if not in fact. The door to opportunity was wide open.

Like their former masters, most of this new middle class were mainly interested in the accumulation of land, as they saw that land was the road to riches and power. Not all of them had the ambition or the ability to achieve this, some preferring to follow their various trades or were content to be small farmers. As some were able to move into the upper class by ability and astute marriages, they were replaced by other newly freed servants. It is estimated that 60 percent of the settlers in Lower Norfolk County had first come to the Colony as indentured servants, designated on ships' passenger lists as "Ship's carpenter" or "Yoeman."

John Sibsey was one of these. As plain "John Sibsey, Yoeman" when he came in 1624, he was "John Sibsey, Gentleman" with a dress sword by 1652! By 1649, he had accumulated 1,820 acres of land, was a justice of the court, a vestryman, and also had the title of "Captain."

Not all were John Sibseys, however. Two who were not destined to become leaders illustrate the variety of early immigrants who came here, for whatever reason, and how they fared in the wilderness.

The Middle Class

Daniel Tanner, "Carpenter," had come to the Colony in 1618 at the rather advanced age of 40, and he is so listed in Lt. Purifoy's Muster of 1624. His land grant, due him as an "Ancient Planter," is missing, but we know that he was living in the County of New Norfolk in 1637 because a grant for William Croutch in that year states: (*Cavaliers and Pioneers*, Nugent, vol. 1.)

> "In the great Cr. on the left hand goeing into the mouth of the Eliz. Riv. about 2 mi. on the N. Side from Daniel Tanner . . ."

Many other land grants of the first half of the seventeenth century refer to Tanner's Creek as either "bound by" or "n. or S. of, etc." Tanner's Creek is now known as the Lafayette River. Tanner evidently hired himself out as a carpenter, but he did have an estate. His will, dated 17 Nov. 1653, shows that his land was adjacent to that of Lemuel Mason as recorded in the Lower Norfolk County Records.

> "Recorded 15 Dec. 1653
> To Mr. Lemuel Mason all estate on Southside of James River and all debts paid.
> To Mrs. Anne Mason Lemuel's wife for her great paynes and care and love towards me, 3600 lb. of tobo. to be paid from estate in hands of John Sherley
> To John Worsham a heifer
> To James Simonds the tobo. he owes and 40 lbs. to be due from Jasper Hoskinson
> To Tho: Sherley the residue of estate in Virginia for the use of his child provided the Child be Christened and named Daniell.
> Exor: Mr. Lemuel Mason"

This sounds rather sweet in its gratitude to Mr. and Mrs. Mason, but the story has a sad little ending. The following year, a John Tanner appeared, armed with this certificate:

> "Dated 10 Aug. 1654
> "Certificate of Wm. Stanly Mayor of the City of Canterbury in the Commonwealth of England Know ye for a truth that Charity Tanner late wife of Daniell Tanner, is the daye of this date living & an inhabitant in this City, and that it has been sufficiently proved to me by the Register booke of the parish Church of St. Paul's in the sd. Citty before me brought that the sd. Daniell in the sd. parish 14 Oct. 1627; which sd. John is compelled to travell to pointes beyond the seas about the looking after the estate of sd. Daniell Tanner his father who died in the Virginia. And for that cause the sd. Charity & John desire this certificate from me."

No one knew that he had a wife in England. Either she had refused to come with him to the New World, or he did not wish her to and chose to forget her. It is amazing how fast unknown or forgotten relatives always appear when the deceased leaves an estate, no matter how small.

Savill Gaskin's case is quite different. He had an abundance of ambition but not enough common sense. His downfall appears to have been the result of over-extension, the wrong wife and, certainly, recklessness. Once a Frenchman, whose original name was Saville Gascoyne, he came to Virginia as a headright for a William Rainshaw, who patented land six miles up the Elizabeth River in 1638. Evidently, he was indebted to Thomas Marsh for 800 pounds of tobacco, which he could not pay. He bound himself to one John Gooch as a servant, on the condition that Gooch pay his debt. But Gooch died in that year and, while he freed Gaskin in his will, the estate was not sufficient to pay Gaskin's debt, and the court ordered him to pay it himself. In debt again to Thomas Mires the same year, he was also in deeper trouble, for he and his wife, Anne, were sued in court for slander against Anne Foster. They had accused her of privately burying a child. Private burials had been banned because some unconscionable masters were in the habit of tossing the bodies of servants, who had succumbed to harsh treatment, poor food or the summer heat, into the river.

> "12 April 1641
> Whereas it appeareth to this Court by the deposition of several persons that Savill Gaskine and Anne, his wife, hath scandalously reported and asserted against Anne Foster wife unto Richard Foster concerning her being delivered of a child and that the sd. child was privately made away, the which the sd. Gaskine nor Anne his wife can bring no testimony or proof. It is therefore ordered that the sd. Gaskine shall receive 20 lashes upon his bare back and his sd. wife Anne 10 lashes of the like kind presently to be executed by the Sheriff and also the sd. Savill shall make payment of the charges of this court concerning the proceedings."

Anne was ordered to ask forgiveness of Anne Foster in court and to make her apology again in church, which she refused to do, insisting that she would never apologize to Anne Foster. She was put in custody at the house of Captain Thomas Willoughby, where she was to receive 20 more lashes for contempt, and she was to be conducted to the church for the performance of the order. Again, she refused, but she finally gave in when told that the lashes would be increased by 10 on each refusal. Anne Gaskin was a tough woman but hardly a helpmate to her husband.

In 1642, Savill Gaskin received permission to operate a ferry between three points of the Lynnhaven River. He needed the money, for Richard Foster was suing him for court charges from his trial for slander in 1641.

> "Dated 6 Feb. 1642
> Savill Gaskin hath this day engaged himselfe or a sufficient man for him before Capt. John Gookin Esq. Commander, Edw. Windham, & Mr. Henry Woodhouse to keep a ferrie beginning from ye 28 Jan. last past for a complete year in Linhaven River from ye Quarter unto ye Eastern Shore unto Robt: Cam's Poynt upon notice given by a Hollow or a fire and likewise from ye Quarter unto Trading Poynt upon notice given aforesaid backwards & forwards between both places. Whereof ye sd Gaskin is to have 800 lb. tob. according to ye order of Court to be paid to him by the Sheriff."

This ferry did not turn out to be as profitable as he thought it would, and suits against him for debts continued. Yet, in 1643, he received permission for court to be held in his house and to operate a tavern there. The wording of this order indicates for whom the tavern was intended to serve; court day was the big day of the month, especially for heavy-drinking men. And with all the goings on, the judges had need of imbibing, too.

> "these may testify that Savill Gaskin hath been allowed by the Court of this County to keep an ordinary for their entertainment and the relief of other ordinary keepers in the County ever since December last past."

As the population increased, court, of necessity, had to be held in other sections of the county as well. Gaskin complained that twice-a-year court days resulted in a loss to him, so it was ordered that henceforth court should be held there regularly. This would seem quite a concession, but even that did not help him. He shortly had the temerity to challenge Colonel Francis Yeardley and his wife (Sarah Thorowgood) in court over a difference in the building of a house for her. The record is mutilated, but it appears that Colonel Yeardley was either to cancel the contract "or else give an acquittance therof unto the sd. Gaskin." Either way, he lost out. Next, we see Savill Gaskin buying and selling real estate. In 1652, he bought a tract of land known as Scull Neck, next to his own land—"on the Swd. side with the now Manor House & land of sd. Savill Gaskin."

The following year, 1653, his wife Anne died under peculiar circumstances, which necessitated an inquest. The examiners reported that her sudden death was neither murder nor suicide, but Savill was on the way down. In 1654, the Grand Jury made a presentment against him for overcharging on sack and brandy. Laws for the price of these were set by Parliament. He lost his license to operate the tavern, the court and the ferry. In February 1662, he assigned over to William Hodge, merchant of London, his 250 acres, the 100 acres granted to him in 1648 and 150 other acres, the residue including "all these messuages buildings, lands, tenements, tracts & parcels of land . . . also all Edifices, buildings, orchards, gardens, woods, underwoods, water courses etc. . . ." Savill owed this merchant so much money that it is doubtful he received anything from the sale and possibly still owed him more. In 1668, after his death, the record reveals the following.

> "Date 5 June 1668
> Ordered that the estate of Savill Gaskin be sold at outcry [public auction] on Tuesday next and the Judgments referred to the next Court."

During the next month or so, William Hodge died. He left his estate to his brother, Robert Hodge, who appeared in court here trying to collect the balance of Savill's debt to his brother.

> "Dated: 5 Oct 1669
> Ordered that Robert Hodge bee paid proportionately out the estate of Savill Gaskin 1337 lb tobacco & Caske with costs."

That is the last we hear of Savill Gaskin in the records. But on his land, once known as Scull Neck, stands a gem of a brick house. It now belongs to the Association for the Preservation of Virginia Antiquities, a gift to them in 1971 from the last owners, the Oliver family. It is now called the Lynnhaven House.

Erroneously known for a long time as "The Wishart House," and the road mistakenly named Wishart Road, the Association thoroughly researched it. Since the title descent shows that, without a doubt, it was on Gaskin's land, that no Wishart ever owned it, and, because it was built in the style of the 17th century, it was concluded that Savill Gaskin had built it, especially since it includes a cellar in which were found evidences of casks of sack and brandy. The massive chimneys north and south, the plan of the house with two rooms downstairs, a kitchen and the other, "The Hall," a stairway rising from the back of this "hall" to two bedrooms above, and a steep roof over the attic storeroom all indicate that the house was built in the latter half of the 17th century. It is said that Gaskin was a cabinetmaker by trade in his native France, and details, both inside and outside the house, evince the work of a master cabinetmaker of that time. It, therefore, seemed conclusive that Savill Gaskin had built the house when he owned the property between 1648 and 1662.

But, as we pointed out in the first chapter, dating anything of the past without absolute proof is apt to be refuted by later investigation. We know from the records that there was a house—"The Manor House"—on this property. But now, an expert on determining the age of wood has decided that the great beams in the ceiling of the cellar, which hold up the house, date no earlier than 1728. Perhaps this is not Savill Gaskin's original house, as there is no way in which beams of that size could have been replaced in the 17th century. If it was built in 1728, the builder was Francis Thelaball, who bought the property from Mary Hodge Miller, the heir of Robert Hodge, in 1721.

While the house retains features of the earlier 17th century style, it is actually transitional in architecture, incorporating Georgian features such as the dormer windows upstairs. The Georgian style became more popular as better adapted to the warm climate here, and more preferable as the people became more prosperous.

Under the management of the Association for the Preservation of Virginia Antiquities, and the generous contributions of interested citizens, this house is now an exquisite showpiece of life in the late 17th and early 18th centuries. A fulltime curator lives in a small compatible house nearby, who, with docents in period costumes has instituted an active program of colonial cooking, music, dance and crafts. Candle dipping, spinning, weaving, quilting, broom making and stenciling are demonstrated. Special announced programs are regularly performed.

The only interesting thing about Francis Thelaball is that his father was French and that his surname was "LaBalle" when he emigrated here. This name confused the clerk of the court, and in the earliest records, his name is written as "The La Ball." For convenience, he anglicized it, more or less, to Thelaball.

As for Robert Hodge, in his will leaving the property to his daughter who lived in Norfolk, he directed that she was to allow his favorite slave woman to live there for her lifetime. After her death, Mary sold the house to Frederick Boush in 1806. The Boush family lived there for three generations, until 1859, when Eliza Boush Walke inherited and sold it to George and Joseph Smith, retaining the graveyard. There are four Boush gravestones remaining in this graveyard, all fairly legible and engraved with the charming and sentimental tributes popular in the 19th century.

> Sacred
> to the memory of
> William Boush
> who was born in the 18th of Feb. A.D. 1750
> and expired at Lebanon 6th of Jan. 1804
> He was an eminently useful member of Society
> in all the relations of life; his heart glowed
> with benevolence to his fellow beings and he lived
> in the practice of the precepts of the Gospel
> and of those graces and virtues which exalt
> character, and whose motto was:
> "Deal Justly, love Mercy, and walk humbly before
> thy God."

There is a bronze plaque at the foot of this tomb, attached by the DAR, which says, "A REVOLUTIONARY HERO." Beside this is the tomb of Mary Boush, William's wife. The stone has been broken almost in half, but two of the larger pieces have been found and will be put back with the remaining one. The dates are missing, but Mrs. Sadie Kellam in *Old Houses in Princess Anne* says that they were 1764 and 1822. One or two words are missing also, but we can guess what they were.

> Sacred
> to the memory of
> Mary Boush
> who was born on the -----
> -------------------------
> Wife of William Boush
> She was of a broken - - - -
> When the last summons came
> With serenity she took leave of
> her relatives and domestics, and with
> Unfeigned faith fell asleep in the Lord Jesus.

Another:

> In memory of
> Wm. F. W. Boush
> a Citizen of Princess Anne
> of which County he was a Justice of Peace
> and a Delegate to the Assembly
> In private life without reproach;
> In public attentive to his duty;
> A Christian in heart and deed
> He lived by faith and died in hope
> on the 19th of Dec. 1818
> In the 25th year of his age

Still another:

> Sacred
> to the memory of
> Eliza J. S. Walke
> widow of
> David M. Walke
> and daughter of
> Wm. and Mary Boush
> She departed this life on the
> 9th day of June 1884
> in the 82nd year of her age.

Eliza J. S. (Boush) Walke was married to David M. Walke, son of the Reverend Anthony Walke. He was buried at "Fairfield," the Anthony Walke estate, once the grandest in the county, near Kempsville. His stone and remains were moved to the graveyard at Old Donation Church after the manor house burned and the estate was sold. Eliza, however, chose to be buried in the Boush family graveyard, her childhood home.

Graves do not easily give up their secrets, nor do old houses, but a little imagination can carry us back through 300 years to the lives of these people.

We have digressed with the Boush family, decidedly upper class, but only to tell of Savill Gaskin and this treasure of a house, which he may or may not have built.

Savill Gaskin, as an artisan, was middle class. He was a superior craftsman, as shown in the house, but there were many others here by 1650, good, bad and indifferent. Heavy taxes in England had closed many mercantile businesses, and the beginning of the Civil War in

England had caused many to flee to this new country. There were many carpenters in addition to Daniel Tanner, including Henry Snaile, Peter Porter, John Penure, Thomas Mosier, Thomas Cooper, Edward Holmes and others. Alexander Bell was a blacksmith, Thomas Davis a tailor, Gilbert Dawley and George Valentine fletchers, Robert Hanney a shoemaker, and there was even a bookbinder, John Hill, although he could not have had much opportunity to practice his trade in those early times. Constantine Waddington and John Hotten were coopers, and Anthony Liney a wellwright. George Ashall had a successful tannery and was a shoemaker. There were a few clerks, also, who transcribed the records. These clerks had beautiful handwriting, but it was so fanciful and the spelling so atrocious that reading the old records is an art unto itself.

Artisans tended to be more of a floating population, as there were no towns in this county where a man could settle down and practice his trade. So these men went from plantation to plantation as they were needed.

In that dark age of medicine, most doctors, then called chirosurgeons, were little more than barbers who had picked up the knack of bloodletting and purging as cures for any malady. As the population increased, there were one or two who had some training, but women approaching childbirth preferred the services of midwives as being safer.

Seamen and shipwrights came and went, receiving a bounty of land whenever they entered the Colony and usually selling these headrights. There were plenty of headrights for sale, and they could be bought very cheaply. Each one was still worth 50 acres, and a man could add to his holdings with little expense this way.

Although these artisans and small farmers became more numerous and felt equal to the elite, they continued to be content to leave government with the "ruling class." They sometimes held very minor positions, but complete control remained in the hands of the upper class of interlocking families well into the 18th century.

No history of the beginning of Princess Anne County would be complete without the story of Grace Sherwood, our one and only convicted witch.

Witchcraft, since early in the 17th century, had been rife in England and had spread to the American colonies. The center of this hysteria was in New England, especially in Salem, Massachusetts, where hundreds of women had been arrested and tried, 19 hanged and one pressed to death for refusing to plead guilty.

Virginia took a more sensible view of such accusations. And in Lower Norfolk County, the justices became weary of charges with no proof, which they suspected stemmed from jealousy.

> "Lower Norfolk. At a private Court held the 23rd of May, 1655 at the house of Mr. Edward Hall in Linhaven.
> Whereas divers dangerous and scandalous accusations have been raised by some persons concerning several women in this Countie, terming them to be witches whereby theire reputations have been much impaired and their lives brought in question (for avoiding the like offense). It is by the Court ordered that what person soever shall hereafter raise any such like scandall concerning any party whatsoever, and shall not be able to prove the same, both upon oath, and by sufficient witness, such person so offending shall in the first place pay one thousand pounds of tobacco: and the likewise be liable to further Censure of the Court."

The case of Grace Sherwood, however, by the number of witnesses to her supposed guilt and the persistence of her accusers, forced them reluctantly to take the charges seriously.

Grace had been living for some time with her husband, James Sherwood, and their three sons on their small farm on Muddy Creek Road, but she evidently was not too popular with the neighbors. It is said that she was beautiful, independent and inclined to be flirtatious with other women's husbands. Also, she supposedly danced naked in the moonlight and wore men's clothing when she chose to do so. She must have been guilty of some of these things to arouse such hostility.

In 1698, Grace and her husband brought suit for slander against two couples, John and Jane Gisburne and Anthony and Elizabeth Barnes. The Gisburnes had said that Grace had "bewitched their cotton," and Elizabeth Barnes said that "the said Grace came to her one night and rid her and went out of the keyhole or crack of the door like a Black Cat." Unlike other cases, the Sherwoods lost both of these suits.

Grace won the next suit, which she should have, on 7 Dec. 1705. it was against Luke Hill and his wife, in which she said that Mistress Hill had trespassed on her property and "assaulted, bruised, maimed and barbarously beat her." She was awarded only 20 shillings of the £50 she had demanded.

The Hills were not satisfied. The following February, 1706, they brought suit against Grace for witchcraft. The minutes of this court noted that she had long been suspected of witchcraft. Among other things, the court was told that where she had danced in the moonlight, no grass would grow, that she had bewitched cows to sour their milk, and that she could make herself tiny enough to ride in an eggshell to England, bringing back seeds for her garden the same night. Rosemary, which grows wild in this area, is said to have been started from a small cutting she had brought back in the eggshell. There is a small mound near Pungo, still called Blossom Hill, where wild lupine grows, but it grows wild nowhere else. This, too, she is said to have brought back from England in the eggshell.

A jury of women was summoned to examine her body for certain marks indicative of traffic with the Devil, such as small blue stains or a third teat. The forewoman was Elizabeth Barnes, who was certainly prejudiced because of the former case, and the jury testified that, indeed, they had found such marks. Grace would not deign to answer and made no excuse.

When the court refused to pass judgment, Luke Hill carried his suit to the attorney general in Williamsburg in March 1706. This higher court refused a hearing, saying that the case was a local matter, and sent it back to Princess Anne.

Further examinations and hearings were held in May and June of 1706, and the Sheriff searched the Sherwood house for objects of a suspicious nature, finding none. All the while, Grace kept silent, except to laugh at her accusers, enjoying her notoriety.

Finally, the county court, anxious to bring the case to a conclusion, decided on July 5th to subject her to a "trial by water," to which she readily consented. The order was given for the ducking, but on the day designated, there was a terrible storm, which delighted Grace and caused a postponement as the judges felt that the bad weather might endanger her health! The date was reset for July 10th, at a point in the Lynnhaven River still known today as Witchduck Point.

News of the trial and the forthcoming ducking had spread throughout the Colony, and on that day, whole families came—by wagon, cart, on horseback, on foot and by boat—and crowded the shore.

"Trial by water" was a rather perilous experience. Stripped naked, her right thumb tied to her left large toe and her left thumb tied to her right large toe, she was examined by the women to make sure that she did not carry anything to aid her in the water. She was then carried to a boat in the river in a blanket, and the crowd cheered and jeered.

She only smiled as she was lifted from the blanket and thrown overboard. If she drowned, she would be declared innocent; if she survived, she was guilty. But as we said, Grace just smiled. Few women in those days could swim, but she could, and she also was

Grace Sherwood's trial by water, July 5, 1705. *Drawing by Newton Byrd Miller.*

handy at untying knots. When she floated, one of the men in the boat tied a heavy Bible around her neck and pushed her down again. Freeing herself from the Bible, she swam about the cove, singing and laughing at the people. Everyone had a good time, especially Grace.

Since she survived, according to custom, she was guilty; thus, she spent the next seven years in jail, unbowed and unrepentant. But all the furor over witchhunting had gone out of style by 1715, and she was released. As a sort of recompense, Governor Spotswood granted her 140 acres of land, for which she only paid two pounds of tobacco per acre. This land was "at a place called and known by the name of Muddy Creek, a branch of Corotuck Bay in the Parish of Lynnhaven in the said County of Princess Anne, and adjacent to her own land." Her husband had died intestate in 1708 while she was in jail.

When Grace returned to her home with her additional acreage, no one dared to molest her, and according to all accounts, she lived peacefully with her sons until her death, sometime between 1733 and 1740. Her will, dated 1733 and probated 1740, leaves everything to her son John, with only five shillings apiece to her other sons, James and Richard. John was named executor. She had not much to leave aside from land.

"1 steer & heifer 3 years old
2 heifers at 2 years old
1 hand mill
1 frame table with a draw
1 chest & box
1 Iron spit
1 box Iron
3 low chairs
1 Inglish blanket
1 iron pot
1 pewter dish & bason"

John was also the appraiser, which leaves some doubt about the veracity of this inventory. But it appears that John was the one who stuck by her through her troubles, and James and Richard may have had some doubts about their mother's innocence.

Others did, too, for in 1979, a colleague of Floyd Painter found a small glass phial of brass pins in a yellow liquid buried in an inverted position on the site of a 17th century house on Great Neck Point. This was a part of the original Thomas Keeling land grant of 1635. The bottle, according to English custom, was so buried by the victim of a painful affliction believed to have been caused by witchcraft. The bottle and its contents were supposed to ward off the curse and return the pain to the witch who had cast the spell (*The Chesopean*, Floyd Painter).

So Grace Sherwood lives on, a popular figure of romance and fantasy, with Witchduck Road, Witchduck Point and Sherwood Lane to remind us of this independent woman who was born before her time.

PART TWO

Chapter 4
INDENTURED SERVANTS AND SLAVES

The indentured servant class, hardly a "class" at all, was so varied in background, education and ability that its members ranged from convicts to gentlemen. William Alford advertised the services of his servant this way in 1674.

> "Book E. f. 174
> I doe hereby license and authorize my servant Jonathan Hurst to appear for me or any other that will or shall employ him as an attorney in any Inferior Lower Courts of Indictment in this county of Virginia, the sd. Hurst having served as attorney at Law in England five years."

This servant surely had more knowledge of the law than any of the justices in the local court, who had been appointed by the governor for obvious political reasons.

As the upper class planters became more prosperous, they looked for tutors for their children and often found them among the Scots who, unable to find teaching jobs in depressed England and Scotland, had come in desperation to the New World as servants. There were no schools here, and sometimes a minister would do a bit of teaching. But during this period, there often was no minister at all. Virginius Dabney in *Virginia the New Dominion* says:

> "The indentured servants who were arriving in such large numbers were often persons in good standing in England, even gentlemen. Some of them quickly worked their way up to positions of responsibility. Seven men listed as servants in 1624 were members of the House of Burgesses five years later. Many others were from the 'lower orders,' and remained so. Perhaps 60% of all immigrants

who came (to the whole colony) in the first fifty years arrived as indentured servants."

These men and others like them were in the "voluntary" segment of this group and were called "redemptioners" or "Free-Willers." They bound themselves for a term of three to five years in return for their passage. These "redemptioners" were also apprentices, minors sent voluntarily by their parents to be provided with training in a specific trade in return for services. Chief among the trades to be learned was the cultivation of tobacco, which the parents felt was the best opportunity. Others were apprenticed to carpenters, smiths and weavers.

While there was no stigma attached to the status of these voluntary servants, the involuntary ones were the other side of the coin. In spite of constant protests by the House of Burgesses to Parliament, British convicts were sent in large numbers in commutation of the death sentence. Between 1655 and 1699, 4,500 of these convicts were sent to the Colony by Parliament. For lesser crimes, they were to serve seven years; for felonies, 14 years to life. One can imagine that these were the ones who caused trouble for the colonists, as thieves and runaways were so unwilling to work that they were useless to their masters. If runaways were caught a second time, they were branded with an "R" on the cheek, according to the law, but we find no record of anyone actually being branded in this county.

These runaways roamed about, stealing when they could, fleeing to the frontier or joining the Indians. Not many were caught, but this one was. (Lower Norfolk County Order Book, 1675–1686.)

> "Whereas by vertu of a hue and Cry from one of the Chiefe magistrates of North Carolina in persuite of one Smith, that was formerly apprehended with Roger Michell and his Complices that Robed the house of Nicholas Smith in Pagan Creek, one John Smith was this day apprehended and brought before this Court upon suspicion of being the same person, and It appearing to this Court In all Likelihood that the said Smith Is the same man mentioned in that hue and Cry. It is ordered that the Sheriff take the said Smith into his Custody and him convey forthwith Into the Isle of Wight County where the fact was Comitted, and after also all papers now taken Convey him beefore the Honorable Col. Joseph Bridger, Esq. a member of the Council to be further dealth with as his honor shall think fitt."

Involuntary servants also included a large number of children who had been picked up off the streets in London and kidnapped. These children were easy to come by for unscrupulous ship captains, for the streets of London were full of homeless children at this time. (Charles Dickens—*Oliver Twist.*)

Then there was involuntary servitude imposed by the colonial courts in satisfaction of criminal sentences. Felonies were tried in the Superior Court in Jamestown. There is no record extant in Lower Norfolk County of anyone serving time for a felony, although there are records of murders. For instance, the rich and prominent William Carver, who in 1676 joined Bacon's Rebellion and was hanged for it, was apparently let off. (*William & Mary Quarterly,* January 1895.)

> "On the 25th of July 1672, while laboring under an aberation of mind, he killed Thomas Gilbert, who was sitting next to him at dinner, by stabbing him with a knife. In his examination, August 15, 1672, he deposed that as for his part hee knoweth nothing of it, noe more than the child that is yet unborne, nor of any other action that day, nor severall days beefore or after."

And this:

> "Book C. f. 58
> Court: 15 Oct. 1653
> ... peticon of Arthur Edgerton ... trouble he had in and about the taking upp and burringe of the Corpses of Thomas Leach, who was murdered by John Newman ..."

This may have been a duel, and Edgerton wished to be repaid for taking care of the dead.

Debtors in England were imprisoned at this time, a burden to the State, and they could hardly repay their debts while incarcerated. So they were sent as involuntary indentured servants to the colonies. These men could have been from any class in England, and it is doubtful that they had to serve as much as seven years. But at least, when their term was up, they were free of debt.

Women coming voluntarily were usually hoping to find a better husband than they had been able to catch at home, but some, of course, had been serving jail terms for petty thievery and the like. They were not compelled to work in the fields, as were the men, but mainly did housework. Except for the constant fear of pregnancy by their masters, or another, their lot was not so bad. And they had very little trouble finding husbands when they were free, and they were expected to do so. Julia Sperry Spruill in *Women's Life and Work in the Southern Colonies* says they only received extra clothing when their indenture ended, "a waistcoat & petticoat of Virginia cloth, a new shift of white linen, a pair of Virginia made shoes, stockings, a blue apron and two white linen caps." More often, these were castoff clothes of their mistress. As to having a bastard child, this was indeed frowned upon. If the woman could name and prove the father, he was required to post bond and support the child and "keep the Parish harmless." But she was sentenced to two years extra service by the Act of 1661. If a master begot a child by his servant woman, he was fined but could not claim extra servitude from her. Instead, she was sold by the churchwarden at the end of her term for two years service for the use of the Parish.

For an indentured male servant who had no skills and was put to work in the fields, life was extremely hard. While nominally he could sue or be sued in the local court if he had a complaint, his existence was a dreary round of overwork, poor housing and inadequate diet and clothing. In addition to the unaccustomed summer heat, which killed off many of them, beatings by masters for even minor infractions were common. As a result, there were repeated incidents of drunkenness, runaways and suicides.

The masters constantly had to be on the alert to replenish their work forces, as well as to control the rebellious servants they had. In the more affluent counties of York and Gloucester, these white servants combined by strikes and insurrections to redress grievances, in York in 1659, and in Gloucester in 1663 where four were executed for treason. But there is no evidence that they were able to get together for strikes here. These plantations were smaller and widely spaced, and no one here could afford the hundreds of bound servants as in those counties, where often the servants never saw their master and could only take a complaint to the overseer. These overseers had a decidedly unsavory reputation for cruelty, but they were constantly pressured by the master to produce more and more.

The master, in addition to the constant replenishing of the work force, had to try to choose servants who would be satisfactory workers. The more wealthy had agents in England to choose servants for them, which involved bargaining with the ship captains and voluntary servants over the terms of the indenture. The terms varied according to prospective servants' skills. Also, the overseers had to be watched, as they were prone to cheat the master as well as mistreat the servants. Overseers had been servants themselves, preferring this easier job to trying to wrest a living from the soil by their own efforts.

Numerous laws were being drafted by every General Assembly concerning bondsmen and their treatment. These laws were largely ignored, but they reflect a growing concern about the evolution of an institution, which, with the coming of the blacks, inevitably led to slavery.

The evolution from the indentured servant system to slavery is rather complex, but with hindsight, it seems a logical, though monstrous development given the time, place and circumstances.

We have already noted the attitude of the English toward other races, which was emphasized by the fact that the blacks, unlike the Indians, had come to a strange land, about which they knew nothing, and were completely at the mercy of the whites. Because of the language barrier, it took longer to make the blacks understand what was expected of them. This, of course, was used as an excuse to extend their servitude longer and, for the unscrupulous, indefinitely.

There had been many abuses of the indentured servant system even before the blacks came, as the records show that these English servants had frequently taken their masters to court for ill treatment or for illegally extending their terms. Black servants, who did not know the language and knew nothing of the courts, had no recourse at all. The blacks were shunned by the white servants, forced to do work they did not understand and were not accustomed to, had a miserable existence on food they were not used to, and their vulnerability to the white men's diseases produced a high mortality rate, although not as high as the white servants.

Slavery was not unknown to the free English here. Besides the felons from England sentenced to life indentures in lieu of execution, they had seen the Indians enslave their war captives. The settlers bought a few of these Indian slaves themselves, on the pretext of Christianizing them. One of the Cornick men, in his will, left his "Indian man, Robin" to his eldest son.

Slavery had been established by the French, Spanish and English, too, in the West Indies, including Barbados. Claimed by England before 1625, Barbados was a thriving port for merchants trading between London and the Islands. Sir John Hawkins was the first Englishman to engage in the slave trade. He started by supplying the Spanish Islands, but he soon sold to the British, as the demand for sugar from the West Indies was more easily met by slave labor than indentured servants.

While the importation of slaves into Virginia was slow for a few years after 1619, it gradually increased after 1649, although the total slave population in the Colony was estimated at only 300 then. Before the Navigation Acts, beginning in 1650, most of the trading by the colonists had been with the Dutch, who were not heavily into slave traffic. The Dutch did not consider Virginia as having a high market for slaves, anyway, although slaves were here at this time. Such upper class men as Francis Land and Thomas Walke had come here from Barbados to settle in Lower Norfolk County, and being from well-to-do merchant families, they brought slaves with them to man their ships and to work in the lucrative tobacco fields. Warren G. Billings in *The Old Dominion in the Seventeenth Century* suggests that some free blacks may also have come from the West Indies with voluntary indentures, looking for a better way of life. Certainly, there were free blacks here by 1652, and those who had come earlier as indentured servants had served their terms. This may explain the case of Anthony Johnson, and whether he was from the West Indies or not, his story confirms the innate ability of the blacks to quickly learn the language and customs of this land, as well as its laws.

In the land grants is a record that Anthony Johnson came as a headright for Capt. Moore Fauntleroy in 1650. In the following year, Capt. Fauntleroy had amassed 5,320 acres in Northampton County. That same year, 1651, Anthony Johnson received a grant. (Nugent's *Cavaliers and Pioneers* vol. 1, p. 216.)

> "Anthony Johnson, 250 acs. Northampton Co. 24 July 1651 At great Nasawartock Cr. being a neck of land bounded on the S.W. by the maine Dr. & S.E. & N. by two small branches issueing out of the maine Cr. Trans: of 5 pers. Tho. Bemrose, Peter Bugby, Antho. Cripps, Jno. Gessarro (?) Richard Johnson."

(Nugent's vol. 1, p. 296.)

> "Richard Johnson, Negro, 100 acs. Northampton Co. 21 Nov. 1654, on S. side of Pongoteague Cr. Ely. upon Pocomoke, Nly. upon land of John Johnson, Negro, Wly. upon land of Anthony Johnson, Negro, & Sly. upon Nich. Waddilow. Trans: of 2 pers. Wm. Ames, Wm. Vincent."

(Nugent's vol. 1, p. 338.)

> "John Williams, 250 acs. Northampton Co. 17 Mar. 1635. On S. side of Pongotegue Riv. Ely. upon Pocomoke Cr. Nly. upon land of Thomas Teagle, Wly. upon land of Anthony Johnson, Negro, & Sly. upon land of John Johnson, Negro. Trans of 5 pers. Jno. Williams, Eliz. Hobson, Rob Atkins, Tho. Broadway, Alexander ———"

(Nugent's vol. 1, p. 532.)

> "Francis & Mary Vincent, 100 acs. Northampton Co. 20 Mar. 1660. S. side of Pongotage Riv. Ely. upon a br. of same called Pocomock, Nly. upon land of John Johnson, Negro, Wly. upon land of Anthony Johnson, Negro, & Sly. upon land of Nich. Waddilow. Granted to Richard Johnson 21 Nov. 1654 for trans. of 2 pers. and due to above named by assignment from Matthew Pepin 25 Dec. 1660, to whom it had been assigned by sd. Richard Johnson, 2 Mar. 1657."

Later: (Nugent's vol. ii, p. 127.)

> "Geo. Parker, 374 acs. Northampton Co. at Pungat. on SW side of Pocomoke Cr. adj. land of John Williams; land formerly Nich. Wadalow's; & land of Antonia Johnson, Negro, 27 May 1673, 100 acs. granted to Francis & Mary Vincent 20 Mar. 1660 and by one of them her moyery assigned to the Husband of the other & by the other & her husband; sd. 100 acs. assigned to Wm. Chase, who assigned to sd. Parker; 274 acs. for trans. of 6 pers. Anth. Prince, Fra. Sittering, Jno. Dorgon, Geo. Hellard, Mary Heard, Mary Deckan."

As confusing as these grants appear, it is clear that all the Johnsons were Negroes, and those they brought in were Negroes as well. Since they had surnames, they came from Barbados, where they had learned some English and something of the law and their rights. Although the Nasawartock Creek is not now named on the map, the Pocomoke River is, running into Pocomoke Sound, just above the present Virginia State Line.

Since these grants are all listed in Nugent's *Abstracts of Virginia Land Patents and Grants*, this is a good time to explain why this land is now in Maryland.

The original charter of the Virginia Company authorized all the land to the company between 30° and 41° N., that is, from just above Cape Fear to about where Philadelphia is now. But as new colonies were being established, Virginia saw its land being whittled away, both north and south. In 1631, William Claiborne, Secretary of the Council of Virginia, had purchased Kent Island from the Indians and had established a settlement there. However, Lord Baltimore induced Charles I to grant him a charter in 1632 for all the territory north of the Potomac, which included Kent Island. Claiborne refused to recognize the jurisdiction of Lord Baltimore, in which he was supported by the Council of Virginia, resulting in a long feud between the two men which was marked by continual attacks and reprisals. This hostility developed into a long-standing boundary dispute between the two colonies, and then the states.

The dispute was settled in principle in 1877, when both states agreed to accept the decision of a commission of arbiters, but nothing was concluded until 1930 when two investigators were appointed by the governor of each state. On the basis of their findings, the boundary was set to run in a direct line across the Chesapeake Bay from the mouth of the Potomac River, east across the Eastern Shore, from headland to headland, touching in each case the low water mark on the Virginia shore. This does not seem impartial, as usually when a river divides two states, the boundary line is in the middle of the river.

One entry in Hening's *Statutes at Large* testifies to this controversy.

> "Dec. 1656—7th of Commonwealth
> That letters be sent unto Coll: Samuel Matthews and Mr. Bennett that in respect the difference between us and the Lord Baltimore concerning our bounds is as far from determination as at first, that desist in that particular until further order from the country . . ."

As to other early Negro ownership of land, two entries in Nugent's show that Negroes owned land in other parts of the Colony as well.

> "Benjamin Doll, negro, 300 acs. Surry Co.
> 17 Dec. 1656 Beg. on the Sly. side of the Reeded Marsh on Capt. Jordan's line. Trans. of 6 pers . . ."

Alf J. Mapp, Jr., in *The Virginia Experiment*, says that "Anthony Johnson, negro, became the first landowner in Virginia to own a slave for life." This slave was John Casar, who claimed in court that he had come as an indentured servant and that Johnson was holding him beyond his term. He could not produce the indenture, however, and Anthony Johnson said that he had never seen it. Even though George and Robert Parker testified that they knew that he had an indenture in "Mr. Cary's land across the Bay," the court, surprisingly, ordered Casar returned to Johnson and the Parkers to pay all court charges!

Hewing to tradition, the English were zealous in their efforts to maintain the purity of their race, which, by the way, even extended to animals. A law was passed in the first years of the Jamestown settlement that no dogs or horses should be sold to Indians because they would despoil the animal's bloodlines. This could not be strictly enforced, but a stern example was made of Hugh Davis in 1630 to hopefully discourage any miscegenation between humans. That did not succeed too well either, but they tried. (Billings, from Henings, *Statutes at Large*.)

> "September 17 1630. Hugh Davis to be soundly whipped before an assembly of Negroes and others for abusing himself to the dishonor of God and shame of Christians, by defiling his body in lying with a negro, which fault he is to acknowledge next Sabbath day."

Later in the 17th century, it was the Negro woman who received the whipping in such case, with the man only paying a fine, if at all.

As the numbers of blacks increased, fear and suspicion intensified, as did restrictions. The progression of the law concerning this up to 1670 gives a clear picture of the deterioration of the condition of blacks in the Colony.

1640—An act requiring all masters of families to furnish arms both offensive and defensive—except Negroes.
1642—All youths of 16 years and upwards and all Negro women to be tithable. (White women always exempt.)
1662—All children born in this county shall be held bound or free according to the condition of the mother. (Contrary to British law, which stated the opposite.)
1667—The conferring of Baptism does not alter the condition of the person as to his bondage or freedom. (Previously, when slaveds were few, it was a frequent occurrence that they were then freed.)
1670—All servants not being Christian brought in by sea to be slaves for life, the issue following the status of the mother.

Over 50 years had passed since 1619. The Negroes had quickly learned the language and their rights under the existing laws. But the laws were changed as the slave trade increased, and another generation of slaves had been born here and were now adults. Fear mounted among whites as plots for insurrection in the more affluent areas of The Northern Neck and Accomac were discovered. There, with plantations of thousands of acres and hundreds of slaves, the opportunity for slaves to get together and hatch a plot was much more available than in Lower Norfolk County. At this time, the plantations here, with few exceptions, were less than 1,000 acres and employed less than 50 slaves, with the average of five or six to an owner. In some parts of the county, there were only one or two to an owner, or none.

Nevertheless, the following law was enacted for the whole Colony. (Hening's *Statutes at Large*, vol. ii. 481482.)

> "Recorded June 1680
> Whereas the frequent meeting of considerable number of negro slaves under the pretext of feasts and burials is judged of dangerous consequence; for prevention whereof for the future, Bee it enacted by the kings most excellent majestie by and with the consent of the generall assembly, and from and after the publication of this law, it shall not be lawfull for any negroe or other slave to carry or arme himself with any cub, staffe, gunn, sword or any other weapon of defense or offence, not to goe or depart from his masters ground without a certificate from his master, mistris or overseer, and such permission not to be granted but upon perticular and necessary occasions, and every negroe or slave soe offending and not having a certificate as aforesid shall be sent to the next constable, who is hereto enjoyned and required to give the said negro twenty lashes on his bare back well layed on, and soe sent home to his said master, mistris or overseer. And it is further enacted by the authority aforesaid that if any negroe or other slave shall presume to lift his hand in opposition against any Christian shall for every such offence, upon the proofe made thereof by the oath of the party before a magistrat, have and receive thirty lashes on his bare back well layed on. And it is further enacted by the authority aforesaid that if any negroe or other slave shall absent himself from his masters service and lie hid and lurking in obscure places, comitting injuries to the inhabitants, and shall resist any person or persons that shall by any lawful authority be imployed to apprehend and take the said negroe, that then in case of such resistance it shall be lawful for such person or persons to kill the said negroe or slave soe lying out and resisting, and that this law be once every six months published at the respective county courts and parish churches within this colony."

This act became the basis for the Slave Code of 1705.

In spite of the fear which in itself inspired cruelty, a peculiar attitude toward the blacks began to develop. This was that they were not human beings at all, but became personal property as horses or cattle. House servants became mechanical things, in some cases almost pets, to respond to any command, to entertain, to be punished severely for any act which displeased, and to be praised or rewarded as the master saw fit.

A slave for life had nothing to look forward to, except to make himself as comfortable as possible under the circumstances of insufficient food and clothing and miserable housing, to work only as hard as he was forced to in order to avoid punishment and to make himself agreeable to his master, no matter how he felt. Always, of course, there was the possibility of being freed by a will or as a reward for some extraordinary service, such as saving the life of someone in the master's family. Although promises of freedom seem to have been made, they were seldom kept at this time, partly because a master had a pecuniary interest which he did not wish to lose.

Cruel masters were not infrequent. Their slaves, in desperation, yearned to run away, but where would they go? They did not know the country beyond their master's plantation and, possibly, a few neighboring ones, and the color of their skin would make them easy to spot. The penalty for running off was harsh: lashes, branding after the second attempt, and after that—death. Also, there was a law that if a master freed a slave, that slave must leave the Colony at the master's expense, and he could not take his wife or children with him. Nor did the neighboring colonies of Maryland, Delaware and North Carolina allow freed slaves to enter.

The price of a slave was about twice the price of an indentured servant. But as time went on, the planters saw that in the long run the purchase of a black slave was a better investment than an indentured servant, whose term was short and who soon had to be replaced. Besides, so many of the white indentured servants were likely to die before their term was up, particularly of malaria, a disease which did not affect the blacks to such an extent as they had brought with them from Africa some degree of immunity to it.

Even more desirable to the planters was the breeding power of the blacks. After the Law of 1670 was enacted, which declared "the issue following the status of the mother," the children, in a few years, more than doubled the value of the planter's initial investment. In inventories and wills, there is an emphasis on "native born" slaves as having a higher assessment than the new or "unseasoned."

In Lower Norfolk County, where the farms were so widely spaced, the Negro children had the run of the plantation and played with white children in and out of the "big house" and in and out of the cabins without any restrictions. Once they reached the social age, however, interracial playing was over. The heartbreak that this sudden separation caused on both sides has been described in many romantic novels, and it was very real. The rapid increase of mulattoes in the slave population was due partly to this childhood lack of discrimination.

The majority of mulatto births were due to other factors. Until almost the end of the century, white indentured servants still predominated, and the lack of any form of recreation for servants of either race, combined with human nature, created a situation beyond government control. Many white landowners had come first without their wives and children, but they did have servants, and both servant and master were lonesome. Even if their wives were here, these women were so constantly pregnant, or ill, that their husbands were inclined to look elsewhere for their needs, and the slaves were very convenient. Submission to the master's demands was part of the condition of slavery, and the slave woman had no choice. The cruel part of this situation was that in the latter part of this century, as stated earlier, the black woman always paid the price with whippings while the master got off with a fine. If she complained to the court, she ran the risk of further ill-treatment by her master along with the pain of bearing a child not her husband's.

Marriages of slaves were acknowledged by masters, although that did not prevent them from selling a couple separately, since these marriages were not performed by the church. They were performed in the African way. The prospective bridegroom would ask the girl of his choice if she was willing. If so, he would ask her father, and if he agreed and the master was agreeable, the two would jump together over a broomstick and thereafter were considered married. Slave family life, what time there was for it apart from grueling work, appears to have been devoted and long-lasting—that is, unless the master chose to sell one or the other, when each could remarry if he or she wished.

While most mulattoes were born to a slave mother, it was not always so. In the case of Katherine Hawkins, a married woman of Henrico County, she testified in court in 1681 that she had been raped by a Negro slave. The depositions taken show that her behavior was so bad that she had courted such attention on numerous occasions. (Henrico County Deed Book 1677–1692.) The depositions are even more explicit than some of the sexiest best sellers today! Gossip tells us of other cases like this resulting in "a touch of the tar brush." But we believe that most of these cases of miscegenation concerned white servant women of the lowest orders who had been picked up on the streets of London and transported involuntarily.

The case of Elizabeth Key in 1655, a mulatto who was suing for her freedom, dragged on for years. She eventually won and married her attorney, a white man.

Fernando, a Negro, sued his master for his freedom in Lower Norfolk County in 1667, saying that he should serve no longer than any other servant as he was a Christian and had lived several years in

England, and before that was a free man, born and living in Portugal. He was adjudged by the local court as a slave, but he appealed to the General Court. We do not know the result of this case for all records of this period were destroyed, but the two cases illustrate that during this time slaves could sue in court.

The courts were at a disadvantage since there was nothing in English law to cover such a contingency, so a way had to be found to bring statute laws into conformity with custom. The House of Burgesses, with the approval of London, found that way by "stripping the Negro of his humanity and reducing him to a chattel who had neither a legal personality nor freedom of movement." (Billings *The Old Dominion in the Seventeenth Century.*)

Meanwhile, the Church was playing a rather evil part. Always eager to convert "the heathen," acceptance of Christianity was first held out as a means to freedom. By 1667, however, the law denied this possibility. Ministers were encouraged to instruct the slaves along the lines of obedience and subserviency. The Christian teaching of a god who was a loving father figure was very appealing to these poor people, and the prospect of a heaven where they would be free of any injustice was very inspiring. Singing had always been an important part of their African culture, and they at first attended church with the whites, though seated separately, joining lustily in the hymns.

Unwittingly, the Church increased their dissatisfaction. If they would be equal with the whites in heaven, it was hard to understand why God would allow them to be slaves on earth when they had done no wrong. They were told that the Bible says that they were created to be slaves, but even the most ignorant could hardly swallow that, even though they were unable to read the Bible themselves.

Indentures as apprentices were a small minority in the 17th century, but they increased as more artisans arrived and as the import-export business increased. These indentures as apprentices were very explicit, restrictive and binding. The early ones often required that the apprentice be taught to read and write, but other than that, the apprentice was hardly better off than a slave.

Wills in both the 17th and 18th centuries often specified that a son be bound as an apprentice, particularly in the case of a younger son or if the dying father had a small estate or none after his debts were paid. This indenture for an apprenticeship in 1767 is typical. (*The Archives,* Eleanor and Charles Cross.)

> "This indenture witnesseth that Charles Sayer Boush, grandson of Colonel Samuel Boush, president Justice of Norfolk County Court

and first Mayor of Norfolk, with the consent and approbation of the Norfolk County Court hath put himself and by these presents, he the said Charles Sayer Boush, doth voluntarily, and of his own free will and accord put himself apprentice to Cornelius Calvert, marriner, to learn his art, trade, and mystery, and, after the manner of an apprentice, to serve the said Cornelius Calvert from the day of the date hereof, for and during and until the full end and term of five years and four months, during all of which term, the said apprentice his master faithfully shall serve, his secrets keep, his lawful commands at all times readily obey. He shall do no damage to his said master, nor see it to be done by others without giving notice thereof to his said master. He shall not waste his master's goods, nor lend them unlawfully to any; he shall not commit fornication nor contract matrimony within the said term. At cards, dice, or any other unlawful game, he shall not play, whereby his said master may have damage. With his own goods, nor the goods of others, without license from his master, he shall neither buy or sell. He shall not absent himself day or night from his said master's service without his leave, nor haunt ale-houses, taverns, or playhouses, but in all things behave himself as a faithful apprentice ought to do during the said term. And the said Master shall use the utmost of his endeavors to teach, or cause to be instructed the said apprentice, in the trade of mystery of navigation and sailorship and procure and provide for him sufficient meat, drink, cloathes, washing and lodging, fitting for an apprentice, during the said term for five years and four months."

Sometimes apprentices felt that they had made a mistake in their choice of a trade or of a master. If so, it took a court order to shift. (Princess Anne County Loose Papers, Creecy, Box A4.)

"1 Sept 1763
Letter. Johnson Jenkins, brother in law of Mungo Campbell (the signer of the letter), was in 1760 bound to Anthony Walke Junr. to learn the art of navigation, and now has a great aversion to the sea, & wishes to learn the business of Pewterer. Mungo Campbell obliges himself to teach the said Johnson Jenkins that art."

Again concerning Negroes and court, the case of Mary Williamson leaves questions. (Lower Norfolk County Order Book, 1681–1686.)

"Court 1687
Whereas upon the information of mr. James Porter, minister, It hath appeared to this Court that Mary Williamson hath Comitted the filthy sin of fornication with William, a negro belonging to William

Basnett Squire. It is therefore ordered that shee bee fined five hundred pounds of tobacco and Caske for the use of Linhaven Parish for which the said Basnett in open court Ingaged himself, as security. Whereas it hath appeared to this Court that William a negro belonging to William Basnett Square hath Comitted fornication with Mary Williamson and hath very arrogantly behaved himself in Linhaven Church in the face of the Congregation It is therefore ordered that the Sheriff take the said William into his custody and give him thirty lashes on his bare back."

The Church wardens continued to try to control the morals of the people through the court, and particularly to prevent interbreeding between the whites and the blacks.

Boat loads of immigrants increased, bearing homeless children, women of the streets and felons from English jails, as well as good honest men and women. The slave trade also increased as more blacks were being brought from Africa.

The case load for the court became a burden for the justices and the wardens were finding it almost impossible to catch those breaking the laws of the Church, much less get them to court.

PART III
PRINCESS ANNE COUNTY
1691-1775

Queen Anne of England, reigned 1702-1714, by Sir Geoffrey Kneller. *Courtesy of the City of Virginia Beach.*

PART THREE
Chapter 1
DIVISION OF LOWER NORFOLK COUNTY

Settlers continued to pour into this extensive Lower Norfolk County taking up land on both sides of the Lynnhaven and Elizabeth Rivers down to Currituck Sound. They were welcomed but the court agenda became overcrowded and the House of Burgesses was petitioned for a division into two counties. (Deed Book E, f.78)

> "Recorded Sept. 1670
> Recorded at a Grand Assembly held at James City.
> Whereas some part of the people of the County of Lower Norfolk & Rappahannock have desired that Each of these Counties might be divided into two, It is therefore ordered that it bee Referred to bee decided by the plurality of votes in Each County wherein for avoiding Surprisall by a Clandestine Somonds: It is therefore ordered that ye Somonds be Issued from the County Court, and therein Exprest the day and place they to meet att and that the sd. Somonds bee published two Sundays in Each Church or Chapel of Ease before the day apointed that all persons may Consider of theire conveniencies or Inconveniences and be ready to give theire votes, and the result of theire Election to be Returned to ye next Grand Assembly, Under the hand of Sherife & Judge of their courts where the business is to have a final decision."

This petition was not acted upon until 1691, 21 years later, when Lower Norfolk County was finally divided into the two counties of Norfolk and Princess Anne, and the boundaries were set along the lines of the Elizabeth River Parish and the Lynnhaven River Parish. Parish boundaries had been set very early, in 1619, when the House of Burgesses met for the first time. These burgesses were representatives of the parishes, as neither counties nor shires had been created by that time. The practice of following parish boundaries for counties continued. Since the Elizabeth River Parish, whose exact boundaries were set in 1637, was much larger than the Lynnhaven—with two Chapels of Ease to Lynnhaven's one in 1691—Norfolk County comprised the western two-thirds of Lower Norfolk County and Princess Anne the eastern one-third, as laid out by Adam Thorowgood in 1639 for the Lynnhaven Parish. These boundaries are those of Virginia Beach today, with two exceptions.

One is our southern boundary. North Carolina was chartered by Charles II in 1663 to various Lords Proprietors and called Albermarle. As we have seen in Charles II's charter to Lord Baltimore, King Charles was no friend of Virginia as he had chopped off much of this Colony's northern territory for Maryland. He did the same for his Lords Proprietors of North Carolina, giving them the land north of the Albermarle Sound. According to the first Virginia charter of 1606, not only Currituck and Knotts Island were included in that charter, but also the land around the Chowan River. Since the Virginia Legislature had been handing out grants in all of these places in good faith since 1653, there was a great deal of resulting confusion and many protests. (Order Book 1675–1686.)

> "Court: 13 November 1679
> Upon the complaint of divers of the Inhabitants of this County (Lower Norfolk) Living Nigh the branches of Corotuck River who have pattented their Lands and paid Levyes divers years in the same that the officers of Carolina doe threaten to distrevne upon their goods for the payment of Levyes and quitt rents & C. to that Government. It is ordered that the Clerke of the Court draw up sd. Complaint to bee by our burgesses presented to the next Assembly to the End that Course may be taken for the Laying out of the bounds of Virginia to the Southward."

The whole situation under the proprietors in North Carolina was fraught with confusion and dissention, partly due to the passage of the Vestry Act in 1701, making the Church of England the established church. North Carolina had been a haven for large numbers of Quakers as well as Scottish Presbyterians who had immigrated there. Finally, William Byrd II, with representatives from North Carolina, on orders from King George II, surveyed the boundary in 1728, drawing a straight line from just below False Cape and Old Currituck Inlet cutting across Currituck Sound and the tip of Knotts Island, between 36° and 37°, cutting off the mouth of the North River, and westward all the way to the present Tennessee line. The following year, 1729,

North Carolina was made a Crown Colony, and all Virginia grants below that line were voided.

There may have been some suspicion that this division of Lower Norfolk County might happen as, for the first time, names of landowners in Currituck appear as justices in the first court of the new Princess Anne County. They included Benoni Burroughs, son of Christopher Burroughs, whose first land grant had been in 1636. Although this land grant was on the Lynnhaven River adjoining Adam Thorowgood, his son Benoni was living then in Currituck. Others living in Currituck were John Sandford and Evan Jones. The other first justices of Princess Anne County were Malachi Thruston, Argall Thorowgood, John Thorowgood, Francis Morse, Henry Woodhouse and William Cornick.

The two burgesses elected in 1691 were Malachi Thruston, of the northern part of the county, and John Richardson, whose land was near Dam Neck.

Some of the strongest leaders, such as the Masons and Willoughbys, were no longer in this group, as their land was now in Norfolk County, but it was not long before the old line upper class of Thorowgoods, Woodhouses, Keelings and Cornicks regained control. There were powerful additions in the Walkes, Lawsons, Maximillian Boush, Henry Spratt, James Nimmo and William Ellegood, who had come later with large land grants and financial backing and who had married into one or another of the old families.

Although court and vestry records show a fair cross-section of landowners from all over the county, there seemed a lack of interest in the popular vote for burgesses. It is estimated that only 50 percent voted, and to correct this, a fine was imposed, although not enforced, of 300 pounds of tobacco. Either most of the people were willing to see those reelected whom they felt were experienced, or most likely it was the result of general apathy toward the affairs of the Colony as a whole. The courts and the church right here in this county concerned them more as they were closer to home and more interested in their affairs. While immigration continued at a rapid pace, the feeling of a community of neighbors was strengthened by the division.

The people of Princess Anne had more urgent matters to consider, as this was the beginning of the fearsome age of piracy, when thousands of these lawless brigands roamed the seas in search of booty. With the 38 miles of exposed shoreline, from Little Creek to the Lynnhaven River to the Chesapeake Bay, thence around Cape

Henry and down along the ocean, they were extremely vulnerable to attack at any time by these vicious rogues. They could expect little protection from the British men-of-war, as England needed them for their war with France in 1689–97.

The following order from the governor was hardly enough to allay their fears, as the militia was small and hardly a match for the pirates who might strike at any time and any place.

> "Court 18 November 1690
> Whereas by Command from the Right Honorable ffrancis Nicholson Esq. their Majesties Lt. Governor of Virginia, Mr. George Newton, the high Sheff. of this County orders Mr. Argall Thorowgood by himself and others for him to Keepe Continual watch att the mouth of Linhaven River to discover what ships Come In att the Capes, and to give timely notice to the militia officers, and he the sd. Thorowgood having taken that Care & Change upon him from the 26th of Sept. Last to the 17 November following this Court upon the sd. Thorowgood's pett. doe hereby Certifie that same to ye Grand Assembly that pay may be ordered him for his care and trouble therein."

British warships were supposed not only to convoy the fleets of tobacco ships but also to protect all merchant vessels in the Chesapeake Bay. But in the summer of 1699, a pirate vessel, "The Adventure," boldly sailed into the bay and captured two merchantment, while the only British guardship, "The Essex Prize," was becalmed and looked on helplessly. As a result of this, at a council held at James City on August 9, 1699, it was further directed that "the militia of Elizabeth City, Norfolk, Princess Anne and Accomac to provide lookouts, one man to go backwards and forewards between . . . and Linhaven River, one man between Cape Henry & Corotuck, and a man upon Smith's Island or Mackie's Island and along the Coast. If suspicion of pirates, to give notice forthwith to the Next Commissioned officer of the Militia."

"The Essex Prize" was replaced by a larger warship, the fifth-rated "Shoreham" with 30 guns. "The Shoreham" remained on duty, and all was quiet until the following April. Then, the French pirate, Louis Guitar, in his ship "La Paix" arrived in the bay near the mouth of the Lynnhaven River with five prizes on a Sunday afternoon while both the captain and Governor Nicholson, who had been staying on board, had gone ashore for an afternoon's entertainment. Rushing back aboard, Governor Nicholson ordered an attack. At dawn the next morning, "The Shoreham" opened fire on the Frenchmen. "La Paix" got the worst of the battle, with 39 of her crew killed and her lines shot away so that she ran aground at Lynnhaven and surrendered. Mercy was granted because of the many prisoners in the hold, but those left of the pirate crew were imprisoned at Hampton. After the trial, three men were sentenced to be hanged—Houghlin, Franc and Delaunee—and the rest sent back to England in chains.

The court was able to make an example of these three as they had not been on board "La Paix" at the time of surrender and were not included in the terms. Houghlin, the pilot, swam ashore and was captured, and the other two were on board the prizes. The established custom was to execute the sentence on or near the spot where the crimes were committed. The warrant for execution was delivered to the court of Princess Anne County, signed by the Sheriff of Elizabeth City County.

> "You are to cause 3 Gibbetts to be erected in Your County, of Ceedar, or other lasting wood, one at Ye Cape, one where John Houghlin was taken and one near the place where the Pirates first engaged her Majesties Shipp, the Shoreham, which you may easily find out by inquirey. In which Gibbetts You are to cause the Severall Pyrates herewith sent to be hanged up, vizt: ffrancis Delaunee at the Capes, Cornelius ffrank at the place where the Pyrates Shipp first engaged her Majesties Shipp, the Shoreham, and Houghlin at the place where he was taken. You must leave him hanging in a good strong Chaine or Rope until they rott and fall away. All and every of these directions you are to observe and for so doing this shall be your warrant. Given under my hand and seal this 17th day of May, 1700."

The hangings were well-attended by the inhabitants of the county.

For years, pirates had made their base on the island of Madagascar, from which they preyed on all the Orient and any shipping. But that came to an end because of disease, the great distance back to England and the force of four British warships sent to eliminate them. With the War of the Spanish Succession in 1715, they happily joined the British as privateers. With the end of that war and depression in England, they found another base. It was in the Bahamas, and it was there that they resumed their former vocation. This base was New Providence, on the island of Nassau, where the governor welcomed them with open arms. This was uncomfortably close to Virginia and the Carolinas.

Captain Kidd, who had reigned supreme in the first era of piracy, had finally been caught and hanged in 1701. But another arose, the fearful Captain Teach, known as "Blackbeard." Well-tutored by another well-known pirate, Benjamin Hornigold, in seamanship, piracy and brutality, Teach became the most cruel and certainly the most colorful of them all.

After protests from other governors in the Bahamas and a strong report from Governor Spotswood of Virginia in 1716—"A nest of pirates are endeavoring to establish themselves in New Prividence, and by the additions they expect and will probably receive, may prove dangerous to the British commerce, if not timely suppressed"—four British warships led by the neval hero, Woodes Rogers, finally sailed in 1717 to take over Nassau and drive out the pirates from New Providence. (*The Pirates*, Douglas Botting, Time-Life Books.) This was a dismal failure, however, as Captain Teach had already sailed away from this area on his ship, "Queen Anne's Revenge," to become the terror of the American coast.

A master of psychology, Teach consciously tailored his already outsize personality to suit the peculiar requirements of his profession. Daniel Defoe, writing in 1725 *A General History of the Robberies and Murders of the Most Notorious Pirates*, wrote thusly of Teach's bushy black beard that reached down to his chest and up to his eyes, "like a frightful Meteor, covered his whole face, and frightened America more than any Comet that has appeared there for a long time." With his beard plaited into little tails festooned with ribbons, before battle he stuck lighted, slowburning matches under his hat so that his fierce face and matted hair were wreathed in smoke, looking like a fiend from hell."

Violence was his life's blood, and killing was his pleasure. By June 1718, Teach had taken 20 prizes in a cruise which had taken him from Virginia to Honduras. Tales about his treasure buried in the sands of Cape Henry and the island in Lake Joyce, still called "Blackbeard's Island" in belief that this was one of his bases, abound.

But Blackbeard did not bury his treasure. Finding a willing ally in Governor Charles Eden of North Carolina, Eden granted him a pardon in exchange for a share of his loot and allowed him to sell openly his merchandise at cut-rate prices direct to the public in the Pamlico River town of Bath. Most of the other colonies had turned against piracy in favor of legitimate business, but North Carolina was poor, with no appreciable export trade at this time, if this may be called Eden's defense.

By 1718, Teach had four ships under his command, and while the people of Bath wanted the pirate trade, they did not want the loutish

Edward Teach (Blackbeard the Pirate). From "*A General Historie of . . . Pyrates, Charles Johnson,*" *London 1736. Courtesy of the New York Public Library, Astor, Lenox and Tilden Foundation.*

pirates themselves. As the pirates began plundering any trading ship which came down the coastal rivers, complaints multiplied, but they were unheeded by Governor Eden. Becoming desperate, the people appealed to Governor Spotswood, of Virginia, for help.

Hating pirates, and Blackbeard in particular, Spotswood determined to act when he received word that Blackbeard, sailing a ship called *"The Adventure,"* had entered Okracoke Inlet with a captured vessel and was planning to establish a base there. Spotswood procured two shallow-draft vessels at his own expense, with 35 men under Lt. Robert Maynard of the *H.M.S. Pearl* and 25 men under Midshipman Baker of the *H.M.S. Lyme.* On November 21st, they arrived at Okracoke and spied two sloops at anchor further up the inlet.

Blackbeard was not surprised to see them. North Carolina's corrupt collector of customs, Tobias Knight, had sent him word that something was up. Overconfident, he spent the night drinking and carousing. The next morning, the battle began, and at first, it seemed to go Blackbeard's way. He put Baker's ship out of commission, killing Baker, and then came alongside Maynard's, lashing the two ships together and leaping on board, followed by his men. Suddenly, Blackbeard and Maynard came face to face, firing point-blank. Besodden with drink, Blackbeard missed, and Maynard's shot went right through his body. Incredibly, the howling, raging Blackbeard swung his cutlass, breaking Maynard's sword in two. As he drew back for the coup de grace, Maynard's seamen shot and cut at him, and one cut across his throat. Still he fought on, spouting blood and roaring curses. He grabbed another pistol from his belt and cocked it. But the fight was over. He slowly fell to the deck, dead. His body had received 25 wounds, including five from pistol shots.

With the loss of their leader, the other pirates surrendered. Ten had been killed, and all nine survivors were wounded. Maynard had 10 killed and 24 wounded. Ordering Blackbeard's head cut off and tied to the bowsprit of this vessel, Maynard returned in triumph to Virginia. The surviving pirates were taken to Williamsburg, where they were tried and hanged on the trees along Capitol Landing Road.

The death of Blackbeard put a virtual end to piracy along the Atlantic coast, and Princess Anne County was able to breathe more easily. Legend has it that when Blackbeard's body was thrown overboard, it swam around Maynard's sloop three times before sinking out of sight. Okracoke natives delight in giving tourists directions to his grave, which they can never find. Besides more grisly details of the exploits of Blackbeard and the other rapacious pirates of those times, records abound of corruption in high places as well and of honorable men who took to this life of crime on the high seas for riches, or just for the excitement. The last record of pirates in Virginia was in 1727, when Governor William Gooch ordered the execution of two pirates and the reprieve of a third, one John Vidal, "after the recent capture of 7 ships within 40 leagues of land by 2 privateers."

Another problem concerned the people of Princess Anne County. Every county was supposed to have a town, with a courthouse, a jail, a church and a center of commerce. When Adam Thorowgood conceived the first church of Lynnhaven Parish on his own land on the western side of the Lynnhaven River, he had expected it to grow and a town to be eventually established there, called Lynnhaven. But it never did, nor was a courthouse ever built there, as the records show that court was held in one or another private home for some years. These self-sustaining plantations really felt no need for a town, for they had their own wharfs on the navigable rivers from which to ship their tobacco and receive needed goods.

But Adam's grandson, Argall Thorowgood, wanted a town, and as the population on the eastern side of the Lynnhaven grew, he obtained a court order for a frame courthouse to be built on this eastern side in 1689. This, then, was the county seat when Princess Anne County was formed in 1691. It was also called "Lynnhaven" or "Lynnhaven Towne," and early wills and deeds refer to it. As the population moved southward, however, the town was abandoned and the courthouse moved further up the river to what is now called "Witchduck Point," where Savill Gaskin had first operated a ferry across the river and where a settlement had grown up. This was about 1692, for a new brick church was "required to be finished by the end of June 1692." A courthouse was here also, for this is where Grace Sherwood had been sentenced to her "trial by water."

The population continued to shift further southward as the Eastern Branch of the Elizabeth River was attracting influential and wealthy families such as the Walkes, the Kempes, the Moseleys, the Whitehursts and the Lawsons. A town had been established here in 1697, for in February of that year, Anthony Lawson, Edward Moseley, Jr. and William Moseley, Jr. bought 51 acres from Simon Handcock with the intention of creating a town to be called "Newtown." This was part of the land on which Simon Handcock lived, and the Lawsons and Moseleys lived nearby. The deed of sale states, "in hopes and designed to be for building storehouses and other houses thereon, for accommodation of merchandizing and for cohabi-

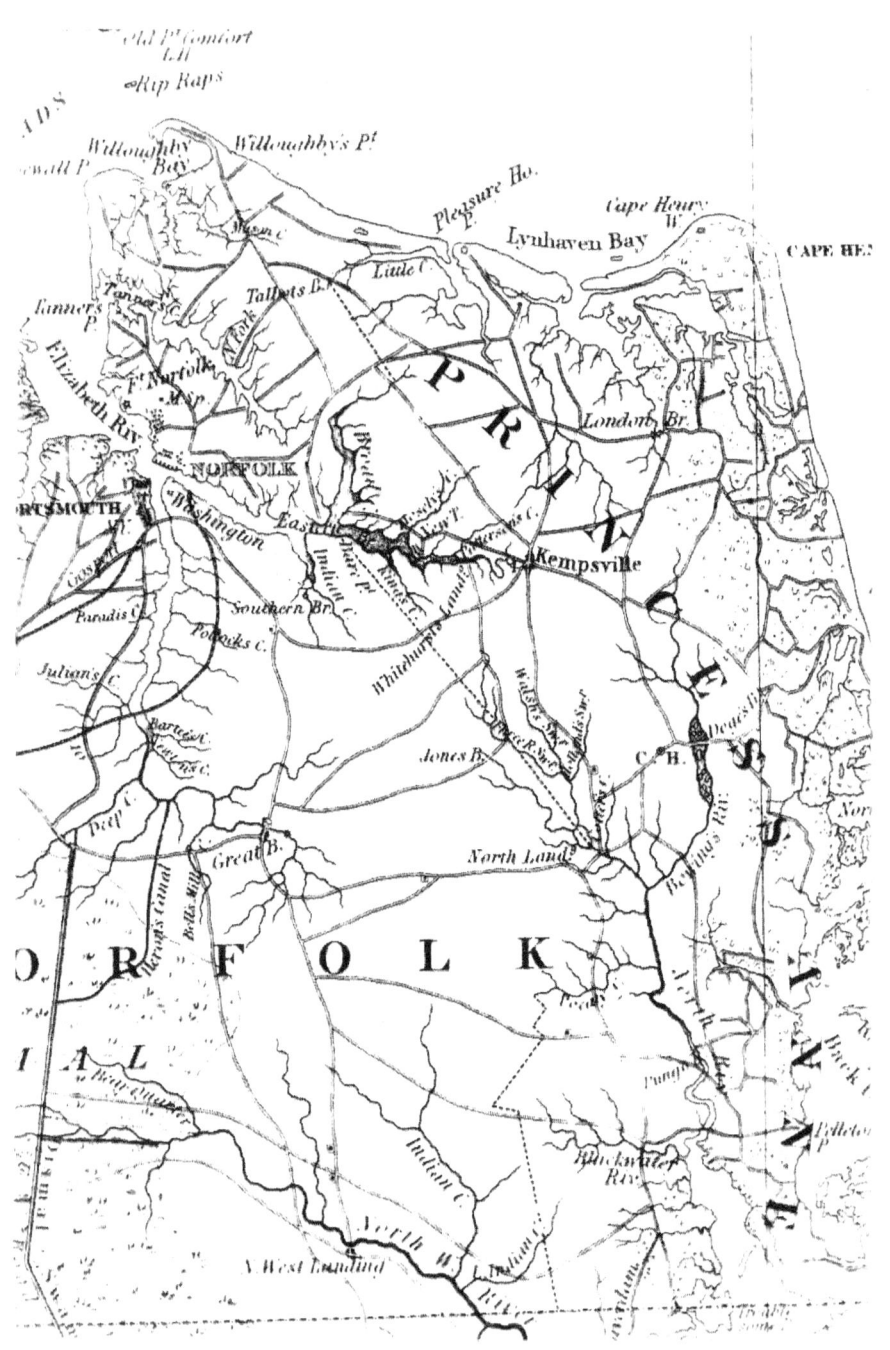

Location of Newtown, 1698. *Courtesy of the Virginia Landmarks Commission's Center for Archaeology.*

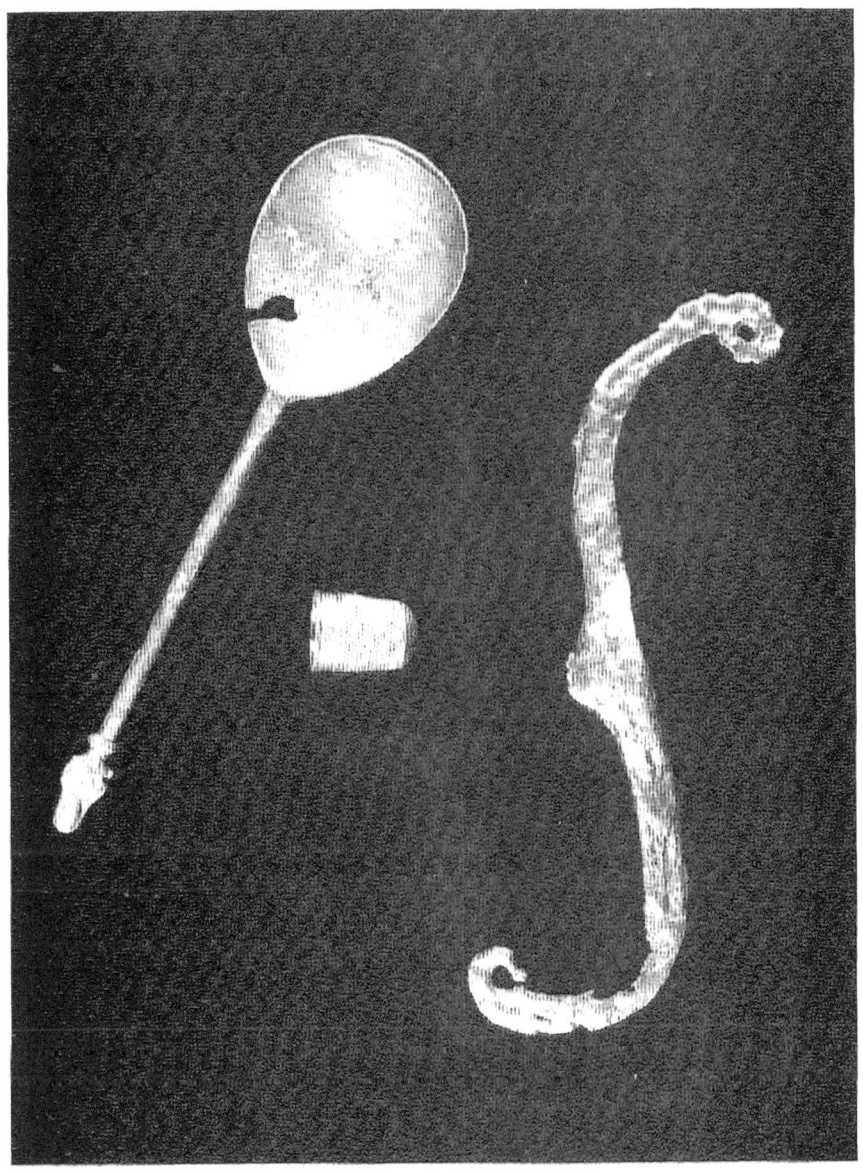

Thimble, sword hilt, and Apostle spoon from site of Adam Thorowgood I house.
Courtesy of Virginia Landmarks Commission's Center for Archaeology.

Adam Thorowgood house, circa 1640. *Photo by Philip R. Morrison.*

John Weblin house, circa 1670. *Photo by Philip R. Morrison.*

Adam Keeling house, circa 1680. *Photo by Philip R. Morrison.*

Lynnhaven house, circa 1725. Built by Savill Gaskin or Francis Thelaball. *Photo by Philip R. Morrison.*

Francis Land house, 1732. *Photo by Philip R. Morrison.*

Upper Wolfsnare, 1759. Built by Thomas Walke III. *Photo by Philip R. Morrison.*

Pembroke Manor, 1764. Home of Captain John Saunders. *Photo by Philip R. Morrison.*

Pleasant Hall, circa 1770. Built by George Logan or Peter Singleton. *Photo by Philip R. Morrison.*

Battle off the Capes, September 5, 1781. From painting by W. Zveg, *Courtesy of the Naval Historical Center.*

Old Donation Church, mother church of Lynnhaven Parish, circa 1782. *Photo by Philip R. Morrison.*

Old Lighthouse, 1792. *Photo by Nancy Braithwaite.*

Old Princess Anne County Courthouse, 1821. *Photo by Philip R. Morrison.*

tation, and a place of pride for buying and selling of goods in the nature or quantity of a town."

The purchase price was 10,000 pounds of tobacco, and the location was on the north side of the Eastern Branch of the Elizabeth River, "beginning at a point of land at the mouth of a small creek, dividing the plantation of Simon Handcock and Edward Moseley, Sr." In 1691, Capt. Hugh Campbell (whose land was on the North River) had offered a gift of 200 acres of land or 6,000 pounds of tobacco toward a "Chapel of Ease and/or a Minister or Reader for the convenience of the Inhabitants of the North River," who seldom had an opportunity to attend church, especially in the winter. Governor Nicholson accepted this offer with gratitude and himself contributed to this worthy cause. Therefore, a Chapel of Ease may already have been built in this planned town.

The half-acre lots were sold at a fixed price for five years on condition that "a good house 20' long and 15' broad be built by or before 1 Mar. 1698/9." Otherwise, the lot would revert to Lawson and the Moseleys. Further restrictions were that no cattle, hogs or sheep be allowed to run loose in the town, and no Indians allowed within its boundaries. Sales of lots were brisk, and it is recorded that Thomas Walke, John Thorowgood and Thomas Lawson had houses there, as well as Christopher Cocke and William Cowles, who were merchants, indicating that there was at least one store here. There also was another, owned by Capt. William Parsons, who received a letter from Edward Moseley requesting credit for Mr. Peter Frasier of Maryland "at your store in Newtown."

Col. Edward Moseley in 1732 gave one of his lots to James Nimmo, a surveyor who had laid out the town. A deed for the same lot states that it was given to Charles Smythe for the purpose of conducting a school in the house already on the lot. Since Charles Smythe is listed in his will as a merchant, it is assumed that he sponsored the school and James Nimmo, Sr. was the teacher.

Finally, in 1740, after a petition by the freeholders, an Act of Assembly confirmed the establishment of the town as "New-Towne" (Journal of the House of Burgesses 1736–1740). Evidence of the success of Newtown was a petition by the residents to the Executive Council of the Colony in 1752 for the removal of the courthouse from its previous location to their community. William Nimmo, Jr., son and heir of William Nimmo, according to the wishes of his father, donated one-half acre for the courthouse. It took two years for the petition to be approved.

"April 7, 1754
The Board having this day resumed the consideration of the petition for removing the Courthouse of Princess Anne County to New Towne, are of the opinion that New Towne is the most firm and convenient place for the Courthouse, with a Good and Sufficient Prison and Pillory to be erected at the expense of the Petitioners."

The town continued to prosper for some years, but in 1778, the courthouse was shifted to Kemps Landing. This move deserves some scrutiny, as it was right in the midst of the Revolution. Although the British were not occupying the area at the time, the merchants operating in Newtown then had departed, as had those in Norfolk, for all mercantile business was ruined, and the prominent Patriot families who had town houses in Newtown were more likely, under the circumstances, to retire to their plantations to protect them from forays by the British and the bands of outlaws which were ravaging the countryside. Also, Kempsville (then known as Kemp's Landing) was further away from the burned-out city of Norfolk, which was still considered a likely spot for British invaders. However, Newtown remained a port of some consequence since it is included on a map drawn for Benedict Arnold, the traitor, when he was General Benedict Arnold of the British Army in command in 1780–81 of the whole area of Norfolk, Princess Anne and Nansemond counties, with his headquarters in Portsmouth. This map shows 12 structures in Newtown and the road leading to it. Later maps continue to show Newtown until 1823, when Herman Boye's map shows only the road.

The 18th century saw many changes in Princess Anne County. Newtown was the third town in the county which had started auspiciously and then just withered away. But it had been, by far, the largest and most important. Perhaps this dream of a real town had been only a fetish of these well-to-do families who had made fortunes and wanted more elegance and sophistication than was available on their farms. At any rate, it rapidly disappeared from the records. By 1950, there was no trace of it, and it was all but forgotten. Only the name of Newtown Road remained, and where the town had been was located the Brock Farm of 1,300 acres, one of the largest in the state.

In 1959, the City of Norfolk annexed this part of Princess Anne County and all the land west of Military Highway, north to just west of Little Creek. With increased housing and industry in the area and rising taxes, Mr. Edwin Brock decided to develop the old site of Newtown in a way which would preserve the history and flavor of its life. As excavation started, such intriguing artifacts were unearthed that he called in the Virginia Research Center for Archaeology. Their findings and further study of the history of the town have been preserved in the Center, and it is hoped that they will soon be displayed with other artifacts of our long history for all to see and study. Some of the most interesting of the Newtown artifacts are a beautiful 18th century wine glass, a fine Chinese export porcelain bowl, seven English delftware punch bowls, two German stoneware vessels with the cipher of George I, and a Spanish silver coil dated 1735.

But the mystery remains. It is almost inconceivable that a well-planned elegant town could disappear into the ground and sleep forgotten for a hundred years while crops were planted, grew and were harvested above it. We have noted the rapid changes in population centers, and then the Revolution had plunged the county into a maelstrom of confusion and desolation. The answer to this puzzle may lie in the combination of circumstances which led up to the Revolution, and the Revolution itself, with the hard times which followed. (Virginia Cavalcade, vol. XXXII, Summer 1982. *Seventeenth Century Virginia's Forgotten Yeomen,* T. H. Breen & Stephen Innes.)

> "Throughout the seventeenth century Virginia's accessible waterways connected her fields with tobacconists of Europe. So long as the ships of the tobacco fleet could sail conveniently to wharves at the leading plantations, the Virginia colonists' recurrent dream of thriving towns and cities went unrealized."

The Chesapeake in the Seventeenth Century, edited by Thad Tate, says:

> "English born inhabitants of Virginia, Henry Hartwell, James Blair, and Edward Chilton, blamed the lack of towns on the native majority in the House of Burgesses, whom, they believed, had never seen one, and therefore could not imagine the advantages."

The Spanish coin which was found by the archaeologists at Newtown leads us to another bit of confusion. For reasons no one has made clear, England had never allowed any of her currency to be taken out to any of her colonies. The result here was that tobacco, the most widespread and valuable crop grown in Virginia, was used as currency as early as 1619. Paper receipts from a tobacco warehouse were used as money. Tithes were collected in tobacco by the church until after the Revolution, and it was used in all local transactions. A small number of coins found here were those of other countries—France, Spain, Holland and Germany—and were greatly overvalued before the Navigation Acts. These Navigation Acts severely limited trade with countries other than England, and merchants of those countries demanded more for their coins than they were actually worth, at least 33 and one-third percent more.

So, the barter system developed. (Lower Norfolk County Book c. f.71.)

> "This indenture made ye Eighteenth day of October in ye yere of our Lord God one thousand fifty & one (clerk's error, should read 1651)
> Between ffrancis Bright of Elizabeth River . . . Lower Norff. planter of these parts & John Lawrence . . . of Nansemond planter . . . consideration of one horse coat and two paire of Shooes . . . one hundred acres of land which he holdeth from William Eyres of Nansemond . . . bought of Edward Selbye. For a terme of Eighteen yeres Rent, one good fatted Capon Yerely on New Yeres Day at ye now dwelling house of ye sd. William Eyres situated in Nansemond."

And another. (Norfolk County Deed Book 6, p. 85.)

> "Dated 15 March 1694/5
> . . . John Tucker & Mary, his wife both of the Western branch of Eliz. River in the County of Norfolk . . . and Andrew Taylor of the Same place . . . for and in consideration of Eight paire of french fall Shoes . . . about four or five acres . . . head of the Said Western Branch, and in part of a Patent formerly belonging to one Capps, and now in the possession of the said John Tucker & Mary, his wife, as in right by her, the said parcel of land lying betwixt the land of the sd. Andrew Taylor and the land of John Whitehall bounded in with two branches . . ."

This barter system worked well within the Colony up to 1650 when England began to impose restrictions on the export of tobacco and any other goods produced by the colonies. These restrictions were designed to eliminate trade by the colonists with any other country, and the major restriction was that no goods from America could be shipped into England except in ships of which the owner, the master and the major part of the crew were English. This act was strengthened in 1660, when Parliament decreed that enumerated articles of colonial growth and manufacture, such as sugar, tobacco and indigo, be shipped only to England on English built ships. In 1673, duties were imposed at the ports of clearance, when enumerated products were shipped from one plantation to another.

There is evidence in many of the larger plantation houses still standing that there was once a tunnel in the basement leading out to a navigable creek nearby. It had long been thought that this tunnel was an escape route in case of an Indian attack, but this is a false notion as the few Indians left were no threat. As stated earlier, tunnels from houses were handy for smuggling. The Mother Country, aware of this, and needing many articles from the colonies, gave bounties for goods other than tobacco in 1705–1709, such as pitch, tar, hemp and other naval stores as masts, yards and bowsprits. They also lowered the duties on beaver skins in 1721, which prior to that time had mostly been shipped to Continental Europe. Beaver hats were high style in Europe at that time.

These acts were resented by the colonists and there were several results, good and bad. The worst for this Colony was the inability to ship tobacco to other countries in Europe. This flooded the English market and the price dropped drastically. Since the planters could not be paid in money but only in English goods, each shipment was accompanied by a list of wanted articles: wearing apparel, furniture, silverware and china. Regardless of the price the tobacco brought in the English market, these requests were filled, and the factor here presented a bill to the planter. This put him in debt to the merchant until the next tobacco harvest. If the next crop failed, or if the price dropped again between the time the tobacco was shipped and it was actually sold, the planter was further in debt because in another year his wants had increased. Always looking for a bonanza crop and a price rise, the planters fell deeper and deeper in debt as their life style became more and more extravagant.

England seemed determined to bleed the colonies dry, but in those years, she had wars to contend with, and to pay for. Other products were encouraged, which was in fact good for Princess Anne County. The time had passed when tobacco grew well here. The sandy soil, almost devoid of the nutrients which tobacco plants needed, did not produce the best quality, and land was becoming too scarce merely to clear another spot and plant again. But the forests were still here and not only produced wood for shipbuilding, but the pines also yielded pitch, tar and turpentine. Bounties were given for these products, and the growing of flax for hemp and linen was encouraged.

The growing and processing of flax was a tedious business and was not widespread. Only Isaac Murray and his three sons, Thomas, David and Isaac, seemed to have made a fortune in this operation on their land surrounding King's Creek on the southern side of the Eastern Branch of the Elizabeth River. The first Murray, David, had come here in 1651 with a grant of 300 acres. Succeeding sons had acquired more land until Isaac Murray had 777 acres and began his flax business in the shallows of King's Creek. Besides his manor house, Isaac built houses for each of his sons, two on the west side of the creek and one on the east. The one on the east bank of the creek was for Thomas, built in 1791 and meticulously and beautifully restored some years ago by Mr. and Mrs. John Tucker. David Murray's house, across the creek remains, also, but in poor condition.

By the middle of the century, the planters were turning to grain, especially wheat and corn which was sold to New England as intercolonial trade increased.

Tobacco continued to be the main medium of exchange by the court, the church and local businesses. New England began to print paper money in 1690, and by 1720, it was legal in all payments there. Virginia was forced to follow suit during the French and Indian Wars, 1754–70, to pay the troops conscripted here for that war. By law, they could not be paid in tobacco. The people of Lower Norfolk County had resented being recruited to fight the occasional Indian wars in other parts of the Colony, as those other Indians were no threat to them here. When they were required to provide troops to fight England's war, as well as to equip them and pay them, they were indignant, especially when they had to be paid in currency. So they printed £250,000 of paper (Current money of Virginia). Not at all satisfied with this arrangement, Parliament passed "The Currency Act" in 1764, prohibiting issues of legal tender in all the American colonies, nullified all acts of colonial assemblies contrary to its terms and imposed a fine of £1,000 and dismissal from office on any governor who assented to legislative acts in defiance of the law. These acts of "oppression" will be recounted later, as they led up to the Revolution.

PART THREE
Chapter 2
COUNTY LIFE IN THE GOLDEN AGE

As the 18th century progressed, slaves became more numerous, the wealthy became more wealthy, and entertainment of all kinds increased. There is a hint of jealousy in the following opinions expressed by visitors from the Mother Country. Hugh Jones, in 1724 in *The Present State of Virginia*, says:

> "The common planters leading easy lives don't much admire Labour, or any manly exercise, except Horse-racing, nor Diversion except Cock-fighting, in which some greatly delight. This easy Way of Living, and the Heat of the Summer make some very lazy, who are then said to be Climate-Struck."

Another is in the *Memoirs of Elkanah Watson*, from 1777–1842.

> "Dec. 1777.
> Soon after entering Virginia and at a highly respectable house, I was shocked beyond the power of language to express, at seeing for the first time, young negroes of both sexes from 12–15 years old, not only running about the house, but absolutely tending table, almost as naked as when they came into the world. What made the same more extraordinary still, to my unpractised eye, was the fact that several yong women were at table, who appeared totally unmoved by this scandalous violation of decency."

And, in *The Chesapeake in the 17th Century* (Thad W. Tate) is quoted the English view of the colonists.

> "The idea of emigrants growing rich and then passing themselves off as gentlemen and governors seemed to offend the Englishmen's hierarchal sensibilities."

Colonial Farmer and Wife, 1776. *Courtesy of Peter Copeland. From "Everyday Dress of the American Revolution."*

Julia Cherry Spruill in *Women's Life and Work in the Southern Colonies* takes a more acceptable view.

> "Among the chief characteristics of the southern colonists were extraordinary enjoyment of all kinds of gatherings, a great fondness for display in dress and entertainment, and a most liberal hospitality."

The people of Princess Anne County were no exception. From the highest to the lowest, they loved drinking and dancing and welcomed any stranger with the best they had to offer. This "best" was very good indeed. After early morning tea, a sumptuous hot breakfast was served at nine or ten o'clock. The fare for dinner, which was about three o'clock, usually included oysters, several kinds of wild game, ducks, wild turkey or venison, baked ham, a profusion of vegetables, corn or wheat breads, puddings, fruits and nuts. All through the day, there was punch or beer, and a cold supper was served before bedtime.

A "dining room" did not exist as such in the 17th century, except in the most elaborate homes. Breakfast was served in the kitchen, and dinner served outdoors when the weather permitted. Otherwise, for a large number, planks were put on sawhorses in the hall and covered with a cloth; for a small number a table was set wherever convenient.

Popular diversions of men were hunting, fishing, horse races and cockfights. Beginning in the 17th century, the quarter race developed, a diversion unmatched in later times for violence and aggressiveness. The course was a straight and narrow path of a quarter mile and was run by two riders. There were no rules, and as they galloped down the track at full speed, each used whip, knee or elbow to dismount their opponent and drive him off the track. It was a wild ride, and broken bones added to the excitement. There was heavy betting on these races, held on court days or whenever boasting of the prowess of a horse or rider resulted in a challenge to compete.

The quarter horse got its name from these early races. Since that time, it has been bred for speed on a short run and adaptability to quick turns, and it is a favorite of ranchers. Later on, the gentry took over horse-racing on a more formalized style, with oval tracks on all large plantations and regular meets lasting a week at a time, accompanied by dinners, balls and entertainments. But the country people continued their quarter races as before, until today, when they are a sight to behold, particularly the "barrel" race and the "pick up." The "pick up" is the most exciting. The rider at full gallop picks up a

Method of transporting horses in the 16th Century. *From "Horse of the Americas," Denhardt. Courtesy of the University of Oklahoma Press.*

young farm boy and swings him up behind him. Sometimes, the boy swings up too fast and sails over into the wild blue yonder.

Horses had first been brought to the Western Hemisphere by the Spaniards in their conquest of Mexico, and they had wandered north into our western states. The wild ponies of Okracoke and Chincoteague are probably descendants of Spanish horses which had managed to swim ashore after early shipwrecks in the Chesapeake Bay. On a rougher and sparser diet, they gradually became smaller. But most of the horses in these early settlements of Virginia had been brought with cattle from England, Holland, France and especially, Ireland. We believe Daniel Gookin imported a great many. These poor animals had a difficult time suspended in slings, as pictured, and many died en route. The ones that survived did well and reproduced rapidly. A Dutch schooner in 1660 brought 27 mares. By the 18th century, the better horses were kept for saddle and coach use, and the small and inferior ones were allowed to run wild with the herd.

Toward the end of the 17th century, when horses as well as cattle and hogs ran wild in the forests, the horses frequently dropped foals in the woods. These wild horses would belong to anyone who could seize and brand them. A rather cruel sport of the young men was to chase them on horseback, hoping to acquire a spirited steed, often riding their own horse to death in the process.

The English thoroughbred was developed by crossing the native running mare with an outstanding Arabian stallion. "Bull Rock," the first one of these thoroughbreds to be imported to America, in 1730, was crossed with the best mare and was the beginning of the American thoroughbred. Virginia was the leading supporter of this American thoroughbred, and from then on, the fashionable races were run by thoroughbred horses with professional jockeys. Ladies attended these races and were as avid bettors as the men.

The cockfight was another bloody duel. Elkanah Watson also describes this with distaste.

> "The roads, as we approached the scene, were alive with carriages, horses, and pedestrians, black and white. Several houses formed a spacious square, in the center of which was arranged a long cockpit, surrounded by many genteel people, promiscuously mingled with the vulgar and debased. Exceedingly beautiful cocks were produced, armed with long, sharp steel-pointed gaffs, which were firmly attached to their natural spurs.
>
> The moment the birds were dropped, bets ran high, the little heroes appeared trained to the business, and not in the least disconcerted by the crowd or shouting. They stepped about with great

apparent pride and dignity; advancing nearer and nearer, they flew at each other, the cruel and fatal gaffs being driven into their bodies, and, at times, directly through their heads."

This mortal combat became so popular that notices advertised great matches and were even marked in the church calendar of festivals. In a more humane age, this sport was finally outlawed.

Not all entertainment was so bloodthirsty. Both men and women loved dancing. In the 17th century, gatherings were limited to weddings, funerals, going to church and court days. Beginning in 1702, with the death of William III and the proclamation of Queen Anne, a splendid celebration was held at Williamsburg, and social life assumed greater importance. This was of particular gratification to the people of Princess Anne County, who had honored the Queen, then Princess Anne, by naming the county for her. Those who could attended the two-day celebration in Williamsburg, but there was a great deal of drinking, dancing and general jollity on this holiday here.

Dancing accompanied every celebration, even funerals, for once the formality of interment was over and the deceased consigned to the family graveyard, the guests lingered on for several days. Besides feasting, the host provided what entertainment he could, which included music for dancing. Young and old joined in the dancing, which usually started with the stately Minuet, followed by country dances, reels and jigs. Rarely did a dancing master visit this county, although one was engaged by one of the upper class, as in the audit of the estate of Thomas Lawson in 1758, he owed "Mr. Staton the dancing master 10 shillings, 10 pence." But the young men and, especially, the young ladies of the well-to-do did a great deal of visiting for lengthy stays in the great plantations of The Northern Neck or Accomac, where they quickly learned the latest European dances, the English country dances and the reels. When they returned, they taught their relatives and friends. The younger children learned, too, and danced with their companions and the children of the slaves, singing along as an accompaniment.

The black children had learned jigs (a lively jumping dance) from their parents and, in turn, taught the whites. With the blacks' talent for music, they easily learned to play any instrument available to them, from the ever-present harmonica to drums, horns and flutes. Few spinets or harpsicords were in the houses here, but when they were, they were more for concerts of more serious music than dancing. Violins and bass viols were fairly common, and the slaves were very efficient in playing them, being hired out for balls. The banjo, a favorite instrument of theirs, was of Spanish origin and had come to the Colony with Spanish sailors. It was a fairly easy instrument to copy and play.

The concerts on the spinet and harpsicord were designed to show off the accomplishments of the young ladies of the household. Mary Cherry Spruill says in *Women in the Southern Colonies,* "In 1766 one E. Gardner advertised that she had taken a house in Norfolk where she would board young ladies to teach them French and the latest fashions in needlework. Six years later, as E. Armston, she announced that she was continuing her school at Point Pleasant and offered a more elaborate course of study, including painting, and, if her patrons desired, to engage 'Proficients in Music and dancing.'" Sons of the wealthiest, who had been educated in England, had learned there, along with genteel manners, to dance and to play the violin or French horn. Most, however, were merely taught by their sisters, cousins or visitors. The plainer folk did not attend these formal balls, but they had frequent dances of their own, dancing the less ceremonial figures.

Norfolk was growing into an important port in the 18th century, and many prominent visitors from England were entertained by the Scottish merchants, while, in the eyes of the Norfolkians, Princess Anne County remained "country" and rather rustic. But one family here, the Moseleys, was recognized as being "born to the purple," and each generation of that family had been well-instructed in the manners and education of gentlemen. When Norfolk was delighted by a visit from Lord and Lady Dunmore on their coming to the Colony in 1771 as governor, the town was in a flutter over a great ball that was to be given in his honor. On perceiving the elegance of this aristocratic couple, the Norfolk ladies were at a loss for someone to dance with Lady Dunmore who would not step on her feet! Hurriedly, they sent for Edward Hack Moseley, Jr., the "Beau Brummel" of Princess Anne, as the only one worthy to dance with her. Unperturbed, he sailed her around the floor in all the latest dances. At least that is the story told here. But Edward Hack Moseley, Jr., is best remembered as the able clerk of the court through the trying 43 years of 1771–1814.

Games of chance, cards and dice were very popular with all classes. Queen Anne's biographer says she was an avid card player, although invariably losing large sums to her ladies-in-waiting, and the colonists also were inveterate gamblers, sometimes with dire results. At a ball, there always was an adjoining room where the gentlemen could play cards, if they chose, fortified by brandy. The drinking seems heavy, but not as heavy as in England, as the hot climate combined with liquor brought on unpleasant distempers.

Sack, a dry Spanish wine, was popular in the 17th century as is mentioned in many records, such as court records of overcharging by tavern keepers. Sack declined in favor in the 18th century, replaced by homemade beer and cider. Justices in the court were well-provided with drink, and all workers received their allotted "pint" a day.

The law said that there should be only one tavern to a county, and it was to be adjacent to the courthouse. But, in this large county, court at first was held in different areas in private homes. When a courthouse was built in the 18th century these taverns already established continued to operate and the old law forgotten. From a crude affair, with no waiters and for men only they developed into country inns with accomodations for travelers, or those too drunk to make their way home and they were piled in—two, three or more to a bed.

The wealthy drank Madiera, port and other French and German imported wines. These were usually mixed with fruit juices and spices for a punch, the most common drink, and a variety of sizes of punch bowls were kept in every affluent household. Cordials, brandies and rum from the West Indies were the stronger drinks, which the ladies took only for "medicinal reasons," and the gentlemen because they enjoyed them. Whiskey was yet unknown, as they had not learned the knack of distilling from grain. Although heavy drinking had its drawbacks, many lives were saved by indulging in these drinks rather than water from the shallow wells and creeks.

Early in the 18th century, a playhouse was built in Williamsburg, and from time to time, professional companies of actors played there. Between times, gentlemen and ladies put on performances. Amateur theatricals became very popular, not only in towns, but on plantations where the family and neighbors entered into them with great enthusiasm.

Since the beginning of the Colony, apparel for both men and women had been a matter of intense interest and great importance. John Pory, secretary of the Colony, wrote in 1691 that the cow keeper at James City went on Sundays "accowtered all in freshe flaming silks," and the wife of a former collier in England wore her "rough bever hatt witha faire perle hatband, and a silken suite thereto correspondent." *(Narratives of Early Virginia.)*

Certainly, the first colonists' apparel was inappropriate, burdensome and uncomfortable, and perhaps not so many would have died

Capture of Opechancanough, King of the Pamunkeys, by Captain John Smith. *Courtesy of the Folger Shakespeare Library, from their copy of John Smith's "The General Historie of Virginia, 1624."*

Portrait of Pocahontas in court dress, London. *Courtesy of the Folger Library from their copy of John Smith's "General Historie of Virginia, 1624."*

County Life in "The Golden Age"

that first year if they had stripped down like the Indians. But the English had no idea of adapting to the climate and felt compelled to dress as befitting their rank. Only John Smith seemed willing to learn from the savages, and even he, as can be seen in the slightly idealized picture (American Genesis) of his capture of Opechancanough, had not shed his heavy English clothes. The portrait of Pocahontas done in England is a picture of misery, as the formerly carefree young Indian princess was now in the latest ghastly court style. Queen Elizabeth had died in 1603, but styles she had set as most becoming to her remained in fashion in the reign of her successor, James I, at least during the visit of Pocohantas.

In the 18th century, the colonists continued to ape the English, insisting on the latest styles. Satins, silks and laces were worn in abundance. The ladies were laced into their tight stays even for church, and the men paid particular attention to buttons and shoe buckles, which were of silver if they could afford them. Buying ready-made clothes from England was preferable and also convenient, as before towns were established, Hugh Jones says in 1723 that "goods made in London were delivered at private landing places of Virginia gentlemen with less trouble and cost than to persons living five miles in the country in England." Later in the century, materials were imported and fashioned by tailors and seamstresses among indentured servants. Later still, household spinning wheels were common, and many slave women were trained as spinners to make the coarse cloth for the slaves' clothing.

To protect her home woolen industry, England banned the colonies from exporting woolen cloth. If wool was woven into cloth here, it had to be from a farmer's own sheep and used only for that family's needs. (Lower Norfolk County Records, Order Book 1675-1686.)

> "Court 16 Aug. 1683
> Whereas Henry Halstead hath brought before this Court 114 yards of volen Cloath Wch hee Upon Oath declared was of his owne manufactory. A Cett. is therefore granted him for the same according to the Act."

In 1705, Beverly wrote of the Virginians: "They have their Clothing of all sorts from England . . . Yet, Flax and Hemp grow no where in the World better than there. Their sheep bear good Fleeces, but they shear them only to cool them." He was in error about the wool. The only record available of the flax business is the successful operation of the Murray family on King's Creek. Apparently, most of their flax was sold as hemp and for yards and sails to the Norfolk shipbuilders, and scrap was used for stuffing upholstery and mattresses.

We believe that more duels were fought than appear in the records. They were not formal affairs as in England, but since the Gibbs brothers had the effrontery to draw their swords on each other in court, it is likely that other hot-blooded young men, always armed by law, would not be prone to wait for the court to decide a difference. Instead, they would use their arms in a quarrel, especially when under the influence of drink.

Philip Alexander Bruce quotes *Evelyn's Diary*, December 18, 1684: "So many horrid murders and duels were committed about this time as were never heard of in England, and which gave much cause of complaint and murmurings."

The Princess Anne County court attempted to put a stop to this custom by taking Reodolphus Malbone to court for challenging Solomon White "with Sword and pistoll & other misbehavior." Malbone was put in the custody of the sheriff until he could come up with 50 pounds current money for security for his good behavior for 12 months and court costs (Edward W. James, Virginia Historical Magazine.

A more serious side of colonial life was the concern for the education of children. Choosing home sites on the many navigable creeks and rivers seemed an excellent idea at the time of no roads, but these home sights were so far apart that providing schooling for children was indeed a problem. Only a few could, or wished, to send their children to England to be educated. Only one in Lower Norfolk County, Henry Seawell, is recorded as having sent his son there, and he never returned! A few more sent their sons across the ocean in the 18th century, but they were usually the sons of English and Scottish merchants of Norfolk.

Alternatives were to engage a tutor or procure an indentured servant who had sufficient education to teach reading, writing and simple arithmetic. A third alternative was to persuade the minister, where there was one, to teach one's children for a fee in his house, but there was then the problem of transporting the children to the Glebe for lessons. Another problem was the young boys who had come as apprentices and whose indentures often included the stipulation that they be taught to read and write.

When the second Lynnhaven Parish Church, on the east side of the Lynnhaven River, was abandoned as a church in favor of the new and larger one at "The Ferry," the vestry voted to use the building as a school, with a paid teacher. It is uncertain how long this school lasted, but it was a start, and in 1715 (Book 9, p. 437), Gilbert Holloday was hired as a schoolmaster.

Although about 50 percent of the freemen could not read or write themselves, as evidenced by the signing of their wills with a mark, their wills often directed that children be educated—girls for two years and boys for three—with funds for that purpose to come out of the estate.

Occasionally, a philanthropic individual would leave bequests for schools in land. Beverly in 1705 in *History of Virginia* wrote: "There are large tracts of land, houses and other things granted to free schools for the education of children in many parts of the country . . . and management left to direction of county court or the vestry of respective parishes."

In Princess Anne County, there were four such bequests of land. Here, there is a dearth of charitable donations in wills of the more affluent. The exception was Thomas Walke III, whose will of 1759 states:

> "*Item:* I give all the land and swamp I bought from Hezekiah Fentress containing about one hundred and ninety-six acres, also that piece or parcel of swamp land I bought of Aaron Fentress, lying between the aforesaid land and Int (?) Shipping Land containing about twenty-five acres to and for the use of the poor and disabled people of the parish of Princess Anne, towards the education and maintaining of them, for the Vestry of said Parish to erect houses thereon for the reception of such poor orphans and others, if they cannot get a more convenient place, but if they can elsewhere provide themselves better, then I desire the said Vestry or Church Wardens, or their successors may sell and dispose of the said land and swamp, and the money arising from said land, etc. be by them laid out as soon as possible for breeding negroes, for the use and uses aforesaid, that is, for the better help, schooling and support of the said poor orphans, etc. from time to time, as the Vestry or Church Wardens of the Parish shall deem proper."

In his way, Thomas Walke was a philanthropist. He had quite a lot of land, almost 7,000 acres, and he left his six children and his wife well-provided for, with land, money and cattle.

Another to bequeath land was Charles Whitehurst, a successful Norfolk tailor who was a member of the Princess Anne County Whitehurst family. He owned extensive acreage west of Kemp's Landing, and in 1760, he gave 25 acres to the vestry of Lynnhaven Parish for the use of the poor. This was part of a tract of 250 acres that was on "the main road that leads from Kemp's Landing over London Bridge," on a branch of the Lynnhaven River which once flowed through the present town of London Bridge. This gift also proves that in 1760 there was a main road from there to Kemp's Landing.

The third was Anthony Walke. In 1762, he deeded 31¾ acres for the use of the poor, to be sold after 1785.

The fourth was the Reverend Robert Dickson, rector of Lynnhaven Parish for 28 years, from 1748–1776. He left a very generous bequest for a free school for orphan boys. He directed that one-half of his personal estate go to his wife Amy, the rest to be sold and the money to go to the vestry of Lynnhaven Parish. After the death of his wife, the balance of the estate was to be sold to "hire an able and discreet teacher of Latin, Greek, and mixed mathematics to teach a number of poor male children, natives of the Parish, for as long as the Vestry sees fit, and to furnish books and other necessaries to poor males." Mr. Dickson was a wealthy man. His inventory showed seven horses, cattle, sheep and beehives and, in the house, fine furniture, china, silver and two barrels of brandy!

The estate was finally settled in 1782, and the money was in the hands of the vestry, who kept one-third of the land for the school, which became known as "Donation Farm" and the church, also on this land, became known as "Old Donation Church" by 1822. The Revolution was now over, and in the separation of church and state in the new Constitution, all unused glebes and church buildings were escheated to the state. We believe that none of this particular property was confiscated, however, as the vestry contended that it would be used for the church and school.

In spite of other beneficent bequests for the education of the poor in former wills, which even go back to the will of Richard Russell of Lower Norfolk County in 1667, who left one-sixth of his estate for that purpose, there is no concrete evidence that these instructions were ever carried out by the vestry until Mr. Dickson's bequest. Even then, it was not until 1785 that a minister was found to teach as well as preach. He was to teach six free students with an additional 16 who paid, giving him an extra £ 40 a year in addition to his salary as minister.

It is said that the school continued for many years, but it appears doubtful. The church was frequently without a minister—thus, no teacher. Without the compulsory tithes collected during the tenure of the Church of England, the vestry had a difficult time finding a minister, let alone one with the qualifications demanded by Mr. Dickson's will. Norfolk Academy had been founded as a private school in that city in 1728, but it was inaccessible to those living in Princess Anne County. Thomas Jefferson, even before he was governor of Virginia in 1781, had urged the creation of a public school system, and he continued to do so. But it was not effected until after 1866, Virginia being one of the last of the original 13 colonies to supply this urgent need.

But despite the lack of schools in this county in the 18th century, many of the inhabitants had a surprising number and variety of books. With the growing prosperity and the increased importation of slaves, from 1690–1740, parents had more leisure to attend to their children's education themselves. While this education did not go much beyond the basics, books were available, and many titles were on the list of articles ordered from England in exchange for tobacco.

As early as 1640, almost everyone had at least one Bible, and in addition, inventories of estates in Lower Norfolk County usually merely stated, "a parcel of ould books," which could number from four to one hundred. Nathaniel Branker had a whole trunk of books in 1684; John Kemp in 1648 had seven books of chirosurgery, five divinity books, Pastell's *Abridgement of the Statutes,* and part of the Court Baron and Leet; and Richard Russell in his will bequeathed 27 books to different friends. William Moseley in 1671 left books in French, Dutch, Latin and English, and Mrs. Thomas Willoughby had in her inventory: divinity books, several Bibles, *Essays of Montaigne,* a *Seaman's Calendar,* a Thesaurus, directions on planting mulberry trees, *Aesops Fables,* a book on trigonometry, volumes of Ovid, Virgil and Cicero in Latin, a *History of Animals and Minerals* and many others. In the 18th century, wills show an increasing number of books on a variety of subjects, and Norfolk even had a bookstore.

As evidence of the prosperity of Princess Anne County, as well as the whole Colony, in "The Golden Age," modern-day Virginia Beach has within its boundaries 20 houses that were so well-built during the 18th century, they have survived the vicissitudes of the last 200 years. One is now owned by the City of Virginia Beach, two are owned by The Princess Anne County Historical Society, and others are privately owned and inhabited. All 20 have been either lovingly preserved by various owners or are in the process of restoration. Research of wills, deeds and other court records has revealed who built these houses and how these people lived. Thirteen others, while historic in part, have been so renovated by the requirements of various owners and changing life styles as to no longer give a vivid picture of life 200 years ago.

The Francis Land House, the one owned by the City of Virginia Beach, was built in 1732 by Francis Land III. Although four generations of Francis Lands lived here, it was Francis III who built the house as it stands today as there was a brick on an outside wall incised with the date 1732, and Francis III died in 1736.

The first Francis Land was here before 1637, for in that year, Adam Thorowgood took him to court in a boundary dispute. Land's first grant was recorded in 1649 for 270 acres, and his second, in 1654, for 1020 acres, was a repatent of the 270 plus additional acreage he had purchased or received for the transportation of others into the Colony. This large holding was on a branch of the Lynnhaven River, now dried up, which flowed to the southwest of the house, but it was navigable at that time for we know that he had at least one ship. He had come from Barbados, where many well-to-do English families had shipping interests.

Although the date of the house implies that it was built by his grandson, we believe that it was built on the foundation of an earlier house, which probably burned, of the same size. There is a marked difference in the bricks of the foundation as seen in the large English basement. They are much paler and more irregular. We are sure, however, that this house was on the land of the original grant, for it states that it was on the Lynnhaven River in Lynnhaven Parish, and Thomas Keeling's grant of 1640 places it "near Francis Land's plantation." William Shipp's grant of 1647 also states, "near Francis Land's plantation." Francis Land was in court several times for not paying his bills, but that did not prevent him from immediately joining the inner circle of the upper class as tolerance had developed early in this community. He was a vestryman and a church warden and was active in church affairs.

This is an elegant house of a wealthy family. Of brick laid in Flemish bond pattern, it has a gambrel roof and large inside chimneys at the east and west ends. The high ceilings, spacious hall and graceful stairway, with a landing lighted by a south window, show a house designed for entertaining. The four bedrooms above, an unusual number for that period, indicate many guests, for none of the Lands had large families and banquets in those days were lengthy affairs. Of typical Georgian design, the nine-foot-wide paneled hall separates two large rooms on the front, the parlor on the left and the formal dining room on the right, with a smaller room behind each: one the family living dining room and the other a library or office. With ancient trees and a sweeping driveway, it is a commanding sight on Virginia Beach Boulevard, one of the oldest roads in the county. Unusual features are the brick firewall through the center of the house, from the basement to the roof, huge beams running the length of the house visible in the basement, and an outside door in the formal dining room.

Succeeding Francis Lands continued to be even more prominent as justices, and in other public offices, and married into other prominent families, such as the Moseleys and Thorowgoods. But Francis V had no sons, only two daughters. They, with their husbands, quarreled over the division of the estate, and it was sold with all contents at a public auction with all the prominent men in the county as buyers. From then on, it had many owners. No outbuildings remain today, but Mr. Colin Studds, the owner in 1952, retrieved enough old bricks lying about to rebuild an outside kitchen where he thought it may have been.

When Union troops occupied the county in the War Between the States, the house was used as a headquarters and, it is said, the large basement a prison for captured Confederate officers. There is no visible ghost here, but there is a strong sense of days long past.

When this beautiful house was in danger of being demolished in 1975, the City of Virginia Beach bought it, along with the surrounding 35 acres. Leaving the three acres around the house clear, the rest has been developed with commercial buildings compatible with its style and period. All the property is officially zoned as an Historic and Cultural Area, and the house is listed on the Virginia Landmarks Commission's List of Historic Landmarks and the United States Department of the Interior List of Historic Places.

One of the two houses built in the 18th century that is owned by The Princess Anne County Historical Society is Upper Wolfsnare, on Potters Road near the present town of Oceana. This substantial house, also of brick, was built by Thomas Walke III, the grandson of the first Thomas Walke, who had come to Lower Norfolk County in 1662 (Kellam). He, too, came from Barbados, where the Walke family had already established a prosperous shipping business, and he evidently came here to expand that business in the Colony.

Thomas Walke I first bought land at the head of the Elizabeth River, but a grant is not recorded for this until 1689. This was for 450 acres, and another for 194 acres was recorded in 1693, the year he died. These acres he left to his son Thomas, and he left another plantation nearby to his son Anthony, with directions that it be sold and, with an addition of 100 £ sterling from his estate, his executor to buy him "a more suitable plantation."

This first Thomas Walke had come here well-supplied with money and fine furniture, including 18 Russian leather chairs and a Spanish olivewood chest. His silver included a pair of "silver hilted pistols" and "a silver headed cane." He quickly established himself, marrying the daughter of Colonel Anthony Lawson, already prominent in the colony.

The first court record to mention his name was in 1680, when he refused to serve as a juryman, either because of his maritime business or because he felt it beneath his social status, and he was fined. In 1691, he was sworn in as a justice of Norfolk County, as his land at that time fell within the boundaries of Norfolk County.

Although his wife had died before him, Thomas Walke, characteristic of later Walkes also, left nothing to chance. He stipulated that his wife's relatives were to have mourning rings purchased out of the estate, and to his friend William Moseley—"40 shillings to be paid him out of my own wareing clothes and unto Margaret Moseley, the wife of sd. Wm. Moseley, 40 shillings to be paid her out of my wives wareing cloathes." Fine clothes were very expensive. Either each was to choose something of that value or to be paid in cash after a sale. He did not forget his relatives in Barbados: he left his sister and each of her children £5 apiece and directed that mourning rings be bought at 20 shillings each for his other two sisters and his brother there. The balance of the estate was to be divided equally between his two sons and his daughter Elizabeth, with all his household goods "which are not perishable." His ships were to be fitted out and "this year's goods to be shipped off in them to Barbados" and sold by his executors "as they shall see fit."

The startling items in the inventory were the amounts of ready cash, "£578 in good Spanish money" and "£400 in several sorts of other foreign money. Few planters had ever seen that much "real" money. Tobacco was the currency, and either that or receipts for it from a tobacco warehouse were all they knew. The estates of Thomas Lawson and Adam Thorowgood II were also indebted to him in the amount of over £800. This was a wealthy man.

We are not sure where Thomas II lived. He left his eldest son, Anthony, "all that land & plantation on the eastern branch." As his will was probated in Princess Anne County, this must have been the

Eastern Branch of the Elizabeth River. His wife Katherine was to have "use of the whole during her widowhood only" and "not to be molested or hindered by my said son." He also gave Anthony one lot in Norfolk but does not mention any house there.

Then, "I give and devise to my son Thomas Walke my land and houses in New Town . . . my tract of land at the head of the Lynnhaven River . . . also my smith's tools that belong to the smith's shop in Newtown and that shall hereafter come from England." It would appear that while Anthony, as the eldest son, received most of the land, it was his son Thomas whom he considered the most reliable. The houses in Newtown included at least one warehouse, possibly a shipyard, and the smith shop with all its tools, as well as those coming from England. The appraisal includes two sloops, the *Hope* and the *Mary*, with "all their fittings, apparel and furniture," along with "206 barrels of pork, 257 bushels of peas, 80 bushels of Indian corn," all obviously for export. He also had a store there, for in the appraisal are hundreds of bolts of cloth of all kinds and quality. The 24 pounds of beeswax and 27 pounds of myrtle wax evidently were made here. The 166½ pounds of feathers for feather beds were from wild birds— ducks, turkeys and swan—because there were a great many of them, and nowhere are chickens mentioned. He left 15 slaves not including the crews of his two sloops to his wife and four children by name.

Old maps show that "the tract of land at the head of the Lynnhaven River" left to Thomas III was on Wolfsnare Creek, which once flowed to the west of the house and joined the upper reaches of the Lynnhaven River. When Thomas II bought this land, it was already cleared, as there is evidence that there once was an Indian village here. Thomas Walke III probably lived in the house in Newtown while building this house, which was not quite finished when he made his will in 1759, two years before he died in 1761.

While he continued with family shipping and mercantile business, Thomas III was more interested in the acquisition of land and cattle and the affairs of the county. His father had been a burgess in 1712– 14, but Thomas III was not a burgess until 1756–60. This third generation Walke, like other people in the county, had absorbed the same feeling of isolation from the rest of the Colony and had come to feel a great love of land and the acquisition of it. His interest in the business lagged, as his will shows that he had only a half interest in the sloop, *Endeavor*, owned but one small schooner, *The Humming Bird*, and left the management of the two stores he had an interest in to others—the one in Kemp's Landing to his brother Anthony's sons and the other to his son-in-law Charles Williamson. But he knew what he had, and his inventory is one of the longest on record.

A family man who left his six children well-provided for, his other great interest was the church. He was a vestryman and a church warden, instrume ntal in building the Eastern Shore Chapel on Cornick land nearby, and he was one of the few wealthy men of the county who left a charitable donation. He could well afford it, for when he died, he owned over 7,000 acres, many herds of cattle, horses and hogs and a mill "at the bay side," in addition to his interest in the two stores and sloop and 55 slaves. He named his wife and five others as executors, and they must have had their hands full. The appraisal of the estate runs to eight closely written pages, and characteristically, he left detailed instructions. Even his son Thomas, who was only a baby at the time, did not escape directions.

> "*Item:* I bequeath unto my son Thomas Walke my plantation, lands and houses whereon I now live (at the Eastern Shore) and desire the houses to be finished, furnished with glasses, maps, one desk, all the walnut and cherry chairs, three good beds and furniture, also my one-third part of the Wash Banks and Marshes about Old Currituck Inlet (which may be about one hundred head, great steers excepted), a roan mare and colt, 20 ewes & lambs, 10 sows & pigs, 2 yoke oxen, . . . etc. etc."

This is a masterful will of an astute business man, a devoted family man, a pillar of the church and one active in the community—he had been High Sheriff and was a major in the militia. If he had any faults, one may have been that he did not quite trust his brother Anthony's perspicacity, as in his will he forgave Anthony his debt to him but left his interest in the Kemp's Landing store to Anthony's two sons, instead of to him, along with two slaves. Perhaps Thomas was too careful and meticulous to suit his wife Mary Anne, for within a year, she had remarried, to John Phripp. After Phripp's death, she married Dr. Michael Hackett, who died a year later.

Thomas Walke IV finally grew up and received his inheritance, but he was the end of the direct line. He married Elizabeth Newton, and they had no children. He was a delegate to the Virginia Constitutional Convention in 1787, but he soon died, in his early 30s, ten years later.

His will is short, leaving his wife half of the home tract, marshes and plantation utensil, all the household and kitchen furniture, one female slave and her children, 10 cows and calves, 20 ewes and lambs and six sows and pigs. He left the other half "of the plantation I now live on, not before disposed of" to two of his half-sisters, Margaret Thorowgood Hamilton (daughter of his mother's first husband) and Anne Phripp Ramsay (daughter of his mother's third husband). He does not mention any Walkes. And after the death of his wife and these two sisters, the estate was to be divided between John Murdaugh, Wright Westcot and Thomas Willoughby, sons of the other half-sisters.

To friends, he bequeathed: "Major Adam Keeling my pistols which are in the house, my sword and gun, and my pistols at the Bayside; to William D. Woodhouse as a mark of my esteem, a sword in the possession of his brother John." Also, "on account of Mr. James Norris' fidelity I give him the house and ten acres of land where he now lives rent free for six years."

His appraisal is equally short, only two pages. Except for six spinning wheels, which may have been for sale, everything else appears to be household effects and a few farm implements, the cattle mentioned in the will, six horses and 36 slaves, including children.

Since by this time there was fine mahogany furniture and a large quantity of silver among the household furnishings, one may think this will and appraisal show a dissolute young man who wasted his family fortune. On the contrary, they tell a pitiful story of a frail young man trying to cope with external conditions beyond his control.

The three preceding Thomas Walkes rode the general wave of prosperity before the Revolution, but the war came before this Thomas had even reached his majority. Not old enough to take an active part in the fighting, he was helpless as both the Continental and British armies confiscated his cattle and anything else they needed or wanted. Even before the occupation of Princess Anne County by the British, in 1781, bands of outlaws had been constantly on the prowl, stealing, killing and burning. The British blockade put an end to the shipping business, and his appraisal shows no boats of any kind—they had either been recruited by the Virginia Navy or taken by the British. It is amazing that he was able to hold onto five horses and any cattle, and he obviously was not a Tory as he was elected to represent the county at the Virginia Constitutional Convention. And while his father had left him only 16 of his 55 slaves, it seems unusual that Thomas IV still had 36 when he died, as, it was said many of the local slaves had run off to join the British on the promise of freedom or had been stolen by them.

Thomas Walke IV really did the best he could, but his will was ignored in 1802. His widow and half-sisters sold all the property, including the house, and it passed out of the hands of the Walke family.

In the hard years following the Revolution, when the struggles of the new United States of America continued until after the War of 1812, Thomas Walke III's house had many owners, and the land passed through many hands. But its history was not finished.

When Dr. Enoch Dozier Ferebee came to Princess Anne County before the War Between the States looking for a likely farm, he bought Broad Bay Manor on Broad Bay and, later, Upper Wolfsnare, which he gave to his son George Emory Ferebee with 343 acres. George was commissioned in the Confederate Army when the war broke out, and while he was away fighting and the Union Army was occupying all of Princess Anne County, Union officers suddenly galloped up to the house and demanded it for their use. Forced out, Mrs. Ferebee and the children moved in with Dr. Ferebee at Broad Bay Manor. After the war, finding the house intact, George and his family moved back in and lived there until Dr. Ferebee moved back to North Carolina. Then they took over the Manor. A later owner of Upper Wolfsnare found a Confederate uniform and some old Confederate money under the floor of an upstairs closet.

After this, many owners came and went until the house was finally donated in 1964 to The Princess Anne County Historical Society. Through wars, adversities and the proximity of the United States Navy jets, which fly over daily, this house has remained a living symbol of life over 200 years ago. Not as majestic as the Francis Land House, it was built by that careful and meticulous Thomas Walke III to last, and it has. With later additions removed, it reflects the character of the builder in its excellent proportions, 14-inch-thick brick walls and fine inside paneling. Even if the builder did not live to see it finished, his son Thomas IV is still there—in spirit. There is not only a "presence" felt there, but a young man in a white ruffled shirt and dark knee-britches has been seen three times, by three different people. He fades as soon as noticed, but the description is always the same. Perhaps it is the spirit of that unfortunate Thomas Walke IV which has kept the house intact through all these years!

With the help of the Virginia Beach Arts and Humanities Commission, the Virginia Landmarks Commission, the Virginia Beach Garden Club and the Junior Virginia Beach Garden Club, along with many interested citizens, work is progressing toward complete restoration and period furnishings. It is open to visitors once a month from April through October.

The other house owned by the Princess Anne County Historical Society is Pembroke Manor, built in 1764, but we will tell of that one in a later chapter, as well as others of the upper class.

It is amazing that so many frame houses built by the middle class in the 18th century—nine in all—remain virtually untouched by the ravages of time or renovated beyond recognition. One of the most interesting is a sweet little house near the center of Kempsville, on traffic-laden Witch Duck Road. It was built, we believe, in 1774 by John Carraway, the grandson of the first John Carraway who had come here in 1644. It is now an antique shop, beautifully restored and furnished by the present owners and open to the public every day except Wednesday. It is a saltbox with a sloping roof to the back, unusual in this area, and is well-proportioned, with the one huge exterior chimney on the north side and the entrance door on the east corner to balance.

The first John Carraway came to Lower Norfolk County as an indentured servant to Colonel John Sidney (Nugent's, vol. I. p. 155). He could neither read nor write, as when he witnessed William Moseley's will in 1655, he signed with his mark, "IC." He had been a juror for a Grand Jury case in 1654 and, again, in 1663 and 1664 in a long drawn out suit against the Quakers. He was a witness in the 1664 case, having seen the accused at a Quaker meeting. He had also been one of the appraisers of the estate of Colonel Francis Emperor in 1662. Jurors and appraisers were carefully chosen for their reliability and knowledge.

He owned land in 1663, for in that year, a grant was recorded for John Porter in Lynnhaven Parish, "E. by N. to John Carraway's land—on the south side of the Eastern Branch of the Elizabeth River." His own grant for 100 acres was finally recorded in 1695, "in Princess Anne County, south of the head of the E. Br. of the Elizabeth River . . . to Kemp's patent." In 1706, his son, now entitled "Mr. John Carraway, Sr.," was granted an additional 447 acres.

The Carraways had done well, buying other land around the county, until in 1773, John Carraway III bought for £ 20, "a tract of land on the Western Shore called 'Labour in Vain' containing 67 acres." (*Antiquary*—James.) This had been the land of William Johnson, deceased, and was sold to John Carraway by his widow and his two sisters, co-heirs, but, he built the house now standing in Kemps Landing. At first, it had only the hall and one room downstairs, with two rooms upstairs. Later, an additional room was added on the back, and still later, the outside kitchen was moved and attached to the house. But from the front, the house looks as it did in 1734, with the original shutters on the windows, which contain many panes of the old hand-blown glass. While the bricks of the chimney are laid in the Virginia, or American pattern, some are decorated as in the 17th century, and beneath the large roof overhang on the front is decorative molding. Small as it is, it was built with care and taste. It was continually occupied by descendants of the first Carraway until 1975.

The only early Carraway will extant is Ann Carraway's, dated 1689, and it shows extremely few possessions. (Lower Norfolk County Order Book D.)

> "daughter Mary Lovett—an iron kettle
> daughter Elizabeth Nichols—bell mettle mortar & pestle
> son Bartholomy Williamson—one shilling
> son John Carraway—one shilling
>
> Signed: Anne Carraway
> her mark."

John Carraway had obviously died first and distributed his property in his will, so this is all that poor Anne had to leave.

The story of John Carraway and his descendants is, we like to think, the story of America through the centuries: a success story of a man who started with nothing but strong character and ambition, and who learned and prospered through hard work and intelligence. His descendants were as upright and hardworking as he. A visit to this charming house is an inspiration.

The other houses of this middle, or small farmer class are privately owned and not open to the general public. Many of them, however, can be spotted by sharp eyes from county roads, and we hope that they will be preserved. For more about the houses in this county, see *Old Houses in Princess Anne Virginia*, by Sadie and V. Hope Kellam.

No houses remain of the lower class, as they were poorly built and soon destroyed. Also, cheap land had become unavailable for newly freed men as the population increased. Some worked as laborers or overseers for others, thereby being given a place to live, but others left to seek their fortunes elsewhere, especially in the frontier, which had been opened up by Governor Spotswood. Land was available there for little or nothing, as it was in eastern North Carolina, which was still sparsely settled at this time.

But it is unlikely that many people left Princess Anne County. The population figure of 1690 for tithables (no women or children) for all of Lower Norfolk County was 1,097 (Back of Book 5, 18 Nov. Court). In 1783, the population count of all inhabitants of Princess

Anne County alone was 6,655. This was quite a jump, even though it included women and children by this time. (Calendar of State Papers, vol. 3, p. 552.) The great surge in the importation of slaves from 1690 to 1740 accounts for a large part of this increase, for the count at this time was 3,999 whites and 2,656 blacks.

From wills and inventories, we find several interesting items which throw some light on this small farmer class. (Princess Anne Will Book, 1, p. 72.) In 1785, Thomas Brown left 150 acres to be divided between his two sons. Each of his three daughters received one slave, and the rest of the estate was to be sold to pay debts. Of the balance, £ 32 Virginia money was to be reserved to board and educate the four eldest children.

(Princess Anne Deed Book, 1, p. 251.) John Evans in 1700 left his estate after all debts paid to be divided between his wife and his son John, instructing John not to meddle with anything until all debts were paid. He also left John one broadcloth coat and a pair of plush britches, and to his wife all the crop of wheat then growing.

In 1790, John Henley left his seven daughters two cows, five shillings, a feather bed and a pot, with the two eldest daughters as executors.

The bequests in these wills seem very meager, but, in fact, there was little poverty, and high and low enjoyed life.

Two statutes enacted by the House of Burgesses on orders from the King had little effect on the population here. One was designed to discourage the importation of slaves. From Nugent's *Cavaliers and Pioneers*, introduction: "April 15, 1699, the practice of allowing headrights for blacks was discontinued. His Majesty's land in this Colony ought not to be granted to any others than His Christian Subjects coming to reside here." Slave labor was a bonanza for planters, and they were not inclined to have it, nor the means of acquiring more land, hampered.

The other was to encourage settlement beyond the Blue Ridge mountains in the valley and beyond to the Ohio River.

> "On June 13, 1699, the Governor and Council established a treasury right whereby a person paying five shillings to the auditor gained the same liberty to take up and patent 50 acres of land which he would otherwise have had for the importation of any of His Majesty's subjects into this Dominion."

In 1770, an interesting petition was presented to the Honorable William Nelson, Esq., President of the Council and Commander in

Chief as acting governor of the Colony of Virginia. Until within a few years past, the wild stretch of sand dunes, swamp and pine barrens near Cape Henry known as "The Desert" had been open to grants, but this petition hoped to stop any more.

> "Petition of Subscribers, Inhabitant of the County of Princess Anne in behalf of themselves and other inhabitants. (That) No Patent be granted, that the same may remain a common for the benefit of inhabitants of the Colony for carrying on a fishery and for such other public uses as the same premises shall be found Convenient.
> (Signed) James Kempe   Frederick Boush
>   Thomas Wishart   Horatio Woodhouse
>   Lemuel Newton   Robert Richmond
>   Samuel Boush   Charles Hill
>   William Woodhouse"

The area close to the shore was taken over by the United States government for a coastal defense post in 1916. The land was donated by the state of Virginia.

Although the threat of pirates attacking from sea had long since disappeared, there is a left-over feeling of security with the Army post guarding Cape Henry. In spite of efforts by lumber companies to cut timber in the interior, it is now a state park, where small animals live among plants native to both North and South, and Spanish moss drapes the great cypresses growing in dark pools between high dunes.

The rural life in Princess Anne County was a pleasant and democratic one, where the pursuit of pleasure was more important, for most, than the pursuit of profit. Dancing, drinking, hunting and gambling were their passions, and hospitality to all comers was the rule. Page Smith in *The Shaping of America* says, "The Virginian is remarkable for his colloquial happiness, loses no opportunity for knowledge, and delights to show his wit. . . ." Almost everyone was in debt due to his love of dress and ornament, but what matter? Next year's crop would pay for any extravagance. The outside world did not concern them. Only the condition of the established church bothered them, and that, too, they thought, would right itself.

PART THREE
Chapter 3
THE CHURCH AND THE GREAT AWAKENING

The Church of England, heretofore always known as "The Church," steadily lost power in the 18th century. Although the oath of allegiance, required of all new immigrants, continued to include fidelity to the Church of England as well as to the King, and the church wardens continued to attempt to enforce the church laws and work closely with the court, dissatisfaction grew.

As Richard B. Morris states in his *Encyclopedia of American History*, "The influence of the Church was restricted by the predominately mediocre quality of the colonial clergy, by oversized parishes, low salaries, neglect of discipline, and lay control. In the absence of a resident bishop confirmation and ordination could not be administered in the colonies. The latter served to discourage the growth of a native ministry." Here, in Princess Anne County, the vestry system was at fault, also. Instead of a general election at regular intervals, the upper class continued its control by allowing the vestry members to serve for life, and at the death of one, they themselves appointed another, usually a son, brother or other relative. Granted, the duties of the vestry were heavy and required the service of men superior in ability and those who could contribute financially. Still, all males were taxed for the support of the church, and this "taxation without representation" made those of the middle and lower classes restive.

As the population shifted, the mother church was moved from the original site on the western side of the Lynnhaven River at Church Point to the eastern side, then further up the river at the presently named Witchduck Point, then to the present location and is now called Old Donation Church. The Eastern Shore Chapel of Ease was not established until 1726. That also was in the northern part of the county, ignoring the difficulty in attending service for all those living in the larger part of the lower county.

Since all were required by law to attend church every Sunday, those who could make the long journey from Pungo and around Back Bay found an archaic, though English, seating arrangement rigidly enforced by the vestry. (From the Vestry Book of Lynnhaven Parish.)

> "At a Vestry held the 10th of July 1736. For preserving order, decency, peace & Harmony in the New Church 'tis resolved & the vestry doe hereby assign & appoint the two upper opposite great Pews (in the Chancel) for the Magistrates & their wives: the next adjoining pew on the north Side of the Church to the family of the Thorowgoods as their priviledge in consideration of the gift of our glebe (minister's land) by that family: the third great pew on the north side for the vestrymen & their wives: the pew on the north side of the Communion Table is assigned to the family and Name of the Walkes as a benefit formerly granted them in Consideration of gifts & services made & done by Col: Thomas Walke 111 deceased & Col: Anthony Walke the Senior: the next great pew on the South side for the Elder women of good reporte & magistrates daughters: the other great pew on the Same Side for Such Women as the Churchwardens with the approbation of the vestry shall think fit to place them."

Edward Moseley had already requested permission to build a hanging pew for himself and his family, and at this same vestry meeting, another request was considered.

> "On the motion of mr: William Robinson Liberty is given him to build a hanging Pew on the North Side of the new Church (and in case the family of the Moseleys who have had the first liberty refuse to accept thereoff, then the said Robinson to have his liberty of building the first Pew as aforesaid not obstructing the light of the windows."

Ordinary people were seated in the back of the church. If there was a minister, which was rather infrequent, and the church was crowded, they stood. This was discouraging, when in other aspects of life at that time, democracy was rapidly gaining ground, having begun in 1619 when Governor Yeardley had convened the first meeting of the House of Burgesses with representatives elected by popular vote. The famous and sensible Judge St. George Tucker wrote of the 18th century, "every man is respectable in society in proportion to the talents he possesses to serve it." That was true, except in the Church. The only possible excuse for these hanging pews would seem that occupying this exalted position in the church put them above the common people or, perhaps, closer to heaven than those below. For whatever reason, these hanging pews were popular with the elite in other counties, also, such as Christ Church in Lancaster, where some of the wealthiest in the Colony lived.

Philip Vickers Fithian, the serious young Presbyterian minister, who, before taking up his ecclesiastical duties, was engaged as a tutor for Robert Carter's four sons at Nomini Hall, was very apprehensive about going to Virginia. Before his departure, he wrote in his delightful *"Journals and Letters, 1773-1774"*:

> "I hope in the Kindness of him who was my Father's God, & has been the Guide of my Youth, that he will save me from being corrupted or carried away with the Vices which prevail in that Country."

He soon discovered that his fears were unfounded, for he was completely charmed by the Carter family and their gracious acceptance of him as a member of the family. He remained as strait-laced as when he came, and while he did not approve of the general custom of the Carters and their friends of turning Sundays into a day of pleasure and using the churchyard before and after the service to conduct business, he was tactful enough to keep quiet about it, except in his diary.

"A Diary of a Lady of Quality" is more outspoken.

> "There is not much religion in their Church of England ceremonies. After the service they spend an hour strolling about among the crowd, giving and receiving invitations to dinner."

And in William Byrd II's diary, who had services at home, Westover, was written: "I rose about six & played the fool with Sarah. God forgive me! However, I prayed and had coffee."

John Randolph declared in his will that his religion came from the Gospel and he had no need of learned doctors who made religion a science of difficulty and mystery. (*Virginia Gazette*, May 6, 1737.)

In the meantime, some of the wealthy and prominent had also joined the ranks of dissenters. William Tayloe, of the prominent Tayloe family of The Northern Neck, was a trustee of the Presbyterian Church in 1753. Some of the large and prominent family of Porters who owned land near Kempsville were Quakers. That was another matter altogether, and they tried to keep quiet about it. But when John

Porter was elected to the House of Burgesses, he confessed when accused that he "was loving toward the Quakers" and refused to take the oath of allegiance. He was then dismissed from the House. The Quakers had always been in trouble because of their pacifist principles and refusal to abide by the oath of allegiance, as well as stressing the separation of church and state.

The Presbyterians were the one Protestant denomination which was not only tolerated but welcomed here, partly because many were Scots and, also because their principles were much the same as the Church of England. Their first meeting house was registered as standing on Edward Cooper's land in 1693. The Reverend Josiah Mackie had been the minister of the Elizabeth River Parish (Church of England), but he had been fired because of his "non-conformist practices." The people of Princess Anne were not so uptight, and he and his flock were welcome in the Lynnhaven Parish. He served as their substitute minister from 1684–1691, another long period when there was no Anglican minister available. The following court record (*Lower Norfolk County Antiquary*, James) proves that everything was aboveboard.

> "Att a meeting of the Justices, 4th of Octob. 1699
> Present: Col: Anthony Lawson
>   Mr. Wm. Cornick   Capt. Edward Moseley
>   Mr. Ben Burroughs   Mr. Henry Woodhouse
> There are in the County only two meetings for Religious Worship besides the Church of England as by Law Established. One of which is kept at a house in the eastern branch of the Elizabeth River on the land belonging to Mr. Thomas Ivy Certified for a place of Religious Worship to his Majesties Justices for Norfolk County (which at that time before the last Division of the Counties was in Norfolk) at a Court held the 15 Aug. 1692 & Recorded as appears from the Records of the sd. Colony, the other att a meeting house upon the Eastern Shoar of Lyndhaven River on the land belonging to Edward Cooper being certified to his Majesties Justices for this county as a place of Religious Worship at a court held the 6th of Septemb. 1693 and Recorded in the Records of the sd. county.
>   The preacher at the said place is Mr. Josiah Mackie, a presbyterian minister non-conforming in part (vizt.) as to Rites and Ceremonies, who Since his comeing into these parts hath formerly with the allowance of his Lordship ffrancis of Effingham, his majesties & Lt. Gov. of Virginia been Entertained and officiated as minister of the Gospel in Eliz. River Parish until such time as his present Excellency ffrancis Nicholson, Esqr. etc., then Lt. Gov. was pleased to Discharge him by Order, who since appears from the records of Norfolk County bearing date 1692 under the hand of Mr. Will

Porten, Cl. Cur. hath fulfilled the Law of Indulgence Exempting his Majesties Subjects from penalties of certaine Laws.

As to Wandering Strangers as preachers, or upon any other practice of Religion, there is not any in this County."

This is an interesting document, descriptive of the hospitality accorded any personable strangers, the indifference to any past offenses and, also, the independent thinking of the justices who were also pillars of the Church of England's Lynnhaven Parish. That last sentence is a bit startling, for we suspect that there may have been at least some "wandering preachers" around, although underground. Be that as it may, in 1736, Governor Gooch decreed that Presbyterian missionaries would be protected.

The Reverend Josiah Mackie died in 1716. Besides monetary gifts to his sisters' children in Ireland, he left a considerable estate to his many friends here—Elizabeth and John Wishart, William and Mary Johnson, Thomas and Elizabeth Butt, Richard Butt, Horatio Woodhouse and Mrs. Martha Thruston—and "my more Schoolastick Books of the Learned Languages as Lattin: Greek & Hebrew to be equally divided Between Mr. Henry, Mr. Hampton & Mr. Mackness, nonconforming ministers at Pocamoke or thereabouts."

If separation of church and state was not stressed by the Presbyterians, other Protestant sects were very keen on this. The so-called Great Awakening, which was a series of revivals from 1726-1756, was led by eloquent and impassioned itinerant preachers throughout the colonies. Such leaders as George Whitfield, Isaac Backus and John Leland attracted large crowds, preaching on behalf of religious freedom and the separation of church and state. The Baptist Church, organized by Roger Williams in Rhode Island in 1639, spread to Virginia and was strengthened here by the leadership of the Reverend Samuel Davies. In 1764, the prominent John Whitehead and Mary his wife sold, for just one pound & five shillings current money of Virginia, half an acre near Pungo to the Elders and Rulers of the Baptist Church, "where the meeting house now stands." (*Antiquary*, James.)

Methodism, which began later, in 1766, as a movement within the Church of England, was started by the great intellect John Wesley. "He made his appeal to the conscience in the clearest language, with the most cogent argument, and with all the weight of personal conviction." *(Encyclopaedia Britannica.)* While Wesley never intended to found a church separate from the Anglican, "his crusade was to move the church out of the walls of the church buildings and into the world of the people—all the people" (*Charity, Its Past and Present,* Barbara Murden Henley and Susan Brown Flanagan).

The first missionary of Methodism to come here was Robert Williams, who preached in Norfolk and Portsmouth without much success. Then, a missionary in Baltimore who had preceded him in this county, Joseph Pilmoor, preached with great success in Norfolk, then at the Currituck Courthouse, the Narrows Chapel at Kempsville and at the Baptist Meeting House and the Pungo Chapel. In Portsmouth, in 1772, he formed the first Methodist Society in Southern Virginia. In 1775, Francis Asbury was sent by John Wesley to be the pastor at Norfolk, but his stay was brief.

John Wesley had written a pamphlet, *"A Calm Address to the American Colonies,"* expressing the view that the British position was favored rather than that of the colonists, and many of his ministers supported his ideas. When war broke out, all of the regular Methodist ministers returned to England, except Francis Asbury. Although all Methodists were looked upon with suspicion as being Tories, they survived the war, actually increasing in numbers. And in 1784, the Methodist Episcopal Church was formally established, with Francis Asbury as its first Bishop.

It has been estimated that in the years from 1740 to 1790, 4,000 to 5,000 members of the Church of England in Virginia left to become Presbyterians, Methodists and Baptists. These were people of high and low degree, but the majority were the common people who challenged the authority of the Church of England. It was evident to them now that the resolves of the leading gentry on the vestry were not a strong commitment to them.

The Great Awakening encouraged frugality and industry and questioned the morals of a society in which indebtedness was a way of life and slavery insured a life of ease. The Methodist ministers particularly denounced slavery, freeing their slaves, and many followed their example.

The progress toward true democracy was speeded up as men now questioned their former acceptance of leadership of the gentry, and they voted not for whom they were told, but for the ones they felt were the wisest. Class distinctions had never been very strong in Princess Anne County, except in the church, and now they were even more relaxed.

These were difficult times for the Church of England in Virginia. In 1662, a law had been passed setting the clergy's salary at 16,000 pounds of tobacco a year, a meager amount to begin with and one which did not encourage recruitment in England of able ministers. In 1755, there was a small crop of tobacco, especially in the lower counties such as Princess Anne, where the crop failure was really acute. To enable the planters to pay their tithes, the House of Burgesses passed a law to permit payment in money at the rate of two pence per pound of tobacco. The parsons were enraged, as obviously a small tobacco crop forced the price up to three or four pence a pound, and they complained to England. This act was then dropped. But in 1758, there was another poor crop, and the House again passed the same act. Again, the King voided it, and the local judge upheld the decision. The Reverend James Maury of Louisa County and several others sued for the additional salary, and it was now up to the jury to fix the amount of the damages.

The tax collectors, unable to collect the tithes, engaged the young lawyer Patrick Henry to represent them. This was Henry's opportunity, and in his speech to the jury, he launched an all-out attack on the King as well as the clergy. He is quoted as having said, "These rapacious harpies would, were their power equal to their will, snatch from the hearth of their honest parishioner his last hoecake, from the widow and her orphaned children their last milch cow, the last bed, nay the last blanket from the lying-in woman." Also, "A king, by annulling or disallowing laws of this salutary nature (Two-Penny Act) from being father of his people denegrates into a tyrant and forfeits all rights to his subjects' obedience."

Admitting that the local court had also voided the Two-Penny Act, he suggested to the jury that their decision on the damages "need not be more than a farthing." The jury was out for only 10 minutes and gave Mr. Maury one penny.

While this decision, known as "The Parsons' Cause," catapulted Patrick Henry into political prominence and popularity, it also brought out into the open the many resentments of the ordinary people toward the clergy, whom they felt neglected them. The Church did not change its ways as a result of this rebuff, unfortunately, but it gave the people courage to resist its domination and that of the King in the events which followed.

Some laws affecting the Church had been modified as the Colony moved slowly toward democracy. By 1736, the furor over the Quakers had died down. Laws on the franchise did not mention religion at all, only the exclusion of recusant convicts. Quakers were allowed to vote on making affirmation, which was a solemn declaration by a person with conscientious objections to swearing an oath. But they were not allowed to hold office or serve on juries. The same restrictions applied to the Papists (Roman Catholics), and their priests were ordered to leave the Colony.

As ministers of the Methodist and Baptist faiths spoke constantly for the separation of church and state and for religious tolerance, they preached emotionally to their large audiences of the sin of slavery. Guilt, they had always felt in their hearts and tried to ignore, but fear became even stronger.

PART THREE
Chapter 4
THE CONDITION OF SLAVERY

With the passage of the Slave Code in 1705, slavery, with all its miseries, was now a condition of life in the 18th century. Governor Spotswood as early as 1711 spoke against any further importation of slaves, as did others from time to time, privately, and in the House of Burgesses, but to no avail. Some historians have questioned the economic value of slavery, for slaves were expensive to buy, had to be clothed, fed, cared for when sick, old or inform, and children also had to be clothed and fed until age 16, when they could be put to work.

Taxes did not have to be paid for those too young or old to work, and those in the work force, with no hope of freedom in their lifetime, usually did not do more work than they were forced to do. The only hope of bettering his condition for a field worker was to present such a pleasing and willing face to his master that he might be promoted to a house servant, the elite of the slave world. As a house servant, he would then have easier work and be better clothed and fed. But this was a rather forlorn hope for most field workers, particularly in Princess Anne County where 91 percent of the slave holders owned fewer than five slaves (*Virginia, 1705–1786*, Robert E. and Katherine Brown).

There was no reliable count of property owners here before 1775, when the court appointed tithe takers by precincts, but throughout the 18th century, the majority of taxpayers were small farmers, who more or less stayed that way. Proof of this is in the period of 1750-55 when the white population in other counties decreased while it stayed the same in Princess Anne. Characteristically, like their forebears, they were not much interested in other regions "beyond the water" and seemed rather smug in their contentment with their lot here.

This count of 1775 (*Lower Norfolk County Antiquary*, James), while not too accurate, reveals some interesting aspects. In the Upper

Precinct (actually the lower part of the county), of the 188 reporting, 123 had no slaves at all, 28 had only one, 21 had two and only one had more than 10. That one was John Ackiss, the largest landholder, who had 19. The Blackwater Precinct report was lost, but that would have been similar or even lower for there was no large landholder there. In the Middle Precinct, of 85 reporting, 51 had no slaves, and only one had as many as six. In the Lower Precinct (around the mouth of the Lynnhaven River), of 79 reporting, 24 had no slaves, 25 had one and, slowly working up to the largest slave owner, Jacob Hunter had 28. This was a more affluent and older area in the settlement, as were the Little Creek and Eastern Branch precincts. The Eastern Branch Precinct comprised the Eastern Branch of the Elizabeth River. In the Little Creek Precinct, of 41 reporting, nine had no slaves and Anthony Lawson, the richest man in that precinct, had 26. In the Eastern Branch, of 105 reporting, 17 had no slaves, only four had more than 20 and Anthony Walke, the wealthiest and largest landholder in the whole county, had 83.

Therefore, in this county, where there was practically no poverty and where everyone, it is said, wanted the prestige and ease of owning slaves, there were 224 taxpaying farmers who owned no slaves at all! Making an allowance for cheating—many did not give an accurate count to avoid tax—this is a surprising number, for they were all farmers, even if their land was only leased.

Often, it was more practical to lease land, and according to this report, 207 out of the 508 reporting leased. Some of these lessees not only had a slave or two, but cattle, a horse and a carriage or cart of some sort.

Although we do not feel that these figures are exact, they show that the majority were small farmers, and with so few slaves, there was a much closer relationship between them and the master. This closer relationship worked two ways. A good master, working right along with his slave or two, was inclined to be more considerate and not to expect more of the slave than of himself. But at the same time, he was more watchful and never let the slave forget who was the master. A bad master could make life so unbearable by whippings, starving or overwork that, and it did happen, the slave was driven to run away, suicide or even killing his master. He knew that death was the penalty, but sometimes it was preferable.

Just how many of the Princess Anne slaves entered into the plot for insurrection with those of Norfolk County in 1730 is not known, nor how the Princess Anne slaves had even had word of the meeting, but the total was estimated at about 200. The following account in The British Public Records Office of a report from Governor Gooch tells the story.

> "Lt. Gov. Gooch to the Council of Trade and Plantations. Account of Negro conspiracy (v. 14th Sept. 1736) Since while the negroes in the countys of Norfolk and Princess Anne had the boldness to assemble on a Sunday while the people were at church, and to choose among themselves officers to command them in their intended insurrection, which was to have been put in execution very soon after; But this meeting being happily discovered and many of them taken up and examined, the whole plot was detected, for which the major part of them were severely punished, and four of the ringleaders, on full evidence convicted, and have been executed. This, with the imprisonment and correction of some of the most suspected in the other parts of the country, when the designs appeared not so far concerted, have brought them now to be very quiet and submissive: But as we cannot be too much on our guard against such desperate combinations, I have ordered the Militia to provide twice or thrice in a week, to prevent all night meetings, and every man to bring his arms to church on Sundays and Holidays, lest they should be seized by the slaves in their absence, if the same mutinous spirit should be revived amongst them."

According to the *Virginia Gazette* of January 25, 1770, some of these slaves claimed they had heard that the King had ordered their freedom as soon as they were Christians. This had been true early in the 17th century, but it was eliminated in the Slave Code of 1705.

This was the only threat of organized insurrection in Princess Anne County, but in 1767, alarm was caused by "a mob of negroes" in Frederick County. In 1770, several people were killed in an insurrection of slaves in Hanover County where, it was said, the slaves had been treated with "too much levity and indulgence" and had grown "extremely insolent and unruly." (*Virginia 1705-1786*, R. E. & B. K. Brown.)

By this time, many slaves were "native born" and had not only learned the language, but how to present a smiling and happy face to the white man, while underneath was a consuming hatred of the servile state and those who had imposed it on them. The white man, too, wore a mask—of superiority, kindness and security—but the slave also knew that beneath his white skin, the master had suppressed fear and a conflict of conscience. The clever ones played upon this conflict relentlessly, for always they had the normal, human craving for freedom and the search for some way to achieve it.

The celebrated "Somerset Case," in 1772, demonstrated the ability of one slave to conceal his true feelings and his intelligence in finding a road to freedom and grasping it when the opportunity arose. Somerset was a young slave of Charles Stewart, a Scottish merchant of Norfolk. By ingratiating himself with his master, Stewart became extremely fond of him and trusted him implicitly, which caused a good deal of criticism among the Norfolk townspeople. On a business trip back to England in 1769, Stewart left his daughter in the care of the Ellegood family in Princess Anne and took Somerset with him.

Somerset continued to play the role of pampered pet, but he kept his eyes and ears open. Hearing of a strong abolitionist group, he ran off to them and pleaded his case. Charles Stewart was stunned, but also enraged—he recaptured Somerset and threatened to sell him in Jamaica. This was too dastardly for the abolitionists, whose lawyers took Stewart to court. The result, from *The Journal of Negro History*, vol. LI (July 1966) and Jerome Nadelcroft, follows.

"22 June 1772, Lord Mansfield, Chief Justice of the Court of King's Bench. Case of James Somerset, slave who had run away from his master Charles Stewart while in England, was captured and Stewart was about to sell him in Jamaica.
Lord Mansfield's decision was: 'No master ever to be allowed to take a slave by force to be sold abroad because he had deserted from service, or for any reason.'
Somerset's lawyers deliberately misinterpreted the decision to mean immediate freedom of all slaves in England, and the misinterpretation was cited in newspapers and American Courts, north and south, to mean immediate freedom of all slaves in the Empire, 14,000 of them. Even Benjamin Franklin wrote to a friend in Massachusetts 'England's hypocrisy in priding itself on its virtue, love of liberty and equity of courts, in setting free one single negro, while at the same time encouraging that detestable slave trade.' Slavery existed in England for 50 years after 1772.
Mansfield was on the horns of a dilemma in this case, and Stewart said that he suggested to him that he sell all his slaves!
However, this became an important legal precedent in 1830. John Jay, Jr., son of the first Chief Justice and president of the New York Manumission Society, invoked this decision in another case."

There is nothing in the record as to what happened to Somerset after this. It is presumed that he stayed in England and enjoyed his freedom. Certainly, he did not come back to Tidewater, but it was not long before the news of his case spread. Very definitely, it made more creditable the promise of Lord Dunmore in 1775 that any slaves who joined the British forces would be freed. It did not turn out quite that way, however, as we will see later.

Although in 1750 Princess Anne County had the third lowest percentage of slaves in the Tidewater counties, tension and fear increased among the whites. While slave owners declared that they were not afraid of their own slaves, but of those of others, this was only wishful thinking. As the New England slave ships brought more and more Africans into Virginia, the whites began to worry that they would be outnumbered, and laws restricting the mobility of slaves became even more rigid. While some attempts were made to eliminate the more brutal punishments for offenses, other measures were taken which deteriorated the slaves' conditions even more.

In the 17th century, the slaves had been encouraged to attend church like everyone else. But that was stopped, and they were not allowed into the churches at all. Not content to stand outside during services, they began to meet at night in one cabin or another for their own services. But with Governor Gooch's order to the militia in 1736 to patrol to prevent all night meetings, even that was hazardous. The native-born were, or considered themselves Christians, and for them, the promise of a forgiving God who would give them equality in Heaven was the only hope they had. But their own services, which included their African heritage of much singing and shouting (dancing), were regularly broken up, in spite of the large tub of water they always put in the center of the room to absorb the noise and fool the patrols.

While this patrol duty was supposed to be performed by the militia, instead, poor whites of questionable character were often hired for it. Their cruelty was well-known but overlooked. These patrols were also used to track down runaways. Since the law said that they were entitled to kill any runaway slave who resisted capture, they did not hesitate to use any means, however bestial.

By 1750, as a result of the poor quality of tobacco grown in our sandy soil, farmers were turning to the growing of grain, mostly wheat and corn. Grain was not as lucrative as tobacco, but it required far less labor. Also, they turned to the increased production of pitch, tar and turpentine. As early as 1704, Governor Nicholson had written to the Lords Commissioners for Trade and Plantations in London in answer to their inquiry about the production of pitch and tar and how it may be improved. His answer follows.

"I Humbly Answer:
That I believe there is Annually made in Virginia near 3,000 barrells of Tar in Princess Anne County which containes 97,891 Acres of

Patented Land & part of Norfolk County, about 50,000 acres of low Pine Land, not Agreable for tobacco, And the small quantity there made is of the worst Esteem & soe little value that discourages the Inhabitants to plant And forces them to clothe and Maintain themselves by Manufacturing of Wool and Leather And raising Stocks of Cattle & Hoggs.

What Tar is made, is of the Knotts & Pieces of fallen trees. . . . 'Tis probable treble the quantity can be made out of growing trees in those Counties & it would be much better in the kind & for all Uses and could be made in other parts of the Country not proper for planting tobacco."

He goes on to say that they made use of it for their own houses, boats, etc., sold it to masters of ships and transported it to Barbados, Jamaica and the Leeward Islands. But it was not sent to England.

This condition was soon remedied in Princess Anne with the addition of turpentine and lumber sent to England. The major shift in agriculture from tobacco to grain, in part, accounts for the fact that in 1750, Princess Anne County had the third lowest percentage of slaves in the Tidewater counties. The cultivating of tobacco required far more manuel labor than the cultivation of grains. As a result, the farmers of Princess Anne were not only buying fewer slaves but, in some cases, selling at least some of those they had; unfortunately, they sold them to the slave states in the Deep South where the demand was constant. This often necessitated the breaking up of families, which seems to us the most cruel custom of all.

Family life was very important to the blacks, and truly they had little else to enjoy. While the master often gave the marriage feast and the ceremony and feast were attended by both white and black, the minister carefully dropped from the service the phrase, "till death do us part." All knew that the master could, and often did, break up this partnership at any time, as there was no such thing as a legal slave marriage.

One horrid story concerns a male slave of one of the more affluent planters of Princess Anne County. This slave was such a strong and handsome specimen of manhood that his master decided to use him as a "breeder," selling his wife and children and forcing him to go about from one cabin to another for this purpose.

Another is the story of the son of a slave woman who so resembled the sons of the master, that his mother was sold when he was nine months old, and he was taken into the "big house" to be brought up by the cook who, he was told, was his grandmother. Kindly treated, he grew up in the white family and, although not taught to read and write, was entrusted with as much responsibility as the white sons of the master. After the Civil War and Emancipation, he had his own farm nearby. When he died, one of his old master's sons came to the former slave's daughter, complaining that she should have told him of the death. When she said that she did not wish to intrude since she was black and he was white, he said, "But he was my brother!"

Miscegenation was now taken for granted, but only between a white man and a black woman, not the other way around. The law still held that a child inherited the condition of the mother. Mulattoes remained slaves but became more esteemed than the pure African, and today it is rare that you see a man or woman in this area so dark as to appear of pure African blood. Among the black population, there is no stigma attached to having white blood or to mixed blood of any kind. While discussing the possibility of Indian blood, one sophisticated visiting lady with brilliant blue eyes and light skin laughingly told that she was called, "United Nations," as she was the result of the mixture of so many races, nations and creeds.

Desegregation came easily to Princess Anne County. It was the one area in which the whites of the old families did not show strong resistance to change, nor did the native blacks seem inclined to violence or resentment for real or imagined past injustices as in other parts of the country. We quote: "We have always been friends, and we needed each other."

Spurred on by the Great Awakening, 1726–56, abolitionist groups were being formed in the South as well as the North, and the conscience of men impelled a few to free their slaves. Charles Smith, the first rector of Trinity Church (Church of England) in Portsmouth, decreed in his will of 1771, "I give unto my mulatto woman Mary 3 months of her time, £ 50 in money and my Quarto Bible with the spinning wheel and gears and implements in and about the house with her clothes." But not many manumissions added money and the means of self-support. The few manumissions made in the county before the Revolution were done so in recognition of some heroic deed, such as saving the life of some member of the family, and also needed the permission of the governor, as the law of 1691 stated that no master may free a slave unless he paid for his transportation out of the Colony. For a married man, this was hardly an inducement to beg for freedom, as he would have to leave his wife and family behind, and freed slaves were not welcomed in the neighboring colonies.

If a freed slave could make it to New England, he was no better off. William W. Freehley says in *American Negro Slavery* that the abolitionists, such as John Woolan, prior to 1776 found the North barren soil for antislavery ideas. As John Jay recalled, "The great majority of Northerners accepted slavery as a matter of course, and very few among them doubted the propriety and rectitude of it," and the Northern captains of slave ships continued to supply slaves from Africa, as they had since 1637. Alice Morse Earle in *Customs and Fashions in Old New England* says, "I have never seen in any Southern newspapers advertisements of negro sales that surpass in heartlessness and viciousness the advertisements of our New England newspapers of the eighteenth century. Negro children were advertised to be given away in Boston, and were sold by the pound as was other merchandise." And William Root Bliss in *Side Glimpses from the Colonial Meeting House* says, "It was rum that forced the growth of Slavery in New England. The commerce in rum and slaves—making a circuit from New England to the West Indies, thence to Africa, thence back to the islands with slaves, thence home with molasses and such negroes as had not been disposed of at the islands—furnished nearly all the money that was annually remitted to pay for merchandise brought from England." Of course, not all of the slave ships were of New England. There were some greedy men in Maryland and Virginia as well who participated in this nefarious trade.

Nevertheless, there were some free blacks in Princess Anne who somehow managed to stay, but their lot was not a very happy one. Besides the ones who had been voluntarily freed, there were some who had bought their freedom. They were the ones who had become so proficient in various skills that their masters had "hired them out," and they received a small percentage of the fee each time they worked for someone else. "Virginia-made" furniture is highly prized today, and this was made by slaves on the plantations. But once these artisans were free, those who were anxious for their services before backed off, for freedmen were looked upon with suspicion as the ones causing unrest and insurrection among those not free. Edmund S. Morgan *(American Slavery American Freedom)* says that, "It was made plain to these newly freed blacks and to the white population that their color made freedom inappropriate for them. They were denied the right to vote, to hold office or to testify in court proceedings. These handicaps successfully dissociated them from whites, however poor." Cut off from their own people by jealousy and suspicion, they remained a small factor in Virginia's free society.

At the same time, the white family's dependence on their slaves increased. No longer were the daughters of the household required to do menial tasks, or even to learn how. They were instructed instead in the fine points of needlework, dress and womanly charm. As time hung heavy on their hands, the young girls often taught their playmates to read and write, along with some arithmetic, if they knew any. Not often inspired by an altruistic reasoning, they rather felt that their servants would be more useful to them if they were semi-literate, at the same time demonstrating their white superiority. Since house servants lived with the slaveholders in the same house, they were always together, and the white girls saw no reason to obey the law against this teaching.

What these daughters of the household did not realize was that children taught their parents, and soon, black preachers were appearing who could read and understand the Bible. While the master had been looked upon as the provider and protector, the slaves now began to question this paternalism. These literate black preachers stressed dependence on God rather than master, as only God was their father and master, and to look upon the white man as just another man like themselves. As a result, the slaves became more unruly, more insolent and demanded more privileges. Even a "good master" had to cope with constant irritations of this sort, as he wrestled with his conscience and his fear. As one master of many slaves said when it was reported to him that some of his slaves had run away, "I wish I could run away with them. This burden is becoming intolerable."

PART THREE
Chapter 5
POLITICS—CLOUDS GATHER

Slavery was just beginning to become an acute problem, and other events of the 18th century were of more concern at the time. With the rapid increase in population, particularly in numbers of slaves, the responsibilities of church and court increased accordingly.

Whether Virginians liked it or not, the formation of other English colonies on the Eastern seaboard weakened their position as the most important and prestigious of the colonies. While still the most populous and the wealthiest, compromises had to be made with the other colonies to ensure Virginia's economic advantages.

One of the many accomplishments of Governor Alexander Spotswood, 1710–1722, was the establishment of an inter-colonial postal system, which later facilitated the efforts of the Committee of Correspondence to unite the colonies in protest against the oppressive tax acts of Parliament. Spotswood's successful dispatch of the pirate Blackbeard and his insistence on tobacco inspection were his only acts which directly affected this county, but his expedition of "The Knights of the Golden Horseshoe" across the Blue Ridge opened up the Virginia frontier to rapid settlement in the Valley of Virginia by Germans and Scots who poured down from Pennsylvania. One inducement to settle there for these Lutherans, Presbyterians and Mennonites was that they were not required to pay taxes to the Church of England, partly because there was no Church of England there!

The Indians in that area, tribes of the Iroquois, urged on by the French, who claimed the valley of the Ohio and Mississippi rivers, gave these people a lot of trouble by frequent attacks. As in the past, the men of Princess Anne County were extremely reluctant to go out of this county to fight Indians elsewhere, and they only went under strict orders or paid others to go for them if they could. But the

French and Indian War, 1754-1761, involved a large-scale operation, not only to protect the people living on the frontier, but also to expel the French entirely from the center of the continent—from the Gulf of Mexico to Canada—which the British were determined to do. This was successfully accomplished by the Treaty of Paris in 1763. This war had been further complicated by what was called the Seven Years War in Europe, in which Spain had joined France against England. France ceded all territory east of the Mississippi River, except the city of New Orleans, which remained with Spain, and Spain retained Cuba in exchange for East and West Florida.

The defeat of France and Spain was extremely important for the future of the United States because in the Revolution, a little more than a decade later, the colonists had only one enemy to fight—the British. France and Spain, smarting under their ignominious defeat both here and in Europe, came to our aid in the struggle for independence.

With the French gone from our frontier and compromises made with the Indians, the Shenandoah was safer from attacks, and new settlers poured in.

But Virginia was faced with a huge debt. Here, where tobacco was the currency for almost everything, payment for the soldiers and military supplies which had been required, by law had to be made in money. The House of Burgesses, therefore, issued paper money in the amount of £ 250,000 in 1764. But to the dismay of Princess Anne County particularly, an act of Parliament in 1751 banned the use of this legal tender, nullified all acts of colonial assemblies contrary to its terms and provided for a fine of £ 1,000 and dismissal from office of any colonial governor or any other holder of a government position who assented to legislative acts in defiance of that law.

This, combined with the strict enforcement of the Navigation Acts, which hampered any trade other than with England, plus the post-war business decline, seemed to the colonists calculated to ruin their economy. Massachusetts, whose paper money had earlier been banned, in 1751, at a Boston town meeting denounced taxation without representation and proposed united action by the colonies in protest. The Massachusetts House of Representatives authorized a Committee of Correspondence to contact other colonies, who quickly followed suit by forming their own committees and banning the importation of all luxury English goods.

Then came the Stamp Act of 1765, designed to raise £ 60,000 annually for Parliament to maintain the British colonial military

The Stamp Act, passed in 1764, required that printers place a tax stamp on newspapers and other printed materials. The printers refused to buy the stamped papers and actively worked for the repeal of the tax. In several colonies the stamps were destroyed, and warnings were issued by the Sons of Liberty against their use.

Burning the Stamps as result of the Stamp Act of 1765. *Courtesy of the Virginia State Library.*

establishments here. This was a tax on newspapers, almanacs, pamphlets, legal documents, insurance policies, ships papers, licenses and even dice and playing cards. This direct tax by Parliament, with the clause that any infringements were to be tried by courts of Vice-admiralty (which had no jury), led to Patrick Henry's famous speech in the House of Burgesses in 1764, "Give me liberty or give me death," and his proposal of the Virginia Resolutions. Although the House rejected the more radical aspect of these resolutions, they were published in the colonial newspapers and added fuel to the fire of resentment.

The beloved Governor William Berkeley in his old age had proclaimed to Charles II in 1671 that, "I thank God there are no free schools nor printing (in the colonies), and I hope that we shall not have these hundred years, for learning has brought disobedience, and heresy, and sects into the world, and printing has divulged them and libel against the best government. God keep us from both!" As fine a governor as he was for the young Colony, this later hope was not fulfilled. By 1771, there were newspapers in all the colonies, as well as pauper schools in Virginia. The College of William and Mary had been founded in Williamsburg in 1693, and eight others were founded in other colonies. Harvard had been the first, in 1636, and William and Mary the second. But William and Mary had the distinction of founding the first chapter of Phi Beta Kappa, in 1779, and the first law courses were offered there, in 1726, by George Wythe.

By this time, the majority had learned to read, at least a little, and newspapers were available. The *Virginia Gazette* had been started in 1736 and, under different publishers, has continued to the present day with a wide circulation in Virginia. The *Virginia Gazette or Norfolk Intelligencer* had begun publishing in 1770. Thanks to Governor Spotswood's intercolonial postal system the many newspapers of other colonies were also available, reporting the news of their areas, however biased, for popular consumption. By 1775, as reported by Richard Morris in his "Encyclopedia of American History". There were 37 newspapers in all: 23 Patriot, seven Loyalists and seven neutral or doubtful in loyalty.

As a result of indignation against the Stamp Act and the banning by the colonies of British goods, British exports to America had a sharp decline. Due to a strong protest from British merchants and even protest in Parliament, the Stamp Act was repealed in 1766. The rejoicing in the colonies at first overlooked the statement in the same act that Parliament had full authority to make laws binding the American colonists in all cases whatsoever.

This was a sneaky trick, unfortunately still used by politicians who tack onto a popular bill a proviso which in effect practically nullifies it! But this accompanying statement was not overlooked by the secret organization of The Sons of Liberty, which had been formed in 1765 in New York and quickly spread throughout the colonies. The Quartering Act, passed by Parliament in 1765, required civil authorities in the colonies to supply barracks and supplies for the British troops which were being increased as tension rose.

Under Prime Minister William Pitt, the Townsend Acts were drawn up in 1767 in a further attempt to extract revenue from the colonies, who again turned to non-importation to force Parliament to back down. Led by Samuel Adams, the Massachusetts House of Representatives denounced the acts and circulated a letter to the other colonies repeating his denunciation of the acts and attacking any move by the Crown to make colonial governors and judges independent of the people. The Colonies of New Hampshire, Connecticut and Virginia did the same. After a wharf official in Boston had been locked in a cabin of John Hancock's ship, "The Liberty," while a cargo of Madiera wine was unloaded, the customs officials fled and appealed for troops for their protection. Two regiments were landed in Boston on October 1, 1768, and seige began.

If Virginia seems rather slow in taking the lead in opposition, it should be remembered that this Colony had been settled by staunch Royalists who were not "dissenters" to Crown, Church or anything English, and ever since, they had endeavored to be "more English than the English" in dress, custom, manner of living and governmental structure. It had taken the great orator Patrick Henry to move them away from this closely held concept of the "right way to live." It was different in the Northern states, which had been settled mainly by dissenters and had become industrial, as opposed to the ideal of English country gentry in this predominantly rural Colony, and especially in this county.

When George Washington introduced a set of resolves in the House of Burgesses on March 16, 1769, asserting that the sole right of taxing Virginians lay with the governor and the House of Burgesses and condemning the proposal of Parliament that American malcontents be brought to England for trial, the die was cast. Governor Botetourt dissolved the Assembly, but they met anyway in the Raleigh Tavern and adopted the Virginia Association, which banned British goods, further slave importation, and a long list of European luxuries. Other colonies adopted the same resolutions.

Riots between the Sons of Liberty and British soldiers followed in New York and especially in Boston where, on March 5, 1770, the "Boston Massacre" of civilians by soldiers occurred. Clashes between civilians and soldiers had been increasing ever since the arrival of the troops in 1768, and on this evening, bands of both were roaming the streets looking for trouble. A beleaguered sentry on King Street called the main guard, and as the crowd pressed forward, someone fired into their midst, killing three and mortally wounding two others. Bowing to a demand by Samuel Adams, Governor Hutchinson withdrew the troops to an island in the harbor. At the trial, Captain Preston, leader of the guard, and four others were acquitted, while two of the guard were found guilty of murder. Pleading their clergy, these two were branded on their hands and released.

Next was the Boston Tea Party, on December 16, 1773. This was no "tempest in a teapot." On one side, the British merchants, because of the non-importation resolves, were overloaded with a vast surplus of 17,000,000 pounds of tea of England. In May, the House of Commons had passed a bill remitting all import duties to America except on tea, and the East India Company was given the right to sell directly to appointed consignees, enabling them to undercut the law-abiding colonial merchants who had bought tea through a middle-man at higher prices. With this threat of monopoly, the people of Philadelphia and Boston demanded the resignation of the consignees, but those in Boston refused. When the British *"Dartmouth,"* the first of three tea ships, arrived in Boston harbor, mass meetings demanded that the tea be sent back to England. When Governor Hutchinson refused, 8,000 people assembled to hear the captain of the *"Dartmouth"* relay the governor's decision. Samuel Adams and The Sons of Liberty were ready. Disguised as Mohawk Indians, they immediately boarded the tea ships and dumped all the tea, 342 chests full, into the harbor. Further destruction of tea followed in Annapolis, Maryland, and Edenton, North Carolina.

Decrees from Parliament became increasingly resented and mass meetings everywhere in the colonies began to call for repeal. In May of 1774, urgent demands began for a congress of all the colonies, and in September, they met in Philadelphia with 56 delegates from 12 colonies, Georgia alone missing. The first Continental Congress condemned by resolution all the coercive acts and the presence of a standing army in peacetime, and it set forth the rights of the colonists, pledging economic sanctions. A committee was to be elected in each county, town and city to execute these resolves, and violators were to be punished by publicity and boycott. By April 1775, these committees of the Association were in operation.

During all this excitement, most of the people in Princess Anne County were going quietly about their own business, hoping that the whole affair up North would blow away. They never had taken much notice of what went on in other parts—Boston and New York might as well have been on another planet—and contention in the House of Burgesses was left to those elected to serve there.

There had never been many visitors from other parts to Princess Anne County, as there were in other places, or even in the port of Norfolk, where the presence of the Scottish merchants and officers of the Royal Navy coming and going gave a more cosmopolitan flavor to social life. There is no guest list for the ball given for Lord and Lady Dunmore in Norfolk in 1771, but other than the "dandy" Edward Hack Moseley, Jr., it is unlikely that residents of Princess Anne County who were not merchants, except for Jacob Ellegood, George Logan and William Aitchison, were invited to attend and to contribute to the expense.

With the increased population, more roads and ferries in this county were needed, the court required more justices, more sheriffs and more constables, and the squabbles over property lines were continuous. The Church of England was losing its power as the Baptists and Methodists grew in numbers and strength. The representatives in the House of Burgesses from Princess Anne, 1761-1775, when it was dissolved were, in succession: John Ackiss, 1769-1771, but seldom attending; Edward Hack Moseley Senior, 1761-1771, followed by his son Edward Hack Moseley, Jr., 1772-1774; Christopher Wright, Jr., 1772-1775; and William Robinson, 1775, serving briefly before the dissolution. All of these became Patriots, with the exception of Edward Hack Moseley, Sr. who split with his son over the cause for independence and eventually returned to England.

In spite of the Navigation Acts and other oppressive measures by England, plus uncertainty concerning crops and their market, some people prospered. In the beginning of the "Golden Age," Matthew Pallet had built, in 1715, the fine brick house of "Wolfsnare Plantation." We have already discussed the Francis Land house, built in 1732, and the Richard Murray House, built in 1736. Richard Murray had established the successful flax cultivation on King's Creek. Thomas Walke III built his house in 1759. In 1727 Joel Cornick built a fine house near the present Oceana Boulevard. A long line of Cornicks had been living on this land since William Cornick received a grant of 1,736 acres in 1671. In the grant the land was named "Salisbury Plains," and the name remained over the years. The Cornick family became prominent in the life of the county, and especially in the Church, one of Joel's sons giving part of this land near the house for the Third Eastern Shore Chapel.

The house, with its fine interior woodwork, survived until 1951 as did the Chapel where services were held regularly, with Cornick men serving as lay readers in the absence of a visiting minister.

All of the other houses noted above have survived and are occupied today, but, in 1951, the United States Naval Air Station at Oceana needed to extend their runways for the jet planes, and unfortunately Salisbury Plains and the Chapel were in the way. This announcement caused much consternation, but the Navy paid for the removal of the Chapel and graveyard to its present location on Laskin Road. Descendants were found of all those who had been buried there so long ago, except for one. Since he could not be moved, a bronze plaque was set in the concrete runway with his name and dates. May he rest in peace as the jets roar overhead.

All of these had been well built in "the best of times"—The Golden Age—but three others were built a little later. Thurmer Hoggard built the beautiful "Poplar Hall" about 1760, as did William Woodhouse, and Lemuel Cornick built the imposing "Broad Bay Manor" in 1770.

A few frame houses built before the Revolution have miraculously survived. They are the Carraway House, 1713, now an antique shop, The Charles Henley house, 1771, and the Anthony Fentress House, 1765. Another frame house, which is on Kempsville Road, we believe to be the Nathaniel Nicholas house, built as early as 1671, but it has been so renovated that we cannot be sure of its date or the builder.

If it seemed to be "business as usual" in this county, the leaders of the upper class began to worry. Many felt, hopefully, that the differences between the colonies and the Mother Country should and would be resolved, and this feeling was reinforced by the clergy of the Church of England who were almost solidly behind England. If it came to open rebellion, it was inconceivable that England, the greatest seapower in the world, would not suppress it. And, yet, they felt that England was not being fair to her colonies. The status quo, with all its shortcomings, was still preferable to the possibility of danger to themselves, their way of life, and, above all, their land.

As they pondered, the first Continental Congress was held in

Philadelphia in September 1774, and the delegates from Virginia were Peyton Randolph, Richard Henry Lee, George Washington, Edmund Pendleton, Richard Bland and Benjamin Harrison. All these men were from Northern Virginia, and although their ability and leadership in the Colony was unquestioned, none were from lower Tidewater. While apprehensive, the leaders here adopted an attitude of wait and see.

The Declaration and Resolves passed by this Congress denounced the Coercive Acts and the Quebec Act. This Quebec Act extending the boundaries of Quebec to the Ohio and Mississippi rivers, antagonized the colonies, especially Virginia, by claiming Western land under charters to Virginia and was termed unjust, cruel and unconstitutional. The Declaration made by the Continental Congress criticized the revenue measures imposed since 1763, the extension of vice-admiralty jurisdiction, the dissolution of colonial assemblies and the keeping of a standing army in peacetime. The resolutions set forth the rights of colonists, among them "to life, liberty and property," and of the provincial legislatures to the exclusive power of lawmaking "in all cases of taxation and internal policy," subject only to the royal veto. Thirteen Parliamentary acts since 1763 were declared to violate American rights, and economic sanctions were pledged until they were repealed. This Declaration and the Resolves were to be presented to the King.

The leaders here did not have long to wait. At the first Virginia Convention, at St. John's Church in Richmond (where they would be removed from any interference from Governor Dunmore), Patrick Henry's oratory inflamed the representatives and they passed his resolution, though by a small majority. According to Virginius Dabney in *The New Dominion*, Henry declared that, "A well regulated militia . . . is the natural strength and only security of a free government . . . Resolved therefore, that this colony be immediately put into a posture of defence."

Henry was named chairman of a committee to effect this resolve, and having heard nothing from the King, he returned to attend a scheduled meeting of the House of Burgesses.

The second Continental Congress met in May of 1775, when George Washington was elected unanimously by the Congress to command the Continental Army. While the Congress was in session, Lord Dunmore had become so alarmed that he ordered British sailors to seize the powder in the magazine at Williamsburg, which the colonists had paid for and stored there. As a result of this brazen theft, horsemen were gathering at Fredericksburg to march on the Capitol, and Patrick Henry was leading a group of militia from Hanover County with the same objective. Dunmore hastily produced £ 330 in compensation, but he fled with his family to the British man-of-war "Fowry," anchored in the York River, and attempted to administer his duties from the quarterdeck! When the House of Burgesses met in June, he was courteously invited to attend, but he insisted that they join him on the "Fowry." They refused, and after transacting some necessary business, they adjourned for the last time, on June 20, 1775, dissolving that body which had been formed so auspiciously in 1619—156 years before.

Casting about for a haven, Dunmore soon left for the port city of Norfolk, where he had been so welcome and entertained at the beginning of his term as governor and where the presence of so many Scottish and British merchants would, he felt, ensure his welcome again. Wertenberger says, in his *History of Norfolk*, that "this port of 6,000 inhabitants was a thing apart from the rest of Virginia." To some extent, that was true, for Norfolk County and Princess Anne County had the same origin in Lower Norfolk County, and the people of both counties had the same feeling of isolation and independence from the rest of the Colony.

But this time Dunmore was disappointed. He was no longer the new, elegant and all-powerful governor, but a man fleeing from his responsibilities. His reception was decidedly cool.

PART IV
THE REVOLUTION

PART FOUR
Chapter 1
WAR COMES TO PRINCESS ANNE COUNTY

With Dunmore in the Elizabeth River, the people of Norfolk and Princess Anne held their breath waiting for what would come next. The waiting was not long. On August 17, 1775, the Virginia Committee of Safety was formed, with Edmund Pendleton as chairman and Patrick Henry as Commander in Chief of the Virginia forces. Edmund Pendleton had the following order published in the *Virginia Gazette*, and it was reprinted in the *Norfolk Gazette* and *Intelligencer*.

> "The Committee of Safety earnestly recommends it to the committees of the several counties to lose no time in collecting and forwarding the public arms according to the order of Convention, and also to elect their militia officers where it is not done."

The Committee of Safety for Princess Anne County was immediately elected, 22 of the most prominent men in the county.

Anthony Lawson	Thomas Brock
William Nimmo	Anthony Walke, Jr.
William Robinson	William Keeling, Jr.
Christopher Wright	Erasmus Haynes
James Kemp	Dennis Dawley
John Hancock	James Henley
John Ackiss	Thomas Old, Sr.
Edward Cannon	James Tooley
Frederick Boush	Cason Moore
George Jamieson	Joel Cornick, Jr.
William Cannon	William Woodhouse

Peter Singleton—Commissary of Supply

Virginia was required to produce two regiments. It was up to Peter Singleton to use the public funds to supply the recruits from here with clothes, horses, wagons, arms and food. The duties of the others were first to recruit the required number of men. Quakers were excused but had to pay for substitutes through their church. Methodists and Baptists would not serve side by side and had to be put in different companies. Allowances were to be paid to wives and children of those recruited, also through public funds.

Every white male over the age of 16 was required to declare himself for or against the cause of independence. If he refused, he could not hold any office, nor serve on juries, sue for debts or buy or sell property. As you will see, this oath was actually taken rather lightly, or many changed their minds later. But the oath taken by all recruits into the military left no room for indecision.

> "I do swear that I will be faithful & true to the Colony & Dominion of Virginia, that I will serve the same to the utmost of my power in defence of the just rights of America against all enemies whatsoever, that I will, to the utmost of my abilities, obey the lawful commands of my superior officers, agreeable to the ordinances of the Convention, and lay down my arms peacefully when required to do so, either by the General Convention or General Assembly of Virginia. So help me God."

One of the most difficult and continuing tasks of the Committee was to seek out the "disaffected" and prevent them from aiding the British in any way. It was more difficult in Norfolk, where such a large number of British and Scottish merchants was involved in business, with marital ties with the local inhabitants. But there were many here in Princess Anne County who were in sympathy with the British because of an inbred feeling of loyalty to the Crown, fear of losing their property or, particularly, their land. Some were openly Loyalists, some secretly. It was a time of suspicion and fear. Friendships were irrevocably broken, and in some cases, families were forever split by their dissenting views.

When the Sons of Liberty was formed in Norfolk in 1766, there were 57 signers, including many merchants whose businesses were being severely hurt by the Navigation Acts, especially the Stamp Act. But when the Committee of Safety required an oath of allegiance to America, most of these merchants dropped out, including James Parker, William Aitchieson and Jacob Ellegood. John Willoughby, who had been named chairman of the Norfolk Committee of Safety, demurred at taking the oath of allegiance to America, and although he finally signed, he was under such suspicion that he resigned, and with one of his sons, he joined Lord Dunmore's fleet in the harbor. The old and prominent family of Willoughby had always been merchants with close ties in England, but that did not prevent some other family members from taking an active part in the Patriot cause, and another John Willoughby was a captain in the Virginia Navy. The elder John Willoughby had been a close friend of Lord Dunmore, as was Edward Hack Moseley, Sr., of Princess Anne, who broke with his son, Edward Hack Moseley, Jr., over this difference. Both were interrogated by the Committee, but Edward Hack Moseley, Jr., was already a respected Clerk of the Court, and his father was left alone on his own recognizance. An invitation to dinner with General Benedict Arnold in 1781 to the elder Moseley has come down to us, and he may even have attended.

This disruption of families was not unique here. The wealthy and prominent John Randolph of Roanoke, who was Attorney General of the Colony, resigned and left for England, but his brother Peyton Randolph was elected president of the first and second Continental Conventions in Philadelphia, and his son John stayed and worked hard with his uncle Peyton for independence. Richard Corbin, connected by marriage with the Lee family and Receiver General of the Colony, also resigned and left for England, but his wife stayed behind and was an ardent Patriot, an unusual show of spirit in a woman of those days.

These family divisions were not confined to the upper class. The farmers of Princess Anne County, threatened with the poor harvest of that year and the foraging expeditions of Dunmore, were finding it difficult to keep their hot-headed young sons from enlisting for independence when they preferred to keep them home to protect their property.

A ban on all goods imported from England had been imposed by the First Continental Congress in 1774, and it was up to the Committee of Safety to confiscate any goods coming in after this ban. Colonel Anthony Walke turned over a large quantity of china, James Braithwaite an anvil, and in February 1775, George Logan, a merchant of Norfolk who lived at Kemp's Landing and had a store there, cheerfully submitted to a sale of "four casks of nails, one bale of Oznaburg cloth, one box of linens and a cask of saddlery." The money realized from the sale of these goods was used by the Committee for expenses of the troops.

These were small annoyances compared with the activities of Lord Dunmore in that summer of 1775. In response to his urgent request to Lord Dartmouth, Secretary of State for the Colonies, for reinforcements, Lord Dartmouth had sent four warships and several smaller sloops and tenders to Norfolk with a shipment of arms and 60 regulars of the army. Foraging raids on the countryside increased. While the Committee of Safety had already made heavy demands for provisions for the troops, they at least had given pledges for repayment, but the British raiders merely plundered the plantations of livestock, grain and Negroes. Most of the plantations were on navigable waterways, and these raiders could, and did, pounce at any time, day or night. The leader of this foraging campaign was the infamous Captain Matthew Squires of the HMS Otter, whose wanton destruction and cruelty to the inhabitants in the whole Chesapeake area turned many would-be Loyalists into Patriots. One recorded account was in Northumberland County near Accomac at night. (*The Researcher*, Robert Armistead Stewart.)

> "The marauders first broke all the glass in his windows, tore off all the shutters and then battered down his doors. Having entered the house, they demolished every piece of furniture which could not be carried off, and then proceeded to secure for themselves the remainder of his property . . . including his daughter's whole wardrobe, wool, hogs, geese, etc."

A Virginian wrote from Norfolk, "The Governor sails up and down the river, and where he finds a defenseless place, he lands, plunders the plantation and carries off the negroes."

John Norton, Jr., of the respected mercantile firm of John Norton & Sons, London, wrote to his father from Yorktown on October 14, 1775, *John Norton and Son, Merchants of London and Virginia* (Frances Norton Mason):

> ". . . I have hitherto been silent about our Governor's operations, but I cannot help saying something of them as they are marked with almost every species of cruelty that a wicked mind could suggest. After pillaging the Plantations on the River for some time past, taking Negroes, burning Houses and the like depravations, he hoisted his Standard and issued a Damned, infernal, Diabolical proclamation declaring Freedom to all our slaves who will join him, & obliged great number to take an Oath that they will arm themselves & assist him with their lives and Fortunes."

Powerless against these raids, for the militia and recruits had been sent North to assist General Washington, the people of Princess Anne begged Williamsburg for protection, which was unavailable. Virginia had no navy, as the only naval power in the Colony was British, commanded by Governor Dunmore. But as the situation became more and more intolerable, those who had hidden their own small boats began to use them to harass the British in their operations, inspired by the three Barron brothers of Hampton.

Lord Dartmouth had commanded the *Fowry* to be sent elsewhere, and Lord Dunmore was forced to make headquarters on the *Otter*, a smaller vessel. Dissatisfied with these accommodations, Dunmore commandeered the *William*, which belonged to John Brown & Company of Portsmouth. He had it refitted, armed with 13 guns and the stern reconditioned as a suite for himself. This work was done at the small private shipyard of Andrew Sprowle in Gosport. Andrew Sprowle was a Scot, a British Navy agent and intensely loyal to the Crown. But he did not anticipate that Dunmore would be his guest gratis, especially since Dunmore complained that Gosport was "a dirty little village, infested with flies and an obnoxious odor from a small distillery." He lived well there, however, compared with his ordinary seamen. The shop owners of Norfolk were reluctant to sell victuals to ships which might at any time train their guns on the city. The work on the *William* was finished in August, it was rechristened *The Dunmore*, and Lord Dunmore moved aboard.

Shortly after this, Captain Squires was on board one of his tenders when it was blown ashore at Hampton in a great storm. He fled into the woods while his crew, who had managed to swim ashore, found shelter with a local farmer. It is said that the crew suggested that since the tender had been abandoned, their host and his neighbors had every right to salvage it and its cargo of muskets, powder horns and lead. Making his way back to the *Otter*, Squires wrote the Hampton Committee to return the tender and its cargo. They refused, suggesting that his men had sold them to a local merchant. Enraged, Squires seized every Hampton vessel he could reach. When his activities were reported in the *Norfolk Gazette & Intelligencer*, he sent 20 armed soldiers into Norfolk on September 30 to seize the press and its owner, John Holt, and to carry them to the "Dunmore" where Dunmore intended to print the paper himself with the "true story" of the events.

Then the Hampton Committee said that they would see what could be done about the return of the cargo if they were granted a pledge that the King's men would stop molesting their farms, that all shipping in Hampton Roads would be allowed to proceed without hindrance, and if all boats and persons now in custody would be returned to their rightful owners. Squires refused to negotiate, and Dunmore threatened to burn the town. Learning of this, Williamsburg ordered all inhabitants to evacuate the town and sent down 100 regulars to their assistance. On October 24, six armed British tenders pulled up just offshore and began a furious bombardment, which damaged many homes and commercial buildings. Under cover of the cannonade, several boatloads of armed men attempted to make a landing, but heavy musketry from the beach drove off the landing parties, the cannon fire ceased and the attacking tenders ran back to Dunmore.

Meanwhile, Lord Dunmore was sweeping the counties of Norfolk and Princess Anne of hidden cannon and other arms. One of these raids surprised a small company of minutemen from Kemp's Landing and captured Captain Thomas Matthews, who later died in captivity. Hearing that Colonel Anthony Lawson was at Kemp's Landing with a company of militia, Dunmore sailed up to Newtown with a party of grenadiers, soldiers, some Tories and slaves, and marched from there to Kemp's Landing. The militia, busy with the harvest, hurriedly came together hoping for an ambush. But they were no match for the British and they were routed. John Ackiss, Jr., was killed, the first to die on Virginia soil, and Colonel Lawson and Colonel Joseph Hutchins were captured. Lawson was imprisoned for a year in Florida before he was exchanged, and Hutchins died in captivity. Dunmore then set up his headquarters in George Logan's house, while his men searched the town for armaments, which had been removed by the Patriots the night before. He set up his standard and called on the inhabitants to come forward and take the oath of allegiance to the Crown. Some had escaped to the sand dunes of Cape Henry, but many out of fear of reprisal took the oath, pinning the required badge of red cloth on their chests. It was a humiliating day for the people of Kemp's Landing, as well as the many who had fled there from Norfolk for refuge.

Dunmore, now confident that Princess Anne County was secured for the Crown, returned to Norfolk, and on November 7, he issued his proclamation declaring martial law, requiring all citizens to take the oath of allegiance to the King and declaring that he would free all slaves who would join him. Terrified by what appeared to be an open invitation to insurrection by all slaves, one-third of the city's inhabitants remaining hurriedly departed for the country. Dunmore enlisted the Scottish merchants, their clerks 'and others who feared the confiscation of their property into "The Queen's Own Loyal Virginians," and the slaves who answered his call into "Dunmore's

Private Man | Officer Captain Taliaferro's Co. | Private Man | Officer Captain Wm. Pickett's Co.

The Minute Battalion of Culpepper County, Virginia. 1775-1776

Ethiopean Corps." The promise of freedom to runaway slaves probably did more to antagonize the people than any of his other mistakes as the women, always fearful of a slave insurrection, urged their husbands to resist.

Then, realizing that the main road from North Carolina to Norfolk was not properly fortified, Dunmore erected a stockade on the north side of Great Bridge and installed cannons and a garrison of 30 whites and 90 Negroes to command the bridge. Hearing that Colonel William Woodford with a large force was on the way to join the militia on the other side of the bridge, he sent all his available regulars, 60 Tories and a few sailors, to join the garrison. He would have deployed more, but he was deluded by a slave of Thomas Marshall, who was fighting with the Patriots, into believing that there were only about 300 Virginians there and they were short of ammunition. He should have known from his other encounter with Colonel Woodford what sort of men were with him. They were the up-county "buckskins," with the long and accurate rifles and their hunting shirts emblazoned with their two mottoes: "Don't Tread on Me" and "Liberty or Death." At the last minute, Dunmore did send a few more reinforcements under Captain Fordyce, who arrived December 8th with orders to attack at dawn December 9th.

They came out marching six abreast over the 1,000 foot causeway toward the Colonials, backed up by the roar of their cannon. No shot was fired in return until they were within 50 feet of the Patriots. Suddenly, Lieutenant Travis gave the order and 90 rifles cracked with faultless aim. Most of the Red Coats fell, dead or wounded, and the others fled back across the bridge. Colonel Woodford followed with his men, driving the British into their fort. Sixty of the British had been killed or wounded and none of the Colonials hurt, except Thomas Nash of Princess Anne County who received a slight wound on one hand. The fight was over. Those who had taken part in the rout at Kemp's Landing were vindicated, and it was the beginning of the end for Lord Dunmore in Virginia. The Colonials allowed the British to carry back their wounded and then buried their dead. Captain Fordyce was buried with full military honors as befitting his rank and the courage he had displayed. In that short engagement, the most conspicuous hero of the Colonials was William Flora, a free black from Portsmouth who had been the last to leave his post as the British approached.

Thomas Nash was already a captain in the Continental Army under Colonel Woodford. He continued in the service, was captured in a

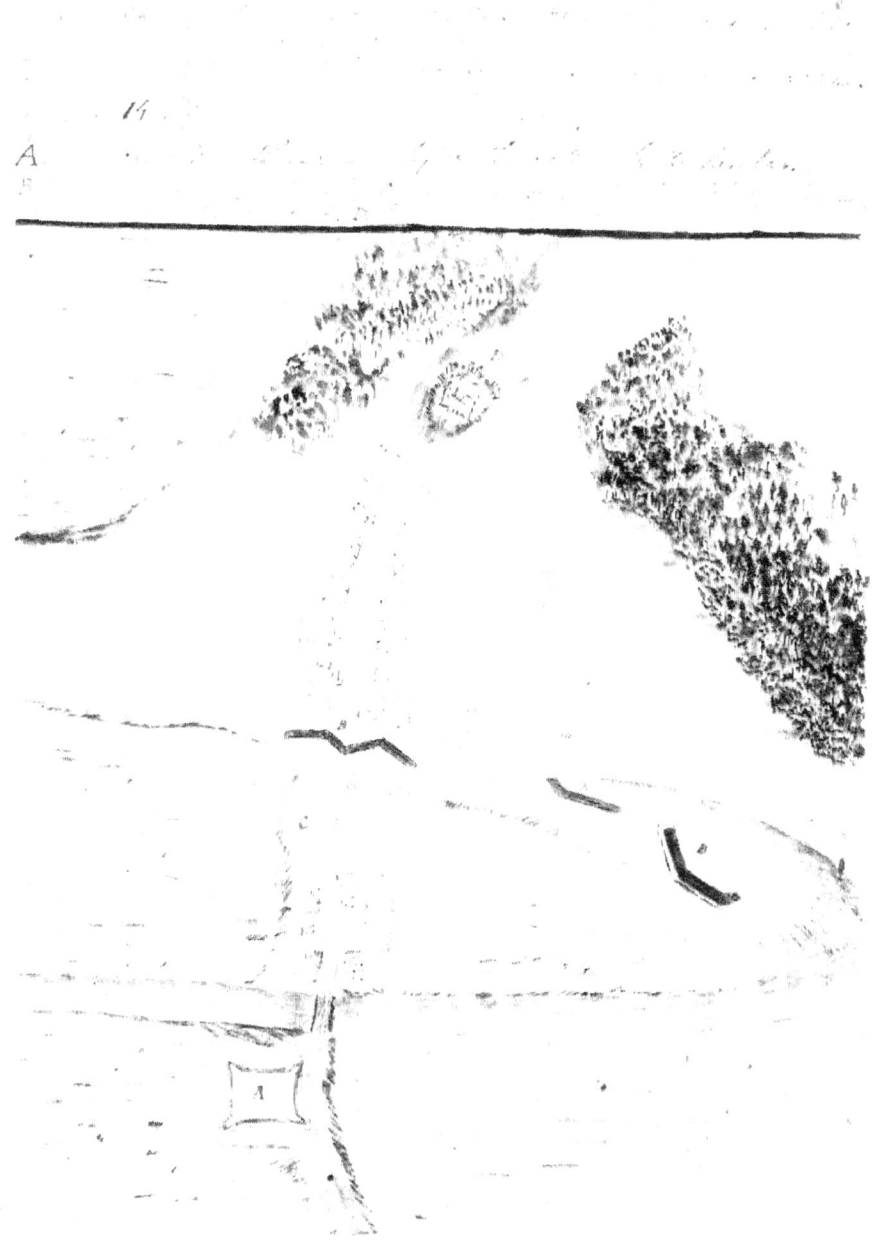

Great Bridge area just before the battle, December 9, 1775. *Courtesy of The Clements Library, University of Michigan.*

daring raid on General Arnold's headquarters in the spring of 1781, and was imprisoned in the Sugar House at Portsmouth. Caught in an attempt to free himself and others, he was confined in Cornwallis' prison ship off Yorktown until after the surrender. This prison ship was described as "a floating dungeon and the condition of the prisoners pitiable." When Captain Nash appeared on deck to be discharged, the only remaining portions of his shirt were his wrist ruffles. He had cut these off and placed them in his Bible, concealed in his trouser pocket.

Surviving this ordeal, he returned to Princess Anne County, married Elizabeth Herbert, also of Princess Anne County, and became a leading figure in St. Bride's Parish, serving as a vestryman and Church Warden.

Not having finished serving his country, Nash was in charge of constructing the gunboats which, with the *Constellation* and the State Troops, defeated the British Admiral Cockburn at Craney Island on June 22, 1813.

After the battle at Great Bridge, the remaining British retreated back up the road to Norfolk. Colonel Woodford's men gathered up the arms they had left behind and waited for Colonel Howe with his regulars from North Carolina, who arrived three days later, before following the retreating British up to Norfolk to the cheers of the country people along the way. When they arrived five days later, they found the city deserted. Stunned by the Great Bridge disaster, Dunmore had moved all his forces, the slaves who had joined him, and Tory sympathizers to his ships in the Elizabeth River. Those who had not already abandoned the city streamed out in haste to the countryside. It was a pathetic sight. Few could find any sort of carriage or horses, so any kind of carts were piled with hastily collected belongings and children, and carrying babies, they trudged along, leaving all that they loved behind. The lucky ones had friends or relatives who would take them in, but Loyalists who had not been able to get on Dunmore's ships hid in the swamps, where they were later rounded up and imprisoned. A few still clung to their houses, and Colonel Woodford wrote to the Virginia Convention: "Some of our people say they received fire from houses. You may be assured the town of Norfolk deserves no favor." Norfolk, the great commercial port, which had more in common with New York, Philadelphia or Boston than with the rest of this mainly agricultural Colony, had achieved a bad name as "a nest of Tories." Colonel Howe also broadly hinted that the town should be destroyed before its strategic position should fall into enemy hands.

The resulting complete destruction may not have happened if Dunmore, angered by his defeat at Great Bridge, had not made another mistake. He announced that on New Year's Day, January 1, 1776, he would bombard the city of Norfolk. Humiliated by his failure at Great Bridge and driven to distraction by the crowded situation on his ships, this was Dunmore's retaliation.

When Dunmore had invited Loyalists to join him on board his vessels, he had not anticipated that whole families would come along, black and white. Crowded together, short of food and water, disease had broken out and smallpox was rampant, particularly among the blacks who seemed to have no resistance to it. Bodies of victims were thrown overboard, and they were washing up on the shore where no one dared to touch them. The troops stationed in the town were getting edgy and picked off any sufferers who dared appear on deck.

Finally, at 4:00 p.m. on January 1, 70 guns were trained on the town and commenced firing, while parties were sent ashore to set fire to warehouses where food or ammunition were apt to be stored and to destroy a warehouse containing a large shipment of salt. The cannonade lasted seven hours, and the flames quickly spread to houses. Inspired by this act of Dunmore, and with the compliance of their own officers, the men in town looted the houses of Tories while drinking all the rum and wine they could find. When the order came on January 16 from the Committee of Safety to "finish the job" (Journal of the Virginia Convention Jan. 6, 1776—"Demolish all that may be of use to our enemies."), they continued the destruction. All told, 1,333 houses of Norfolk were destroyed, leaving the city in ashes. Only 54 had been destroyed by the British, the rest by the American forces.

An item in the Orderly Book for the Virginia Second Regiment January 13, 1776, shows how poorly equipped these troops were.

> "The Commanding Officer is Very Sensible that many of the men were suffering for the want of Shoes in this Bad Weather which is not in his power to help and Cannot Forebear Expressing his Great Pleasure at their bearing this well. Capt. Markham is Gone up to Suffolk for the purpose of Providing Shoes. It is hoped that they will make the Best Shift in their Power till he returns."

The following day, January 14, at Suffolk, Field Officer Major Spotswood (grandson of former British Governor of Virginia, Alexander Spotswood, 1710–1712) wrote: "Notice has been given to all Tories in this town Notwithstanding they have been examined and Acquitted, are ordered to Remove out of Town and not to be seen within one mile of Town during the time that the Troops remain here."

After the total destruction of Norfolk, Colonels Woodford and Howe were ordered to deploy their troops to Kemp's Landing, Great Bridge and Suffolk. This, however, was only temporary protection for Princess Anne, as these troops were soon moved out to the North and South where they were urgently needed. Colonel Woodford was sent to Charleston, where he and his whole Second Virginia Regiment were captured. He died in captivity on May 12, 1780.

It took Dunmore six months to make up his mind to leave, and the suffering of everyone was acute. The Patriots of Princess Anne who had taken in refugees from Norfolk were crowded and hungry. There was just not enough food to go around with all these additional mouths to feed. As these uninvited guests stayed on, their hosts were at the mercy of the Committee of Safety who suspected them of being Loyalists, or the British raiders who took vengeance on them for harboring those from Norfolk who had not taken Dunmore's pledge. And the British foraging raids continued with increased ferocity. Captain Squires' men were noted for nasty tricks such as destroying mills and even filling up wells so that they could not be used.

The Loyalists' families living in Princess Anne whose men had joined Dunmore's legions were reduced to begging from former friends and neighbors. Prices had gone sky high, and no one wished to sell to them anyway for fear that provisions would go to the enemy. The bonds of kin and friendship, once so strong, were stretched to the limit.

The neutrals were hard put to maintain that status as they, too, were looked upon with suspicion. As these neutrals saw lands of Loyalists being escheated to the state and men hauled into court to be tried for treason, sometimes because of just a careless word, they tried to keep quiet and out of trouble, submitting to demands of both sides with whatever little they had. Even those who came in the night pitifully begging for a little food might be spies of the Committee of Safety or brigands attempting to gain access to the house for some foul purpose. Every word, even in casual conversation, had to be carefully thought out before spoken. One Charles Henley, although another Charles Henley in his family was already in the Virginia Army, was accused of being a loyalist by the Committee of Safety for saying he was loyal to the King. In his confused defense, he quoted from the Bible, Romans 13.

"Let every man be subject to the governing authorities. For there is no authority except from God, and those that exist have been instituted by God. For rulers are not a terror to good, but to bad . . . Would you have no fear of him who is in authority? He is God's servant for your good."

The Committee was not impressed and sent him to Williamsburg, where he was imprisoned. The following is his letter to the Virginia Committee of Safety, dated 6th June 1776.

> To the Honourable the Gentlemen of the Committee of Safety
> Gentlemen:
> I beg leave to inform you that my Evidences arrived yesterday from Princess Anne County & humbly desire your Honours to bring me to trial as soon as possible, I am
> Gentlemen
> Your most obed't & Very
> Humble Servant
> Charles Henley"

On June 7, the Convention resolved that Henley had been "guilty of giving information to the enemy and that he should be punished as by law provided." He was imprisoned for four years. An old man, it seems unlikely that he was in a position to give any information to the enemy, but the Committee could take no chances. Others were convicted on more evidence as being "inimical to America." Among these others, Andrew Stevenson and William Faller were both convicted of having been on board Lord Dunmore's ship without permission and corresponding with the enemy.

It seems, however, that the difficulties of the people of Princess Anne were as nothing compared to the misery of those Loyalists and slaves who had joined Dunmore on his ships. If it had not been for the secret Loyalists from Portsmouth and the outskirts of Norfolk who, under cover of night, rowed out to the ships with provisions, many would have starved. As it was, they were crowded into these ships not equipped to carry passengers, there was a scarcity of water as well as food, and many were victims of "jail fever" and the dreaded smallpox. Still, Dunmore lingered on, even though Lord Dartmouth had given him permission to leave at any time. What he hoped to accomplish now is anyone's guess, but after receiving a few more reinforcements, he was able to go ashore under cover of his guns at the tiny hamlet of Tucker's Mill, west of Portsmouth. Erecting some crude shelters, he put most of his followers ashore for a bit of relief from their discomforts aboard the ship.

This respite did not last long. On March 6, Major General Charles Lee, a former British officer and no relation to the famous Lee family, had been given command of all Virginia forces, and he was determined to oust Dunmore. Moving on Portsmouth, he removed all inhabitants, burned Gosport and most of the waterfront of Portsmouth and then the houses of notorious Loyalists. These were Andrew Sprowle, John Goodrich, Neil Jamieson, Robert Spadden and one Hopkins. It is said that he forced these men to watch as their homes went up in flames. After this, Dunmore removed himself and his followers back to the ships.

In January, the Convention had ordered the removal of all citizens of Norfolk and Princess Anne counties to the interior, but it had not been effected. On General Lee's insistance that this be done, members of the Princess Anne Committee petitioned that this order be modified because of the distress and ruin it would bring to the 5,000 people of the county. It was agreed that the Committee would make strict inquiry into the temper of all inhabitants to determine who had taken an active part in behalf of America, who had remained quietly at home, and who had appeared inimical to America. On their certification, the General was to allow all such as had been friends or neutrals to remain at home with their families but to give up all their livestock except such as the Committee should adjudge necessary for their immediate subsistence; and that all the enemies of America be compelled to remove at once with their families and effects, according to the former resolution (Journal of the Committee of Safety of Virginia). Nevertheless, there were exceptions made. The people of Princess Anne had always been pretty independent of orders from Williamsburg, and several families of known Loyalists were allowed to remain, such as the families of James Parker, William Aitchison and Jacob Ellegood. The Committee just did not carry out these strict orders when it concerned those of prominent families, connected by marriage, or whom they liked.

Finally, at the end of May, Dunmore decided to leave. He, with his fleet, his followers and the Negroes who had not died of smallpox, sailed out of the Elizabeth River into the Bay.

Relieved, the people watched them go, but Dunmore intended to go only as far as Gwynn's Island in Gloucester County, near the Piankitank River. Here, he planned to encamp for further operations in the northern part of the Bay. This island of about 2,000 acres was sparsely settled but with a considerable amount of livestock and was well-watered. There is a legend that the original owner received this island as a gift from Chief Powhatan for saving the life of his favorite daughter, Pocahontas. She had attempted to swim across the Piankatank but was caught in a cross current and was drowning when a local settler saw her, pulled her out and returned her to her father.

The progress of the flotilla up the Bay was slow, but it arrived at Gwynn's Island about May 31. Putting all his wretched passengers ashore, Dunmore set to work erecting breastworks, which he felt could withstand any attack, and scoured the countryside for food. But there was little there for those still sick and miserable people, and in a month, they had picked the island clean. At last, Lord Dunmore admitted in his dispatches to the Ministry that his efforts to rally the Tories and set the Colony aflame with slave uprisings had been a failure. Further raids up the Bay had to be thrust aside as he attempted to keep his decimated band alive. Then, he received the news that all his personal property at the Palace in Williamsburg had been auctioned off, as well as his other estate at Porto Bello, which had netted the new state the tidy sum of over £ 3,000 in good English money. On top of that, the reinforcements for which he had been waiting impatiently had been captured at sea by Captain James Barron of the Virginia Navy.

During this time, General Andrew Lewis, the ranking general of the Virginia Militia, had been gathering troops on the mainland across from the island and was awaiting news of the Continental Congress' action in Philadelphia on the proposal for complete independence before attacking. As soon as the news reached him of the adoption of the resolution, he gave the order to start the bombardment of the British positions on the island and afloat. The very first shot crashed into the cabin of *The Dunmore*, the second hit *The Otter* and the third tore through the cabin of *The Dunmore* again, throwing a splinter into his Lordship's leg. "Good God," he cried, "that I should ever have come to this!"

As the entire fleet in confusion began to slip their cables and move out, there was a rush to get on board, and in their hurry, the sick were left behind. The next day, the Americans, having secured some small boats during the night, crossed to the island where they found a shocking sight—bodies strewn about, the sick gasping for help and some burned to death in the brush huts accidently set on fire. The Norfolk Tories had paid a terrible price for joining Lord Dunmore.

When out of range of General Lewis' guns, Dunmore lingered in the Bay for three more weeks, during which time 200 more souls died. He burned 30 to 40 of his dilapidated vessels and departed for New York with half of those remaining, while the rest sailed south. This was the last that Princess Anne County heard of Lord Dunmore. His performance at Norfolk had been the last straw. Now, it was all-out Revolution, and there was no turning back.

PART FOUR
Chapter 2
THE LOYALISTS

All eyes had been on Dunmore's fleet as it sailed out of the Elizabeth River, through Hampton Roads and into the Bay. The decks were crowded with the Loyalists for a last look at the devastated city of Norfolk. Most were glad to be gone, and those who watched from the shore were equally glad to see them go. Most of these on the shore looked hopefully toward the future. Some on the decks were leaving behind all they had known and loved for an uncertain future.

One of those who had already left to join the Queens Rangers was John Saunders, the handsome young bachelor, scion of an old and honorable family of Princess Anne County. He had been commissioned a captain in the British Army as soon as he had offered his services to Lord Dunmore on November 16, 1775.

He was descended from Jonathan Saunders, who had come to Princess Anne County from England to be the rector of Lynnhaven Parish in 1695. Jonathan had married Mary Bennett Ewell, the widow of Thomas Ewell, a substantial landowner and connected with other prominent families. They had two children, John and Mary, and after Jonathan died, his widow married Maximillian Boush of Norfolk, a wealthy merchant. Although Mary had 12 more children by Maximillian Boush, John Saunders' stepfather was good to him, giving him land in Princess Anne County and making him captain of one of his merchant ships. John married one Mary, and when he died, he left their son Jonathan his county plantation. This Jonathan eschewed the mariner's life, preferring to increase his land holdings and to take a prominent place among the planters. In 1764, he built a fine house, now known as Pembroke Manor, on his large estate of 800 acres, and on his 400 acres of marshland he raised herds of meat cattle, sheep and hogs. Around his house were numerous outbuildings to

Captain John Saunders in British uniform. *Courtesy of Miss Antoinette Montgomery-Campbell.*

support this extensive plantation, two kitchens, slave quarters, silos, barns and storage sheds, as well as an overseer's house.

All of this the young John Saunders had inherited when he came of age in the spring of 1775. His mother and father had both died, and Jacob Ellegood, the husband of his older sister Mary, had been appointed his guardian. As his friend, his brother-in-law and guardian, Jacob Ellegood had exerted a strong influence on the younger man.

John had shown an early interest in law and was attending the College of Philadelphia with a degree in law in mind. However, he returned to Princess Anne County on attaining his majority in the early summer of 1775, just as the Second Continental Congress, meeting in Philadelphia, had resolved to raise a Continental Army with George Washington as Commander in Chief. Excitement was at fever pitch, and meetings were being held here to elect representatives to the forthcoming meeting in Williamsburg for the forming of a Committee of Safety to draft plans for the raising of troops.

Headstrong and steadfast in his opinions, John attended all meetings, loudly expressing his beliefs that what they were doing was not only illegal but insane. His friends tried to persuade him to change his attitude, but he violently refused. Handsome, well-educated, a sportsman and the owner of a large estate and a beautiful house, he was the "catch" of the county, but he was also proud and a bit overbearing. Finally, he was reluctantly declared an enemy. *(Virginia Magazine of History and Biography).*

> "Having declared himself to be a Loyalist and contemptuous of the Revolutionary Party, he was not only regarded as inimical to the liberty of America, but his neighbors were recommended to cease supplying him with necessaries of all kinds, including food."

This young man, who had everything to look forward to in his home county, was now an outcast. Many years later he said that he sincerely believed that it was best for the people to remain loyal to England. (Saunders Papers, Library of King's College, New Brunswick, Canada.)

Now, his only friend was Jacob Ellegood, his brother-in-law. He could not foresee all that this stand would mean, but he was adamant in his convictions. When Lord Dunmore issued his proclamation on November 7, 1775, ordering all persons capable of bearing arms to resort to his Majesty's standard, John Saunders joined him.

Dunmore had included in his proclamation a promise to free all slaves and servants who would come with him, hoping that this would cause widespread insurrections. While some slaves did join him, there were no insurrections, but the frightened citizens of Norfolk began to flee the city. To Dunmore's dismay, the ones who came brought with them their wives and children. He had expected to raise a black regiment to be called "Dunmore's Ethiopean Corps," but it did not materialize. There were enough to make up two or three companies, however.

Jacob Ellegood, who had been the first in Virginia to answer the call (he claimed), had been commissioned a colonel in this regiment on the strength of his promise that, as colonel of the county militia, he could bring 500 men with him. When John Saunders came forward two days later, he was commissioned a captain to serve under Ellegood. He, however, was soon transferred to The Queen's Rangers, a regiment commanded by Colonel John Graves Simcoe, and sent to New York, leaving all that he owned behind.

First stationed on Long Island, where the inaction irked the eager young Saunders, his regiment of The Queen's Rangers in September 1777 fought in the bloody battle of Brandywine Creek, where the Americans were forced back toward Philadelphia with heavy casualties. Saunders was severely wounded but recovered to fight again. His courage was noted by Colonel Simcoe who wrote of him as "an officer of great address and determination." (Simcoe's Military Journal.)

After he recuperated, Captain Saunders returned to Princess Anne County only once, in 1780. He was then with General Leslie, who had easily taken Portsmouth and whose orders were to establish outposts along the coast. Two letters from Captain Saunders to Colonel Simcoe describe Saunders and what he had hoped to accomplish. (Simcoe's Military Journal, Saunders Papers, Public Library, Fredericton, New Brunswick and Private Papers of Family.)

> "Agreeable to your desire I now detail some anecdotes of which was sent under my command with Gen. Leslie: on the evening of the arrival of the Fleet in Lynnhaven Bay, I was ordered by Gen. Leslie to advance with a detachment consisting of a subaltern's command of the guard, and the officers and twelve men of my troop, and to march through Princess Anne for the purpose of taking some of the most violent leaders of the rebels in that county; but the great swell of the sea obliging me to land in a different place from which I had intended, I was, in consequence, constrained to cross the Lynnhaven Inlet, which was unfordable. Knowing that there was a canoe about half a mile on the other side, I asked if anyone would volun-

teer the service of fetching it. Sargeant Burt instantly offered himself and, with his sword in his mouth, plunged into the water, swam over and brought the canoe in which we crossed, and this he did although, on our arrival at the inlet, we had observed a man on horseback, who appeared from the precipitancy with which he rode off, to have been placed there as a vidette. A few days after this, I was sent with a detachment under the orders of Col. Schutz to Suffolk, by Sleepy Hole Ferry. We crossed the ferry at night, and by proceeding under cover of the darkness with my troop and the rest of the detachment, I collected a sufficient number of horses to mount both men and officers. From Suffolk we returned to Portsmouth, when I requested Gen. Leslie to permit me to occupy the post at Kemp's Landing, with the two officers and the non-commissioned officers, and twelve private dragoons of my own troop, which he granted after I had explained to him my intimate knowledge of the people and the country. With this force, I remained there until the general was obliged to embark for South Carolina." (Journal of the Operations of the Queen's Rangers)

A month later, he wrote to Colonel Simcoe.

"My dear Simcoe:
With the heaviest heart I ever felt I sit down to inform you that we are embarking with an intention, after every demonstration with to the contrary, of not only leaving this place, but this Province, to the utter ruin of his Majesty's loyal subjects. I have set them an example of sanity which I hope they will follow. I have warned them of the consequences of a different conduct. I know the country hereabouts and have a grateful sense of the manner I treat them and would be moderate, but the people from the upper part of this Colony, whose interest it is to pursue a different conduct, will treat with great severity this lower country. I am apprehensive that immediately upon our leaving this place the town of Portsmouth and several of the lower counties will be laid waste.

I suppose that my next will be stated from the adjoining Province. Lord Cornwallis is at Cross Creek, I am informed.

Present me to the Gentlemen of the Regiment, and believe me to be with the greatest esteem
Yours most sincerely & truly,
John Saunders"

If John Saunders had been able to stay here longer, he may have had some success with his former friends. But it is doubtful. Having formally been declared an enemy and his property escheated to the state, his presence in the uniform of a British officer was hardly conducive to persuasion.

Arriving at Charleston, Captain Saunders was immediately sent to

Georgetown, some 60 miles north of that city. Frustrated by the unaccustomed guerrilla tactics of Francis Marion, "The Swamp Fox," and disputes among his own officers, Saunders ran out of patience and repeatedly requested that he be allowed to join General Cornwallis farther west in the state. This was denied. Instead, he was ordered to Charleston, after it had been captured, to command the garrison, and there he remained until April 1782, in spite of his intense desire to join the Queen's Rangers in Virginia in the summer of 1781.

Even after the surrender of Cornwallis at Yorktown, October 19, 1781, sporadic fighting continued as the British continued their foraging raids. Finally, Captain Saunders and the garrison were ordered back to New York, where he took command of his old company of The Queen's Rangers—until Captain Armstrong returned from captivity. He then sailed for England, never to return to Princess Anne County.

When he arrived in London, John Saunders was practically penniless. He applied to the Loyalist Claims Commissioners in the following "Memorial."

> "To: The Commissioners appointed by Act of Parliament for Enquiring into the Losses and Services of the American Loyalists:
> The Memorial of Captain John Saunders of the late Queen's Rangers showeth:
> That Your Memorialist is a native of Virginia in North America, that at the beginning of the late Rebellion he resided on his plantation in Princess Anne County in the said Province and that in November 1775 he received from the Earl of Dunmore, His Majesty's Governor there, a commission for a company, which he raised and repaired with to the Royal Standard. Your Memorialist will not unnecessarily take up your time by a circumstantial detail of his services. He will only say that from the time of his joining his Lordship to the conclusion of the War he has constantly been on active and hazardly service, in the course of which he hath been severly wounded.
> To evince his loyalty and services Your Memorialist begs leave to call on:
>
> >The Earl of Dunmore
> >Colonel Balfour
> >Lieutenant Colonel Simcoe
>
> This decided and active conduct of your Memorialist in support of the British Government occasioned him the entire loss of his property which was confiscated and sold by the rebels, a schedule whereof is enclosed. In proof of the justness of which, your Memorialist wishes the following gentlemen to be examined:

> Lieutenant Colonel Ellegood
> Captain James Parker
> Mr. John Crammond
> Your Memorialist therefore prays that his case may be taken into consideration in order that Your Memorialist may be enabled under your report to receive such aid or relief as his losses and services may be found to deserve.
> And your Memorialist is very respectfully
> Your obedient Servant
John Saunders"

The Commissioners also praised him, describing him as, "A man of very extra-ordinary merit." Following is his schedule:

> "Schedule of Captain John Saunders property which was sold by the Rebels or otherwise lost to him in consequence of his active conduct in support of the British Government in America:
> A plantation in the County of Princess Anne, in Virginia, lying partly on the Lynnhaven River within two miles of Kemp's Landing, containing eight hundred acres of very good land with a large and valuable new brick dwelling house, an overseer's house, two kitchens, a barn and other out-houses, two apple orchards of more than seven hundred bearing trees of the best quality, a peach orchard with a variety of other fruit trees, and a great quantity of very valuable white oak and other timber.

This	£4,000
A tract of good meadowland of four hundred acres lying in the same county	320.
A Still, Waggon compleat, Carts and plantation Utensils	69.12
Six horses	48.12
Twelve negroes	401.12
Fifty hogs	20.
Furniture and books	56.
Wine, Cyder, Spirits	20.
One thousand bushels of Indian corn . . . a 2/	100.
Three thousand bushels of Oats . . . a 1/	15.
Fifty bushels of Wheat a 4/	10.
Seven thousand feet of Oak Plank . . . a 12 per G	42.
Debts	200.
Fourty sheep a 8/20 head black cattle a 40/	56.
Three thousand weight of Pork . . . a 20/cwt	30.
	£5,388.4

Slaves

Jack	52.
Sarah	17.12
Sue	32.
Sam	48.
Lewis	56.
George	24.
Essex	8.
Charles	20.
Quash	24.
Harry	48.
Stepney	24.
Somerset	48.
Total	£401.12

John Saunders must have received reparations for these losses immediately for he at once returned to the study of law at the Middle Temple. Also, like all of the American Loyalists who had fought for the British, he was retired at half-pay. In addition, he received an extra bonus of £ 40 a year for meritorious service. He was admitted to the Bar in 1787. In 1790 he married Arianna Margaretta Jekyll Chalmers, daughter of Colonel James Chalmers of the Maryland Loyalists, living in Chelsea, England.

Bitter, and certainly disappointed by the outcome of the Revolution, John Saunders was still not a man to dwell forlornly on the past. Little has been noted in our histories of the thousands of Loyalists in all the colonies, exiled from their homes forever and many penniless, but letters record that some with meager British help were able to rise above their defeat and make a new life. Now, John Saunders shows his determination and strength of character. As we look at his once proud house and the portrait there of its former owner, we forget for a moment our pride in winning our hard-fought independence and wish, regretfully, that this man had been on our side. Nevertheless, he was once one of ours, and he and his house are part of our history. The Princess Anne County Historical Society is painstakingly restoring Pembroke Manor's beauty.

The career of John Saunders after the war was exceptional. One of the few Loyalist officers regarded with respect by the British, he was so highly recommended to the Loyalist Claims Commission that he received full compensation for the loss of all his property, was retired on halfpay and received a bonus of £ 40 a year for meritorious service.

After completing his law studies at the Middle Temple in London, through the recommendation of Colonel Simcoe, Saunders was appointed a junior judge in New Brunswick, given a large land grant, and he eventually became the first Chief Justice of the Province. His house near Frederickton, later washed away when a dam collapsed, was built similar to Pembroke Manor, the only reminder of his life in Princess Anne County.

The career of Jacob Ellegood was quite different, as was his character.

Jacob Ellegood was descended from William Ellegood, who had first come to Princess Anne County in 1704. William had quickly established himself by acquiring 514 acres of land and marrying Mary Pallet, of a prominent local family. Succeeding generations prospered until Jacob Ellegood, fourth in line from William, owned "1,250 acres, 9 slaves and 1 riding chair," and this beautiful house, Rose Hall, was destroyed by fire about 1820 (*Lower Norfolk County Antiquary*, James.)

Jacob was a vestryman of Lynnhaven Parish, a Gentleman Justice and Colonel of the Princess Anne County Militia in 1774–1775. He was a prominent man and, it is said, one of great charm, but his indifference to the burdensome acts of Parliament and the resistance in the North must have been noted for he was not appointed to the Committee of Safety as were most of the other leading men here in 1774.

But Jacob Ellegood kept quiet about his feelings until November 14, 1775, when he decided that it would be to his advantage to answer Lord Dunmore's call. That same day, he offered his services and received his commission as colonel of "The Queen's Own Loyal Virginia Regiment," after "Dunmore's Ethiopean Corps" did not turn out as expected. This was the only Loyalist regiment in Virginia, and it, too, did not meet its quota. But Ellegood retained his rank. We believe that he took part in the battle of Kemp's Landing but not in the battle of Great Bridge.

After the skirmish at Kemp's Landing, fearing for the safety of his family, he, his family, William Aitchieson and his family, and his sister Margaret Parker and her children had set out in a tender to find refuge with Ellegood relatives on the Eastern Shore. (Margaret Parker's husband James had early joined the British Army to serve as an engineer and master of works.) The tender was captured by Colonel Woodford, and while the women and children were allowed to continue on their way, Ellegood and Aitchieson were taken to Williamsburg and convicted as enemies. Aitchieson, because of his good character and age, was paroled and allowed to return home, where he died less than a year later. Ellegood, an officer in the British Army, was imprisoned, then paroled elsewhere.

As was the custom for parolees, Ellegood was boarded out in private homes where, calling himself "a loyal Virginian," he constantly complained of his condition and was described as "a trouble maker." He was moved from place to place as he became unbearable to his hosts, and in only one house did he deign to be civil, and only then because there were other paroled British officers there equal to him in rank. His constant requests for exchange were ignored.

Prodding his wife, Mary Saunders Ellegood, she wrote letter after letter to the Virginia Committee of Safety, stating that everything had been taken from her and that she and her children were practically destitute. Finally, allowed to petition in person, her tears so moved the gentlemen of the Committee that redress was ordered. As it turned out, only two horses had been taken from her, and these were returned with an exasperated letter.

This "destitution" was hardly commensurate with the county list of 1778, wherein Marry Ellegood was listed as having one slave and her husband two. (*Lower Norfolk County Antiquary*, James.) The other seven slaves listed in 1774 had gone with her husband when he joined Lord Dunmore.

> "A Petition of Mary Ellegood was presented to the Convention and read setting forth that she has for some time past been in great distress, all the personal estate of her husband, Mr. Jacob Ellegood, being seized as she understands, for the use of the country and that she, with three children, is by that means, deprived of every necessity of life and obliged to depend on the benevolence of friends and neighbors; that she is advised that there is no provision made for the maintenance of wives and children of those who are judged enemies to the liberties of America, and praying that such allowance may be made her and her children out of her said husband's estate, as to this convention shall seem just and reasonable."
> (*Journal of the Virginia Convention*, June 1776.)

> "25 June 1777
> Ordered that all the effects or property of Colonel Ellegood, now a prisoner of war in this state, whosoever is in possession of, they are to be forthwith delivered to Mrs. Ellegood, his lady, on her order, for the present support of herself and family, and it is recommended to all such persons to pay her (as requested) adequate satisfaction for the use of the same."

This, we feel, was an unusual dispensation in wartime. But in those chivalrous days, the wives and children of enemies were not considered as such, and they lived as well, if not better, than families of Patriot men away fighting under miserable conditions with little or no pay.

It was indeed a wretched time for everyone, but Mary Ellegood did not open her house even to her sister-in-law Margaret Ellegood Parker, who with her children had moved into Eastwood, the much smaller house of William Aitchison in Princess Anne County. It was hardly comfortable living in this house of two small rooms downstairs and two upstairs for Mr. and Mrs. Aitchison, their two daughters, their bookkeeper, and Mrs. Parker, her son Patrick and her two wards, Fanny and Jenny.

William Aitchison and James Parker had been partners in the highly successful mercantile business of Aitchison & Parker, as well as entrepreneurs in other ventures and real estate in Princess Anne County and North Carolina. The fine brick houses of both men had been destroyed in the burning of Norfolk in January 1776.

Mrs. Aitchison is listed as having 12 slaves in the tithe list of 1778, which makes Margaret Parker's letter to Charles Stewart of January 3, 1777, seem an unwarranted bid for sympathy. *Selected Letters From the Parker Family Papers* (Carmeline V. Zimmer.)

> ". . . we spin our own cloaths, Nitt, Sew, raise Poultry, and everything we are capable of doing to maintain ourselves. Everything has got to such prices here that we buy nothing that we can do without. Our girls are all dressed in their Spining even little Molly A assists and your Jenny is as Notable at this Country Work as if she had been brought up to it. It gives me great pleasure that once had other vein submit to every thing that is Necessary with so much cheerfulness and good Nature: tho I am sorry our present circumstances prevent them from improving themselves by reading, Writing, keeping polite Company etc. . . ."

This letter from Jacob Ellegood to Charles Stewart on the eve of Yorktown is in the collection at Williamsburg.

> "Many long and what were thought valuable friendships are now entirely dissolved. . . . I am sure there is been no one given more convincing proofs of loyalty than I have, yet as a Virginian I cannot but feel for the distresses of my poor, unhappy country, when I reflect that I was for five years and four months a prisoner in that very country that gave me birth and that I had not even the smallest indulgences that is granted to the unhappy slaves of that country. . . . My Mrs. Ellegood's behavior on all her trying occasions does her honour. . . . I left her in her own house and in tolerable circumstances, that is, plenty of bread and meat, but I hear that she

had been plundered of everything. God knows how she is going to subsist, as I laid out almost all my little all for her support. A French fleet of 30 sail of the line has lain in Lynnhaven Bay for 6 weeks past, but Mrs. Ellegood was plundered of everything before and still made a shift to get the better and I hope that she still will. . . . The bulk of the people are quite against continuing the war . . . so that I think that Mr. Washington will take himself off as soon as our fleet gets in. . . . I think it would be something in my way, but my own feelings will not admit to my going until my parole is full taken away. I was the first man in America that drew a sword for his Majesty. I am now the oldest commissioned officer in his Majesty's American forces."

This letter tells us a great deal about Jacob Ellegood. His thoughtful concern for his wife and expression of pity for his "unhappy country" speak for the deprecating style of an educated man, but his complaints seem hardly justified. Since he was never exchanged, perhaps the British were not too anxious to have him back.

So Jacob Ellegood remained on parole throughout the war. When it was over, he was allowed to return home briefly to attend to his business but could not stay. He left with his wife and three of his sons and also settled in New Brunswick. England was parcelling out land grants there to Loyalists in order to settle that province, and it is estimated that 14,000 Loyalists moved there.

One of Ellegood's sons, William, remained behind, and it is obvious that he had not agreed with his father. He was in the county militia and later, in 1812, was a county justice. Jacob's will ignored him except for two sheep, leaving his wife and other sons the property in New Brunswick, which was considerable, and his "Rose Hall" plantation here to his "friends," Anthony Walke, Jr., and John Saunders. Neither of them wanted it, as Anthony Walke was an Episcopal minister and had inherited a huge estate from his father, and John Saunders was not interested any longer in Princess Anne County. William had to buy the land from the estate, but in the hard times after the war, he was forced to sell it after only one year.

George Logan was also an older man, a Scotsman and a merchant of Norfolk. His home was the fine brick house in Kemp's Landing, still standing, now known as "Pleasant Hall." He had come from Scotland as a young apprentice to John Taylor, a merchant of Norfolk before 1743, for in John Taylor's will of that year, he stated: "I desire that George Logan, my apprentice and bookkeeper, be paid reasonably to attend to my estate until his apprenticeship is out." It was not long after this before George Logan was himself a partner in a successful mercantile firm.

In 1763, Logan bought from Colonel Anthony Walke "for £ 39 10 sh. 9 d. 42030 square feet of Land Scituate lying and being at the Ware house or Kemp's Landing." Here, he built his elegant Georgian home with two wings—the house of a wealthy man of great taste. The interior, with its elaborately carved woodwork, is the most handsome left in the county. Just to the east on another lot was his store. And 10 years later, he bought another plantaton nearby of 173 acres. He was a prominent man in the county, serving as a justice from 1762–1770 and again from 1772–1775. In May 1775, he was also appointed High Sheriff, an important post, and at the same time Tithe Collector for the Eastern precinct of the county. He listed his own property as 173⅞ acres, seven slaves and two riding chairs. A riding chair was actually a small two-wheeled carriage with one seat.

Holding these important offices he, too, kept mighty quiet about his loyalties, and in February 1775, he had cheerfully handed over to the Committee for public sale the following items, which had been ordered before the embargo: "4 casks of nails, 1 bale of Oxnaburg (cloth), 1 box of linens and a cask of saddlery." James Braithwaite and Anthony Walke had also turned in goods.

George Logan continued to keep his opinions to himself, even when Lord Dunmore declared martial law in Norfolk on November 7 and offered freedom to all slaves who would join him. So it was a great shock to his friends of Kemp's Landing when, after the skirmish there on November 11, he offered his house to Dunmore for his headquarters. Moving in, Dunmore triumphantly raised his standard and demanded that all citizens take the oath of allegiance to the Crown and to wear a badge of red cloth to prove it. George Logan made a slight profit in this, for soon all the red cloth in his store had been sold to the frightened people, including many from Norfolk who had already fled that city.

Now George Logan's fatal decision had been made. This prominent and popular man had gone over to the enemy, and at the moment, it seemed that he may have chosen the winning side. But not for long. Dunmore's confidence that he could subdue all of Tidewater was shattered at Great Bridge December 9th. George Logan's hopes were also dashed, and he and his wife soon left for Scotland. His house, his store and his plantation were taken over by the Committee of Safety and his business and warehouse destroyed in the burning of Norfolk in January. It is ironic that his store in Kempsville was used as a courthouse, and it was there that his inquisition was held. Princess Anne County Records

> "27 September 1779. Inquisition of George Logan. The Inquisition indented and taken at the Courthouse of the said Princess Anne County in the fourth year of the Commonwealth before me, Thomas Reynolds Walker, Escheater of said county, which I have taken by virtue of my commission, the Sheriff of this County, having returned and impaneled the following persons as Jurors, to wit: Charles Sayer, Thomas Ewell, Jacob Hunter, John Matthias, William Thorowgood, Jr., Christopher Whitehurst, George Jamieson, Henry Collins, William Haynes, James Moore, Henry Haynes, and William Keeling, good and lawful men of the Parish of Lynnhaven in the said County of Princess Anne, who being charged and sworn to enquire whether George Logan, late of this county, is a British subject under the Act of Assembly entitled 'An Act concerning escheat or forfeiture from British subjects' and likewise to enquire what property real and personal in the said County of Princess Anne belongs at this time to the said George Logan or which did belong to him at the time the escheat or forfeiture took place, if he by them should be deemed a British subject to say upon their oathe after hearing evidence that the said George Logan is a British subject under said act, by having been an inhabitant of the State of Virginia after the nineteenth of April, 1775, and before the Commencement of the Act of Assembly, entitled 'An Act declaring what shall be Treason,' departing from the said State and joining the said subjects of his Britannic Majesty of his own free will and the following real property does at this time belong to him, lying and being in this County of Princess Anne, to wit: one tract of land containing 173 acres, more or less, one tenement with five lots appertaining to it whereon he lived in Kemp's Landing, and several horses taken into possession by one Henry Herbert of the County of Norfolk.
> In testimony whereof as well, I, the Escheater aforesaid, as the said Jurors have mutually put our hands and seals the day and year first written above."

This lengthy legal document is typical of the process of "escheatment," by which the court approved the confiscation of Loyalist property. These jurors had served with George Logan on the vestry, as justices of the court and had approved his appointment as Sheriff. Many had been his friends. Few of the other British merchants of the area had entered into the social and political life as he had. He never came back, although his wife returned in an attempt to recover his losses from the goverment after the war. There is no record that she ever succeeded. After the Peace Treaty of 1783, the government "suggested" that debts owed to British merchants be paid, but there was no mention of the return of escheated property.

Of these three men, John Saunders appears to be the most unselfish in his conviction that staying with England was best for the people. Also, he was young, with the self-confidence of youth, and his war record was so outstanding that he was one of the few Loyalist colonials regarded with respect by the British commanders who, in general, sneered at the Loyalists who were fighting on their side. This was a serious mistake, because if they had made a greater effort to enlist the help of these men who were sincerely loyal to the Crown, the result may have been different. As for ourselves, we regret that a man of Saunders' leadership qualities was lost to our cause. Even though he had lost his home, his inheritance, his position and his friends, he never regretted his decision and he never looked back.

George Logan, a self-made man, seems motivated by ambition alone. He certainly had risen rapidly in business and esteem. Unfortunately for him, he made the wrong choice.

Jacob Ellegood is more difficult to understand. A wealthy member of an old county family, he had many familial ties to other families here, as well as to the Norfolk merchants. His three sisters—Anne, Rebecca and Margaret—were married to Norfolk Scottish merchants, and Margaret's husband, James Parker, early joined the British Army. Also, Ellegood had been educated in England, which gave him a feeling of superiority over his neighbors. On the other hand, he had many staunch county friends among the upper class. He was on the vestry of Lynnhaven Parish and was so popular that even when he was a prisoner during the war and had to be replaced on the vestry, the record merely states, " . . . in the room of Jacob Ellegood who is out of the country." His office as colonel of the militia was indeed prestigious.

The conclusion is fairly clear. At the time of Ellegood's decision, he shared the British feeling that the "Rebellion" would soon be suppressed, and by assisting the British, his own position would be enhanced and all his relationships would continue as before. He could be considered an opportunist yet he continued to call himself "a Virginian," referring to himself in the most flowery terms. But his will reveals him as an unforgiving father, a snob and a man still attempting to play the game from both sides.

Jacob Ellegood also applied to the Loyalist Claims Commission for the loss of his land, house, slaves; that is everything, none of which he had really lost. He also applied for a pension, having been an officer in the army. He probably received both, as his holdings in New Brunswick at the time of his death were considerably more than his property in Princess Anne County. The British apparently honored all such claims without a thorough check into their validity, or they would have caught him when he sold some land here in 1792. He had received full pay in 1778, half pay in 1782 and even requested an increased allowance.

Meanwhile, those of the middle and lower classes were being constantly scrutinized for any sympathies with the British. In the eagerness of the Committee members to prevent any aid to the enemy, they frequently made mistakes, as was probably true in the case of poor Charles Henley, who seemed merely confused. Nathan Fentress seemed to be another victim of confusion. While he disallowed any feeling of loyalty to Parliament, he claimed that he was loyal to the King. And with the British constantly coming in and out, who knows what pressures and threats were used against these defenseless farmers.

Yet, there were more men of this small farmer class from this county actually in the fighting for independence than those of the upper class. They had come here for the opportunity of a better life, and they did not have the same traditional feeling for the Mother country.

Servants and slaves who had run off to the British could hardly be called Loyalists. They were only hoping for their own freedom, and Dunmore's promise, at the time, seemed their best chance to get it.

In no way was the Revolution a class struggle here. We have related the stories of these three men of the upper class simply because we know more about them from records other than Princess Anne County records, which were moved about to avoid capture by the British. Many of these records were lost. The ones surviving show the usual buying and selling of land and other civil court cases but little pertaining to the war.

PART FOUR
Chapter 3
THE PATRIOTS

Now that we have satisfied the historical critics who have condemned Princess Anne County as being "all Tories" during the Revolution by giving examples of those who actually were and why, we will look at our neglected Patriots. While overshadowed by the great geniuses in the House of Burgesses and the amazing generalship of George Washington, without the courage and resourcefulness of these lesser men of action the Revolution would never have succeeded.

The first to show their mettle were those who quickly followed the example of the three intrepid Barron brothers of Hampton to form the Virginia Navy. James, Richard and Robert Barron were sons of Samuel Barron, who had been commander of the fort at Point Comfort. Growing up on the water, they had all become bay pilots with small pilot boats of their own. In the summer of 1775, they were quick to use their skills and knowledge of every shoal and cove to pick off supply tenders of the British, running them aground and capturing their crews and much needed supplies. Emboldened by their success, they attacked much larger ships of Dunmore's fleet, which had either been foolish enough to stray from the main body of the larger men-of-war or had run aground. These valuable prizes were quickly converted to the Americans' use and manned by other Patriots eager for the chase, including many blacks, slave and free, whose skills on the water and courage under fire were outstanding. It is estimated that at least 140 blacks were serving in the small Virginia Navy.

Captain James Barron is credited with the capture of 70 prizes, and other captains were exceptionally successful. Among these were three sons-in-law of Thomas Walke III, Captain Wright Westcott, Captain John Calvert and Captain Charles Williamson and, also, Captain Jacob Valentine, Captain James Tenant and Captain John Harris, all from Princess Anne except John Harris who was from Hampton. There were more from Norfolk, and younger brothers or sons were enlisted to serve as lieutenants and ensigns. James Barron's two young sons—Samuel, 15 and James, 19—enlisted under their father.

Due to the success of these men and the urging of Captain James Barron, the Virginia Convention in May 1776 appointed a Naval Board to build, man and equip a Virginia Navy. Two shipyards were established: one on the Nansemond River (South Quay), commanded by Captain Christopher Calvert, and one on the Chickahominy, commanded by Captain James Maxwell. When Captain Maxwell's yard was burned by the British on April 20, 1781, he was appointed General Superintendent of the Navy, and in 1782, Commander of the *Cormorant*. Somehow, these yards managed to build two cruisers, which with the converted merchantmen and prizes and the host of smaller boats combined to make a rather respectable navy. However, the casualty lists were high. On the bottom of the James, the Nansemond and Hampton Roads are the wrecks of Virginia ships with the brave names of *Revenge, Patriot, Norfolk Revenge, Scorpion, Hornet, Defiance,* and *Mosquito*. At the end of the war, only one was still afloat—the *Liberty*—and it had been captured.

At the beginning of the war Captain Benjamin Pollard was the skipper of the galley *Hero*, another valiant little craft which was sunk. Captain Pollard survived, became a marine, and was one of the charter members of the Virginia Chapter of the Society of the Cincinnati, formed in 1783 of officers in the Revolutionary forces. He lived in Norfolk, but had a large tract of land near Muddy Creek in this county. Long a prominent family in the area, another Pollard, John Garland Pollard, was the governor of Virginia from 1929 to 1934.

Lt. Thomas Wishart, of the 5th Virginia Regiment, another member of the Society, also survived. He married Peggy Singleton, daughter of Peter Singleton I, in 1787 and inherited his brother William's plantation just west of Little Creek. For a long time it was thought that William owned the Lynnhaven House, and the road to it was erroneously named "Wishart Road," but Benedict Arnold's map shows this other location.

Major William Moseley, serving in the 5th Virginia Regiment of the Continental Line, was captured in the disastrous defeat at Charleston, May 12, 1780. General Benjamin Lincoln's force of 6,000 men was overpowered by a British force of 14,000 men and a British fleet. Two hundred fifty Americans were killed and 5,400 captured, among them

The Patriots

Colonel Woodford who had achieved the victory at Great Bridge in 1775, and who died in captivity. Major Moseley was evidently exchanged as he married Betty Thorowgood in 1787.

Many men were killed or captured in these encounters. Sometimes captives were given the option of joining the British or imprisonment. Those who chose imprisonment were treated with such cruelty that even members of Parliament spoke out in their behalf. The British military's defense was that this "Rebellion" was not a war, so those captured were "traitors," not prisoners of war, as described in *Rebels Under Sail*, William M. Fowler, Jr. Besides being transported to evil jails in England, Florida or Barbados, the British in 1776 began to moor hulks, decrepit and decimated vessels, in Wallabout Bay (site of the Brooklyn Navy Yard) where the prisoners were confined below decks. The only breath of air came when the jailer called each morning, "Throw out your dead!" The most infamous member of this death fleet was *The Jersey*, built in 1736. Hundreds, perhaps thousands of Americans perished aboard this rotting hulk whose stench was so strong that she could only be approached from windward. Years later, bodies were still being washed up on the shore.

One of those unfortunates was Captain Charles Williamson. Before hostilities began, he had been a plantation owner, Gentleman Justice, married to Elizabeth Walke and Commissioner of Loyalists' escheated property. An older man of perhaps 45, he had joined the fledgling Virginia Navy in 1779 as captain of his own ship. He had captured many prizes, but when Sir George Collier entered Hampton Roads with his formidable British fleet and took Portsmouth, Captain Williamson's ship was sunk and he was captured. Sent to the hell of *The Jersey* in revenge for the escheating of Loyalists' property, he somehow survived.

> "December 17th, 1780
> Matthew Halstead of Elizabeth Town, New Jersey, late a prisoner of war in New York, represents and declares, That Charles Williamson Esq. & Lieut. John Smith, both of Princess Anne County, Va., were confined in the same prison with himself—'That the Subscriber was informed by the said Williamson and Smith that they and John Hancock Esq. of said Princess Anne County had been held in close confinement from the time of their captivation, which was in May 1779 sometimes in the Sugar House Prison* and sometimes in the Provost Prison.' . . . That the above named Mr. Wil-

---
*Note: "Sugar House" was the name given in colonial days to a place for punishment of recalcitrant slaves.

liamson had applied to the British Commissary General of Prisoners for a Parole to Return to Virginia to effect his exchange & the exchanges of the other Gentlemen above named, to which no satisfactory attention had been paid—That he (Mr. Williamson) had been informed that neither of the above named Gentlemen would be exchanged or liberated, until a Col. Ellegood in Virginia should be either sent into the British lines, Set at Liberty in Virginia, or some Treaty Concluded respecting him: that Upon Mr. Williamson requesting a proposal in form Respecting Col. Ellegood, he was Informed Proposals must be made from this side: That the foregoing were assigned as reasons for their not being exchanged for some persons sent from Virginia with proposals concerning them, Together with the following Reason, that the Persons sent from Virginia were Naval Prisoners, they citizens, consequently in Different Departments—that from Prisoners who had left the Different Prisons in New York since the first of this month, the Subscriber had learned the above named Gentlemen remain in the Situations before Described—That their Situation is Truly Distressing, friendless, moneyless, with an allowance scarcely sufficient to support nature, and too far Distant from home to procure any Supplies from thence. That in making this Representation, the Subscriber had no other motive than the feelings of humanity towards persons suffering for their attachment to their Country's Interest, whose distress is increased by the Inattention of Their Country to them. That, in describing their situation The Subscriber is restrained by a Parole from saying so much as might with great propriety be urged, and for which he could be withheld by no other Consideration."

"The above representation is made to the Hon. The Delegates of Virginia who are desired to remember that Mr. Halstead is a Prisoner on Parole: his name on that account is expected be kept secret."

Charles Williamson was not paroled in spite of Matthew Halstead's efforts, who had actually endangered his own parole by testifying at all. So few captives of the British survived to receive parole that Charles Williamson's survival was an exception, and he must have been an extremely strong man. He may have learned strength while a partner of his father-in-law, Thomas Walke, an exacting and tightfisted man, and he resisted capture only because his ship was sunk beneath him. None the worse for the ordeal, he returned to his position on the vestry and as a justice.

His wife, Elizabeth, had moved to Upper Wolfsnare with her three sisters, wives of Captain Westcott and Captain Calvert and Captain Murdaugh of the Minutemen. While their husbands were gone, they lived there with their much younger half-brother, Thomas Walke IV. Too young to fight himself, this young Thomas Walke had his hands full trying to keep their various estates intact. This he did very well, as after the war, Charles Williamson had as many slaves as he had before, and Thomas Walke had even more horses according to the tithe lists. Elizabeth, however, did not long survive the struggle, and in 1792, Charles Williamson was married again, to Frances Henley.

It is unfortunate that we do not know more of our Princess Anne heroes, or at least a surviving portrait, but as we have said, they were men of action. Joseph Hutchins, who was captured at Kemp's Landing with Anthony Lawson, died in captivity, as did Colonel Woodford, the hero of Great Bridge. William Robinson, a member of the House of Burgesses, is said to have challenged Lord Dunmore to a duel at Kemp's Landing after the battle, but apparently nothing came of it. He was captured and then exchanged. Peter Singleton, Commissary for the Committee of Safety, was forced to flee when Admiral Collier was in Portsmouth. Captain John Harris was captured and imprisoned in England. He escaped, returned to America, and captained another vessel in the Virginia State Navy.

The exploits of John Paul Jones, the naval hero, were amply recorded, and deservedly so from 1777 on, especially when he was in command of the *Bonhomme Richard* in 1779 off the Yorkshire coast in the Baltic Sea. He had encountered a British convoy of 40 ships led by the *Serapis*. The battle raged for over three hours, and when the *Bonhomme Richard* received a particularly galling broadside from the *Serapis*, her captain called out. "Has your ship struck?" Jones' reply is history and the motto of the United States Navy—"I have not yet begun to fight."

Yet, the Virginia Navy eventually cleared the Chesapeake Bay of British invasion and saved Norfolk from becoming a main port for the British fleet. But this was at the cost of many lives and many ships. The inventory of the state fleet at Turkey Island in the James, March 22, 1781, is pitifully short.

"1 ship—16 6 pounders & 22 men
4 brigs
1 sloop—Capt. Westcott, 1 howitzer & 8 men
2 duck guns
1 open river craft belonging to John Cooke of Petersburg with 5 negroes on board."

Heroes abounded in the army, in the militia, Minutemen, regiments of the Virginia Army, and the Continental Army. There were 26,678 Virginians in the Continental Army, more than any other Colony except Massachusetts, which had 67,907. Of state troops and militia, Virginia had the most of all—30,000. Five Thorowgoods were in the fighting, including Colonel John Thorowgood who was a captive in 1781 *(Calendar of State Papers)*.

> "Sept. 17th, 1781. Thomas Newton, Jr. to Gov. Nelson
> The County of Princess Anne has neither civil or military law in it. They are striving to collect their militia. Tomorrow will determine their numbers to turn out. Murder is committed & no notice is taken of it for want of some support up the Country. A few desperate fellows go about on the sea Coasts and large swamps and do mischief in the night. everyone who appears active against them is an object of their fury. A few riflemen with An Active Officer in exchange for some militia from this, might render great service & keep up the authority of the Civil justice . . . Colo. (John) Thorowgood, the life of the county being a prisoner makes life go on very heavily. If he could be exchanged matters would alter & delinquents brought to justice—I pray your Excellency if it can be done to do it—it is impossible to conceive the advantages it would be to these parts."

The leader of the "few desperate fellows" referred to above was Josiah Phillips, the notorious leader of about 50 men who ravaged the countryside, committing untold horrors on their victims. Thomas Reynolds Walker finally raised a company of men with the inducement of $500 reward, and with Colonel Amos Weeks at its head, Phillips was captured and hanged for his many crimes. Colonel Weeks had to flee the state during Collier's invasion because of this.

We know that Thomas Nash of Norfolk County sustained the one injury to the Americans at Great Bridge—a slight injury to his hand—and that Guilford Dudley of Princess Anne also fought in that battle. William Moseley was captured at Charleston. There were several Thorowgoods besides the Colonel John who was so sorely missed in the county, 10 Brocks, several Whitehursts and Murdens, at least two of the Woodhouse family, two Henleys, a Thomas Keeling, Obediah Capps, at least three Cornicks, Colonel Dennis Dawley, William Nimmo, Jr., and John Willoughby. Also, two sons of Anthony Lawson had enlisted while he was a prisoner in Florida. There is no complete list of those who were killed, and the list of those who petitioned for bounties is not complete, as many did not bother or did not go to the trouble or expense of petitioning.

At the beginning of the war, enlistment was for only three months, but if a man continued his service for three years or to the end of the

The Patriots

war, he was entitled to a bounty of land on a scale according to rank. Privates or able seamen received 100 acres, all the way up to Captain James Barron, who was later commissioned Commodore and whose heirs received 7,777⅓ acres. However, in lieu of that, they took money amounting to accumulated back pay. Those who had served for the duration of the war were entitled to more. In the Archives of the Virginia State Library are a few petitions from Princess Anne County presented to the State Legislature for back pay or aid before the Federal Government began hearing them in 1833. They tell a sad tale.

> "To the Honourable Speaker and House of Delegates 1784
> The Petition of Amy Barrett of the County of Princess Anne humbly showeth that Jonathan Barrett, the husband of your petitioner, acted as sailing Master on board the Brig Raleigh, Capt. Edward Travis, belonging to this state when the said brig was taken by a British Frigate and carried into New York, where your petitioner's husband was confined with many others of the said Crew, and died with the prevailing disease on board the prison ship Jersey. Your petitioner is now old and infirm and unable to support herself, therefore prays your honourable house to take her situation into consideration, to renew her pension or grant her such relief as you in your wisdom shall think proper, and she will, as in duty, bound pray. . . ."

Celia, the widow of Isaac Barnes, and Mary the widow of John Tripp, petitioned for aid in 1784. Both had been under Col. Thomas Matthews in the Army and had died in the service. Col. Matthews certified that they had been in the service under his command, and had died serving their country. These petitions were approved.

Jacob Valentine seems to have been a victim of red tape. 1874.

> "To the Honourable the Speaker and Members of the Assembly of Virginia. The Petition of Jacob Valentine your petitioner humbly showeth That your petitioner was a Capt., commanding a Company in what was called the 1st Virginia Regiment commanded by Col. George Gibson. From the situation of the war at that time, the State thought it advisable to direct the Regiment to join the Army in the North. Accordingly, it was effected. In the year 1777, after the battle of Germantown, the British Army, being in possession of Philadelphia, caused the American Army to lay on their arms watching their motions till the latter end of January 1778 before the American Army got into quarters. It was at a place called Valley Forge, on the banks of the Schuylkill, a fatal place to the American

Army, much to be lamented, as many thousand fine fellows lay there buried from their sufferings in being compelled to lay out. It was on these Banks that your Petitioner met with the loss of that invaluable member, the right eye of your petitioner, which baffled all attempts of the Physicians, as will more fully appear by the certificate and oath of the Doctor John Roberts, Surgeon to the Sixth Virginia Regiment and the certificates of several Field Officers.

Your petitioner in the year 1792 prayed for a compensation for the loss of his eye. The prayer of your petitioner was referred to the Committee of Claims, as will more fully appear from the resolution in Nov. 1792, Col. Nathaniel Wilkinson in the Chair.

The resolution was not fully carried into effect, your petitioner was directed to make application to the General Government for compensation as Gibson's Regiment was in Continental Service, though raised for defense of the State. In the year 1778 the Assembly of Virginia passed a law that Col. Gibson's Regiment should supply the 9th Virginia Regiment, which was entirely out of the battle of Germantown, until the same should be again recruited. Therefore, Gibson's Regiment, to which your petitioner belonged, was continued in the Continental Service.

Your petitioner, in consequence of this resolution on the 3rd day of December 1792 made application to the General Government for a compensation for the loss of his eye, by appearing in Richmond before Judge Cushin and Judge Griffin, two of the judges of the United States and it was by them determined agreeable to an order of that day as will more fully appear from the record of the Court of the United States, that your petitioner should be entitled to receive a compensation of $100 per annum for life and $200 arrearage for not applying sooner.

Your petitioner under a copy of this order made application to the General Government for payment. Your petitioner was referred back to the State of Virginia for payment as belonging to a State Regiment. Your petitioner being thus situated hath never received any compensation for the loss of his Eye.

Your petitioner now prays that your Honourable Body will take his case under your tender consideration and grant to your petitioner which in your great wisdom may seem meet, and your petitioner will ever pray. . . .

Then the following:

"It appears by the books in this office that a certificate was issued on the 14th of March 1803 for $240 in the name of Jacob Valentine being the balance of his full pay as a Capt. in the State Service. Aud. Office, 18 Dec. 1807.

Note: This petition was not acted on in the Dec. session 1807."

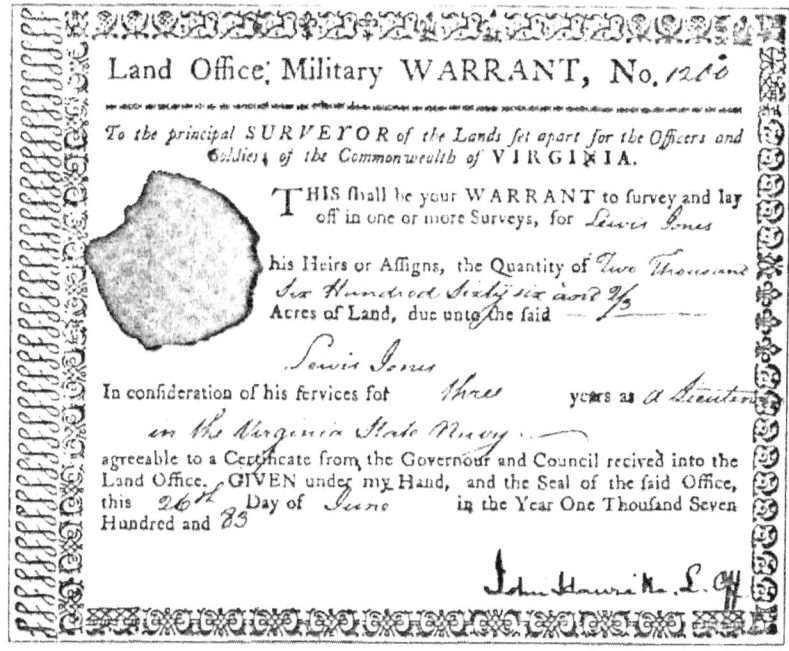

Land Office warrant for land as bounty for military service in the Revolution, 1783. From "*Revolutionary War Records*, Gaius Marcus Brumbaugh."

No wonder more veterans did not apply for compensation!

The following is an additional list of those men of Princess Anne County known to have fought, but the whole story of each can only be found if they or their heirs applied for pensions. All 80,000 are listed by name and state service in *The National Archives, Revolutionary War Pension Applications* (Washington, D.C. National Genealogical Society, 1976) However, this is a start.

OFFICERS IN THE VIRGINIA STATE NAVY

Boush, Charles Sayer, later appointed to Board of Naval Commissioners.
Boush, Goodrich, brother of above
Boush, Wilson, son of Goodrich
Boush, William, tombstone at Lynnhaven House
Boush, Robert Goodrich, son of William
Ewell, Charles
Ewell, Thomas
Gunter, John
Sayer, Thomas
Tenant, James

OFFICERS AND MEN IN VIRGINIA REGIMENTS AND MILITIA. Virginia had more men in the regular army than any other colony except Massachusetts, and more in the militia than any other.

Brock, Allan
Brock, Elias
Brock, Henry (2)
Brock, Jesse
Brock, John (2)
Brock, Mayor
Brock, Matthias
Brock, Nathaniel
Brock, Thomas
Brock, Uriah
Capps, Obediah
Coleman, Whitehead
Cornick, Henry
Cornick, John, Lemuel, Henry—All captains in the militia.
Davies, William
Dawley, Dennis
Denny, George,—captured, possibly died in captivity
Delby, William,—loss of eye. Petition approved.
Doud, William
Ewell, Charles
Ewell, Capt. Thomas
Fentress, Nehemiah, William
Godfrey, Matthew, Capt.
Hancock, John—captured.
Henley, Charles, Cornelius, James, Robert
Hoggard, Daniel
Hunter, Jacob—captured
Jones, Robert
Keeling, Thomas
Land, Edward, John, Louis, Moses, Thomas, William
Matthews, Capt. Thomas
Murden, John, Peter, Edward
Murray, Abraham, Alexander, David (surgeon, Virginia State Navy)
Nimmo, William
Smith, John
Thorowgood, (Now spelled Thoroughgood) Lemuel, John, Mitchel
Waterman, Solomon
Wiles, Reuben
Whitehead, Samuel
Whitehurst, John, Jonathan, Samuel (Virginia State Navy)
Williams, Moses
Wilson, William
Woodhouse, Henry, John, William

Blacks who had served three years received their freedom and 100 acres, more if they had served longer, which some did. William Flora, a black, who had distinguished himself at Great Bridge, fought again at the Battle of Craney Island in 1814.

But identifying names of blacks eludes us, as unless they were free blacks, they are not listed, except with given names. For instance, on the illustrious Captain Benjamin Pollard's ship, he had four blacks—Abraham, Boston, Daniel and Will—all listed as just "negro", But ones whom we know were from Princess Anne County were: Cuffey, a slave of Elinor Boury, whom she enlisted, Nimrod Perkins, a "free man of color", James Jackson, Nathaniel Anderson, and Aaron Weaver, all free blacks. In the army were also Marshall, Demce and Isaac Anderson Joseph Ranger and Jesse Whitehurst. Samuel Kelly and James Murdin performed important duty as spies for the Americans Joseph Ranger was also in the Virginia Navy.

Evidently Aaron Weaver was a free black. His petition for relief in 1811 follows: (from the Archives, Virginia State Library, Richmond)

> "To the Honourable Speaker and Gentlemen of the House of Delegates That your petitioner, Aaron Weaver, during the Revolutionary War enlisted as a sailor on board a Galley called The Protector in the service of the Commonwealth, commanded by Capt. Conway, and then by Capt. Thomas, that he served fully three years in that character, being first on board the said Galley and afterwards transferred to the ship Tarter, commanded by Capt. Richard Barron, and your petitioner being put on board the Boat Liberty to go to his Ship, the said Boat was attacked by the enemy near the mouth of the York River, and your Petitioner received two dangerous wounds in that attack. He is now old and infirm, and very indigent and has not received any of that portion of land bounty to which the sailors in the service of the commonwealth, in the said Revolutionary War who served three years were by law entitled. He is also informed that no land can now be found to satisfy his said just claim. He, therefore, appeals to the justice and gratitude of his Country, and prays your Honourable Body to make him a pecuniary recompense; by allowing him a sum of money for his present relief, and also by placing him on the Pension List with such annual allowance as is reasonable and necessary for his support, and your Petitioner will ever pray, etc. . . . (Presented and sworn to by Wm. Casady before Anthony Walke, Justice of Princess Anne County)

This application was approved.

Loyalists left from all of the colonies for New Brunswick, and more went to England or relocated in Barbados or elsewhere. Their loss of property is recorded in their petitions to the Royalists Claims Commissioners in London for redress, which were honored, but damage and theft by the British foraging raids went unnoticed. There was an attempt by the Americans to regain stolen slaves, as the British had discouraged any importation of them to England, but few were recovered. Most had been sold in the West Indies, and finding them was impossible.

As in any war, there were many so-called "neutral" inhabitants who had managed to avoid outright allegiance to either side. If necessary, they complied with orders of whomsoever was in command at the time, turning over what was demanded and keeping as quiet as possible, feeling that discretion was the better part of valor. After the war, they were hardly in a position to apply for any damages sustained from either side.

For some reason, no complete list exists of the names of those Americans killed in battle. Switched back and forth from one regiment to another as the need arose, we can only guess at numbers and names. For instance, how many Princess Anne men were killed when Colonel Woodford's regiment met with disaster at Charleston and he was captured, or actually how many died a miserable death in captivity? In the distress of those times, family records either were not kept or were destroyed in fear of the British learning of relatives fighting against them.

There were many desertions in this fratricidal war of men with a common heritage fighting each other. Although the penalty was death if caught, both sides were guilty of courting these desertions.

For the half-starved Americans, poorly clothed and often not paid, the temptation to defect was particularly strong after a defeat. There were even mutinies. In May of 1782, 400 veterans of the Pennsylvania division left their quarters, seized arms and artillery, wounded several officers who tried to stop them and marched toward Philadelphia. They had been provoked by the appearance of recruiting officers who were paying $25 to new enlistees, and although concessions were made by officials, half of them left the service.

A Virginian writing home reported that one man caught trying to desert was immediately shot. And in June 1782, at a General Court held in Richmond, three men of Princess Anne County were convicted of treason *(Calendar of State Papers)*. They were John Caton, Joshua Hopkins and James Lamb. After conviction, they were "severely sentenced to be hanged for the said offenses by the Sheriff of Henrico County."

Virginia had ratified its Constitution in 1781, and in Article 3, section 3, treason was defined as to "consist only in levying war against them (the states), or in adhering to their enemies, giving them aid and comfort." Who these three men were or what they actually did to be convicted is unknown, but the charge was "bearing arms in the service of the British or assisting the British forces". Apparently the sentence was never carried out. In 1786 John Caton was presented again to the Attorney of the Commonwealth with twelve others on the same charge. Also, in *Virginia Antiquary Vol. I* Princess Anne County Loose Papers 1700–1789, ed. John Harvie Creecy, James Lamb in 1787 won a case in court to collect a debt owed him, and in the same year, 1787 Joshua Hopkins was called as a witness in another court case.

All men are not born to be heroes, or even respectable citizens, and the people of Princess Anne County had their share of all kinds, as did the other colonies. Before the British took New York, there had been riots there against the draft. Here, given the circumstances of almost constant occupation and/or harassment throughout most of the war and their inbred aversion to disruption of their ordinary lives, the majority, though unsung, showed a remarkable endurance and character.

If Lord Dunmore had not chosen to land on their doorstep, threatening not only their property but their way of life, it may have been difficult for the people of Princess Anne County to drop their laissez faire attitude and indifference to what was going on outside their borders and, in fact, it was impossible for some. But many were aroused to resist this arrogant threat and fought and died for their independence. No other state suffered such almost constant humiliating occupation and harassment "by their own people", nor such betrayal of their inherited values.

PART FOUR
Chapter 4
YORKTOWN

Washington wrote to Congress in 1777: "Our sick naked, our well naked, and our unfortunate men in captivity naked." His pleas for food, clothes and equipment went mostly unanswered by that hard-pressed body. Small successes at Trenton and Princeton revived spirits, but on September 26, 1777, the British occupied Philadelphia and the Congress fled.

Then came the long, agonizing winter for Washington at Valley Forge, when suffering was so acute that hope was almost lost. But the arrival of the Baron von Steuben was a lifesaver. This German, with his good humor and broken English, raised morale as he enforced military discipline in the disorganized troops. It paid off. General Clinton, the new commander of the British forces, evacuated Philadelphia June 18 on hearing reports that a French fleet was heading for America. The next day Washington pursued, and after the battle of Monmouth, the British retreated to New York. Washington then marched north and took up a position at White Plains, north of New York City.

Things were not going well in the South. On December 29, Savannah fell to the British, and on May 12, 1780, General Lincoln surrendered Charleston. Feeling now that South Carolina was secured, General Cornwallis moved into North Carolina. Stopped by the superior marksmanship of the backwoodsmen under Nathaniel Green, Cornwallis retired to Winnsboro, South Carolina for the winter.

Concerned over the plight of the South and his homeland of Virginia, Washington learned of Cornwallis' plan to completely subdue Virginia and thus drive a wedge between the colonies. His anxiety increased when in May 1780, Clinton sent an expedition under Admiral Sir George Collier to Virginia. Portsmouth was taken with little opposition and also Suffolk, Virginia's chief depot for military supplies. Great quantities of naval stores and food were destroyed, with a great deal of sacking, burning and pillaging. Belatedly, Governor Jefferson called out the militia, which had been reserved for fighting in the North, but Collier was soon ordered back to New York. This, alas, was the beginning of the Virginians' disappointment in their beloved Thomas Jefferson, leading to the embarrassment of investigation of his governorship and his resignation. Later, the people regretted their repudiation of him, and he was restored to power and leadership, and elected President of the United States in 1801.

As the war dragged on through 1777, 1778, 1779 and 1780, the people of Princess Anne County tried to go about their daily lives. With the departure of the merchants from Norfolk in 1775 and 1776, business was at a standstill, and the depleted farms were barely producing enough to sustain their owners as demands from the army increased. After the capture and execution of Josiah Phillips by Colonel Amos Weeks in 1779, attacks from his gang of brigands had abated somewhat, but there were still dangerous pirates in the bay and raids from British ships.

There were more funerals than marriages, and any celebrations were rare and only half-hearted. Horse racing and cockfighting, the two favorite sports, continued and relieved some of the tension. The buying and selling of land continued at a rapid pace, and auctions proliferated as farmers gave up the struggle or wives of the landowners who were away fighting could no longer maintain them.

Destitute women were forced to accept charity from their neighbors, their church or, in extreme cases, the state authorities. Elizabeth Cometti, in *Women in the American Revolution*, says, "One woman complained that her husband had received no pay for four years, and that she had three small children, and for want of assistance, her Household goods, even her bed, was seized and sold for rent, which brought her and her children to very great distress, having neither wood nor bread." (This from the Papers of the Continental Congress.)

With the arrival in Hampton Roads in December 1780 of the traitor Benedict Arnold, now a Brigadier General in the British Army, accompanied by a large fleet and 1,600 troops, Cornwallis' plan to completely subdue Virginia was now clear. For Virginia—the richest, the most populous and the acknowledged leader of the colonies—Arnold's presence was humiliating. Adding injury to insult, he landed at Westover and proceeded unhindered to Richmond, the new capitol, burning public buildings and destroying tobacco warehouses and military stores. The government fled to Charlottesville, Momentarily satisfied, Arnold, with the addition of 2,000 more troops, took up winter quarters at Portsmouth.

General Benedict Arnold exhibited the cruelty of his nature while in Portsmouth. He, who had been a favorite of General Washington and a splendid officer in the American forces, emulated the worst side of the British in his treatment of prisoners. Captain Willis Wilson of Princess Anne County had the misfortune to be captured when his ship, the *Dasher*, was destroyed in Lynnhaven Bay. When he was released after the surrender at Yorktown, he made public the "secrets" of the "Prison House" at Portsmouth in the following deposition from *The Researcher*, Charles Armistead Stewart.

> "The deposition of Willis Wilson, being first sworn, deposeth and saith. That about the 23rd of July last, the deponent was taken a prisoner of war—was conducted to Portsmouth (after being plundered of his clothing, etc.) and there lodged with about 190 other prisoners, in the Provost. This deponent, during twenty-odd days, was a spectator of the most savage cruelty with which the unhappy prisoners were treated by the English. This deponent has every reason to believe, there was a premeditated scheme to infect all the prisoners who had not been infected with the small-pox. There was upwards of one hundred who never had that disorder, notwithstanding which, negroes, with the infection upon them, were lodged under the same roof of the provost. Others were sent in to attend upon the prisoners, with the scabs of that disorder upon them. Some of the prisoners soon caught the disorder, others were down with the flux. And some with fever. From such a complication of disorders, 'twas thought expedient to petition Gen. O'Hara, who was then commanding officer, for a removal of the sick, or those who was not as yet infected with the small-pox.
>
> "Accordingly, a petition was sent by Doctor Smith, who shortly returned with a verbal answer (as he said) from the General. He said, the General desired him to inform the petitioners, that the law of nations was annihilated that he had nothing then to bind them but bolts and bars, and they were to continue where they were, but that they were free agents to inoculate if they chose. About thirty agreed with the said Smith, to inoculate them at a guinea a man; he performed the operations, received his guinea from many, and left them to shift for themselves, though he had agreed to attend them through the disorder. Many of them, as well as those who took it in the natural way, died. Col. Gee, with many respectable characters, fell victims to the unrelenting cruelty of O'Hara who would admit

of no discrimination between the officers, privates, negroes and felons, but promiscuously confined the whole in one house.

"This Deponent further saith, that the Prisoners were often refus'd the liberty of going out to answer the Calls of Nature, which obliged them to do their Occasions in Their Respective Rooms. They also suffered often from the want of water, and such as they was very muddy and not fit to drink.

Sept. 21, 1781

This day came before me Capt. Willis Wilson, and made oath that the above is true.

Signed
SAM'L THOROWGOOD"

Tobacco was the only source of credit the Continental Congress had for the purchase of arms and military supplies, and the Virginia Navy, up to this time, had done a pretty good job of protecting these tobacco ships on their way to the West Indies. But Arnold was determined to cut off this traffic. It is presumed that the maps made for him by his staff of Nansemond, Norfolk and Princess Anne counties were to aid him in this destruction by locating the houses of leading citizens who either had tobacco stashed away or could be made to tell where it was. A question remains as to why there is no differentiation between those houses shown on the maps of Patriots and those of Loyalists. Forage raids increased in intensity to feed the 3,600 troops and crews of the British ships, and fearing starvation, the people hid their small supplies as best they could.

Meanwhile, with the occupation of the area by Arnold, some of the merchants who had fled Norfolk in the conflagration of 1776 began to come back, confident that the war would soon be over and they could resume business as usual. To Patriots who had fled only as far as Princess Anne County and who were living in whatever make-shift houses they could build quickly, this was discouraging as they watched these merchants rebuilding their businesses and fine houses, for at this time they knew that Cornwallis was moving toward Virginia. They were further shocked to learn that Colonel Simcoe, with a detachment of his Queen's Rangers, had surprised General Thomas Nelson's militia at Charles City Courthouse, killing several and capturing 50. A captured slave had been the informer.

Washington had sent Baron van Steuben with a small contingent to protect Richmond, but he could only delay action. Lafayette then marched to Richmond with a fairly large force of Pennsylvanians to assist him but, unfortunately, these were the same veterans of the

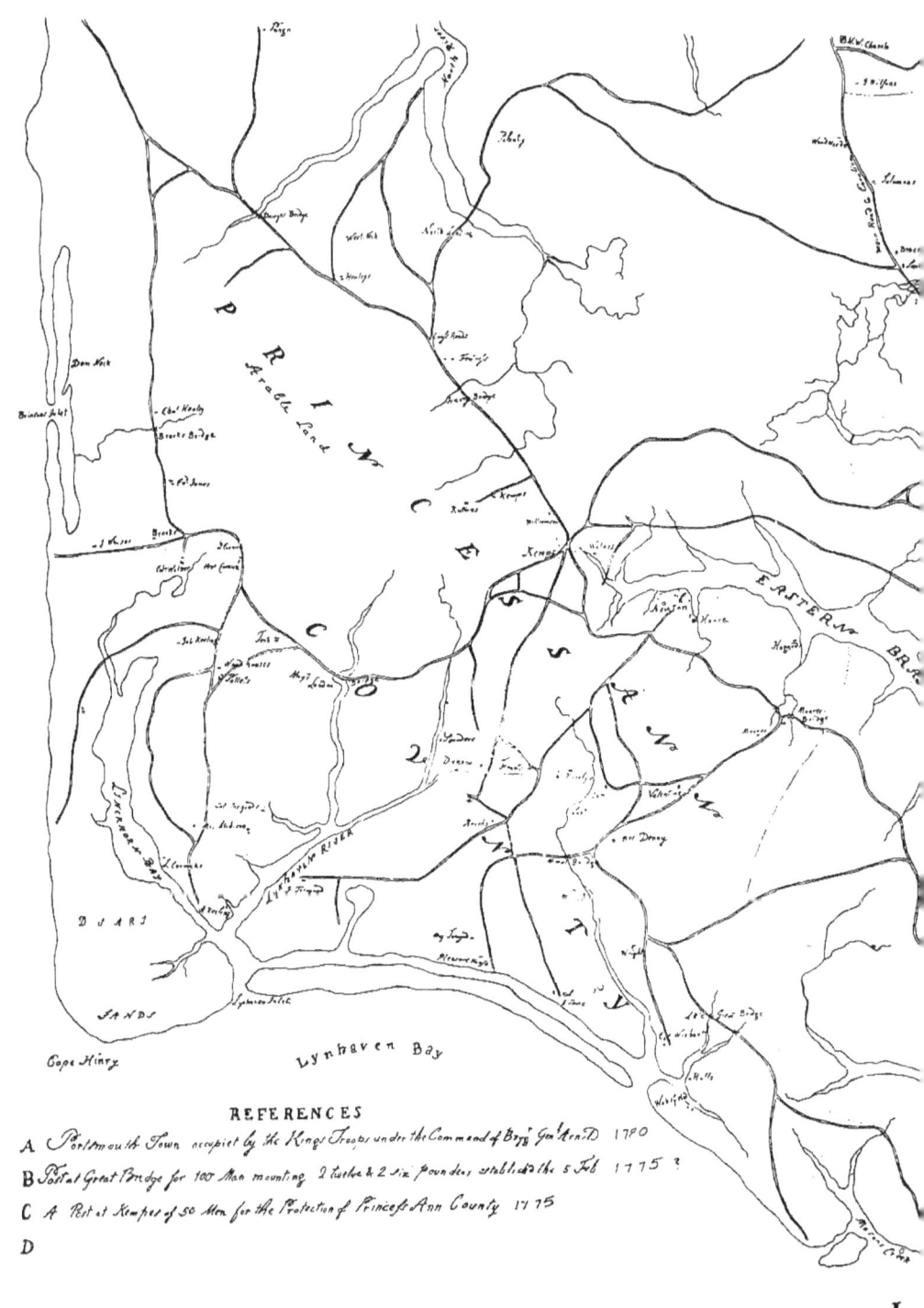

Map of Princess Anne County, drawn for General Benedict Arn

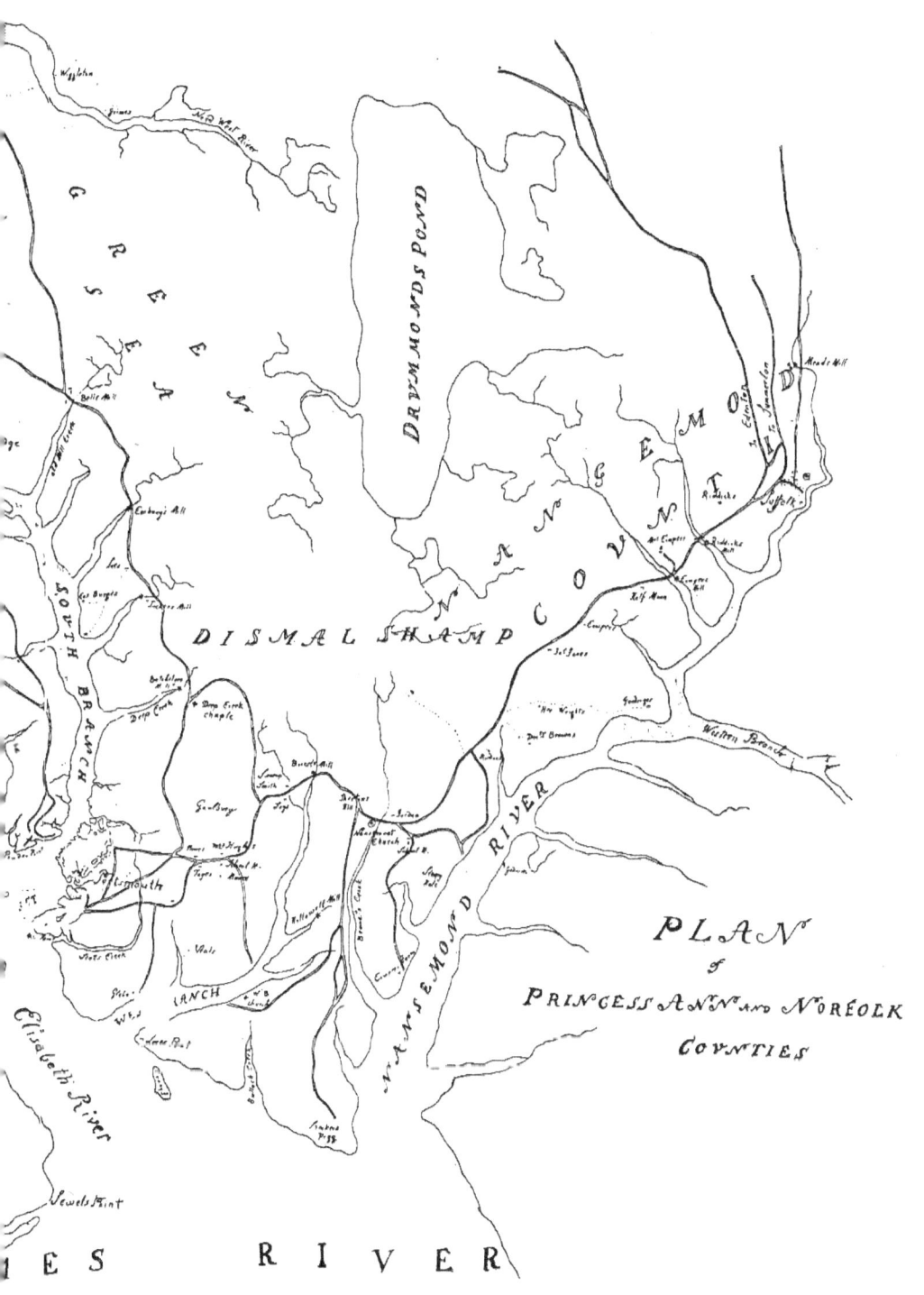

1781. *Courtesy of The Clements Library, University of Michigan.*

Pennsylvanian line who had mutinied on January 1, and neither Lafayette nor von Steuben felt sure that they could be trusted. Reinforcements of French troops had been promised, but they were intercepted by a British fleet.

When Cornwallis arrived at Petersburg with 5,000 troops plus Colonel Tarleton's cavalry legion of 800 mounted on stolen Virginia thoroughbreds, Lafayette and von Steuben decided on a series of skirmishes and to avoid a large-scale confrontation with their only 1,000 ill-equipped troops. Again, this was only a delaying action, but their feints, twists and turns served to baffle Cornwallis.

After burning warehouses and a military depot at Chesterfield Courthouse, Cornwallis was joined by Arnold, and he next moved on Richmond, reaching the village of Manchester on the opposite side of the James. But nothing happened. The British believed it unwise to attempt a crossing of the river under fire, and Lafayette felt too weak to attack until the expected arrival of General Nathaniel Greene. He wrote to Washington, "I am not strong enough even to be beaten." Cornwallis is reported to have written, "The boy cannot escape me."

During this time, Lafayette was searching for black spies. A slave named James, owned by William Armistead, Commissary for Military Supplies, volunteered. By July, James had infiltrated Cornwallis' headquarters. Acting for Cornwallis as a forager, James was able to carry instructions to other spies and to slip through the lines to acquaint Lafayette with information about projected movements by Cornwallis. It was he who told Lafayette of Cornwallis' planned move to Yorktown with the intention of making it his base, and this information was quickly relayed to Washington. To allay any suspicion, James pretended to spy for the British. He was so valuable to Lafayette that the Marquis, after the surrender at Yorktown, gave him a document in gratitude.

> "This is to certify that the bearer by the name of James has done essential services to me while I had the honour to Command in this State. His intelligences from the Enemy's camp were industriously collected and most faithfully delivered. He properly acquitted himself with some important Commissions I gave him, and appears to me entitled to every reward his Situation can admit of. Done under my hand, Richmond, 21 November, 1884.
>
> Lafayette"

But for James, it was back to slavery with William Armistead. Finally, Armistead agreed to his petition for freedom and that he be paid £ 250 as compensation. The House of Delegates, then the Senate, impressed by Lafayette's testimonial, granted James his freedom on New Year's Day 1787. He took the surname of Lafayette and by 1816 had acquired two tracts of land adjacent to William Armistead's in New Kent County. In 1818, at the age of 70 and ill, he petitioned the General Assembly for "a small sum for immediate relief, and such moderate amount for the remnant of his days as in your wisdom may seem just." He received $60 for immediate relief and $40 annually for his pension.

In 1824, when Lafayette returned to America for a tour of the 13 original states, he recognized James in the crowd around his carriage in Richmond. The Marquis embraced his former spy with the greatest affection as they recalled old times together.

After failing to provoke Lafayette into more than a skirmish, Cornwallis returned to Portsmouth. From there, he sent Colonel Tarleton with cavalry and mounted infantry to Charlottesville—where the government had fled to reconvene—hoping to capture Governor Jefferson and the Virginia legislators.

Accidently learning of this plan, Captain Jack Jouett, a young officer, instructed the tavern keeper at the Cuckoo Tavern near Richmond to delay Tarleton as long as possible, then rode 40 miles at breakneck speed from there through the woods to warn the Commonwealth's leaders. Cutting through the woods at a mad gallop, his clothes torn by lashing branches, he dashed up to the steps of Monticello before sunrise to warn Jefferson and then the legislators. Thanks to him and the tavern keeper, who took an inordinately long time to serve dinner to Tarleton's officers, the British found that their birds had flown and the "coup" unrealized.

Now Cornwallis held the area at the mouth of the James. Ordered by Clinton to fortify some point suitable to command a harbor for his Majesty's ships, he decided on Yorktown with its deep harbor. Seizing Yorktown and Gloucester Point, just across the mouth of the York River, August 1, he started moving his men from Portsmouth and erecting fortifications.

Washington, torn by his desire to rescue his home state of Virginia, still felt—as did Comte de Rochambeau, who had joined him at White Plains with his French army—that the best plan was to capture New York City. But before a large-scale attack could be mounted, Washington had a letter from the Comte de Grasse that he was leaving the West Indies with a large fleet and 3,000 French troops for the Chesapeake Bay. Jubilant, Washington immediately scrapped the New York plan and headed with Rochambeau for Virginia, while still put-

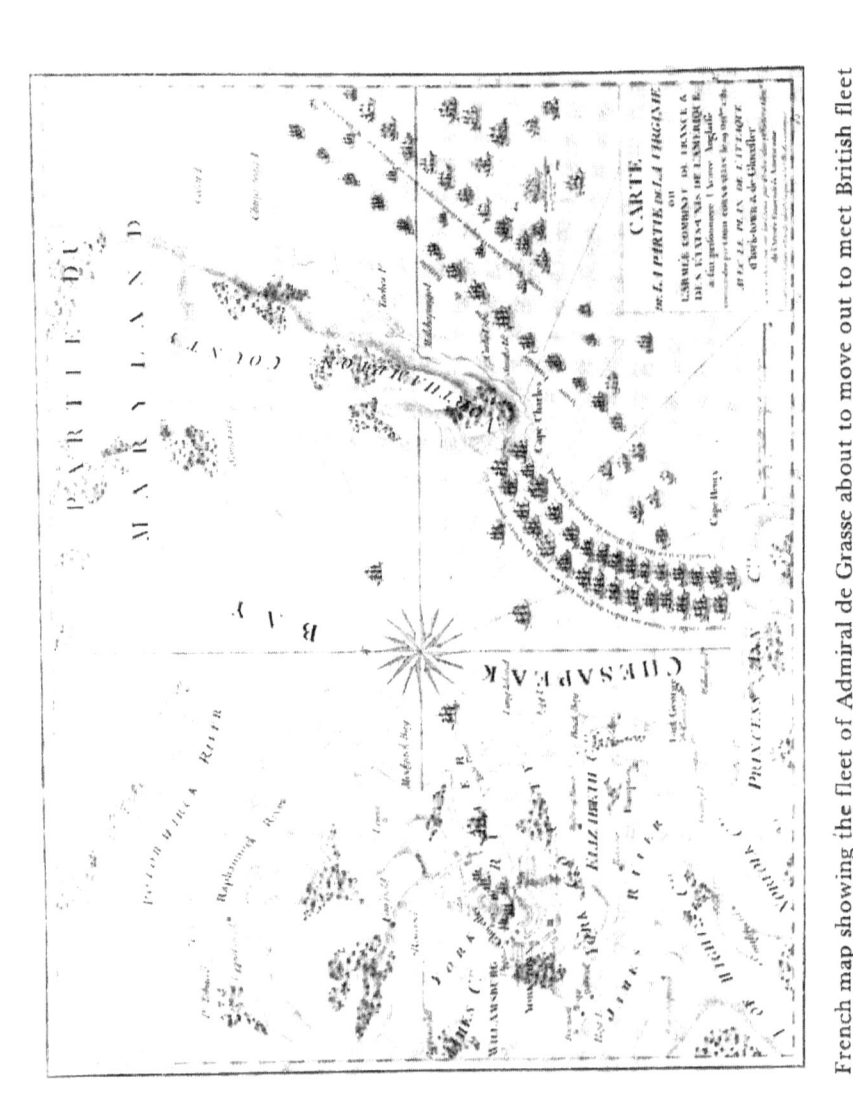

French map showing the fleet of Admiral de Grasse about to move out to meet British fleet of Admiral Thomas Graves, September 5, 1781. *Courtesy of The Mariners Museum.*

ting out the word that he was preparing to attack New York. It was a long, grueling march of more than 400 miles in the heat of the summer with few stops, and Washington was worried about the arrival of de Grasse. But at Chester, Delaware, he received news that de Grasse was at the mouth of the Chesapeake Bay. Rejuvenated by the news, Washington moved toward Williamsburg.

On August 30, de Grasse arrived off Yorktown, set up a blockade of the garrison with his fleet and landed his troops to join Lafayette's forces, hemming in Cornwallis by land. Cornwallis had sent off urgent dispatches to General Clinton in New York to send help, and on September 5, a British fleet under Admiral Thomas Graves appeared. De Grasse sailed out to give battle. The two fleets maneuvered for three days, exchanging cannon balls while trying to catch a favorable wind and eventually drifting southward. The British ships were more powerful than the French, but the French were better marksmen, and they inflicted heavy damage on the British. It is estimated that 600 men were killed in this encounter, in which there were no Americans. The British fleet finally withdrew to sail back to New York for repairs, but it was an inconclusive naval battle for the French. Nevertheless, this battle was crucial to the victory at Yorktown. With the French fleet of 36 ships blocking any reinforcements by sea and the combined armies of Washington, Rochambeau and Lafayette closing in by land, Cornwallis was trapped.

This "Battle off the Capes" has been much neglected by historians, perhaps because in itself it was inconclusive, no American participated, and the British were embarrassed by the bungling tactics of Admiral Graves. Although de Grasse is now recognized as one of our heroes and his contribution vitally important to our victory, the French could not forgive him for being captured in a later battle with the British in the West Indies. After imprisonment in England, he returned to France in disgrace. This seems strange, for when Cornwallis returned to England after his surrender, he retained the respect of the British and continued his military career.

Now de Grasse is remembered, and with gratitude. In 1976, the Bicentennial of the Revolution, a bronze statue was erected in the sand dunes of Cape Henry, gazing out to sea. We are proud and happy that this statue of our friend was given to the City of Virginia Beach by the French Government. We see with his eyes those great sailing ships of long ago, tacking back and forth, and hear their cannon booming. At the base of this statue is a bronze plaque:

FRANCOIS JOSEPH PAUL DE GRASSE

This statue, a gift from France, is placed here overlooking the waters where Admiral Comte de Grasse successfully engaged the British Fleet on Sept. 5, 1781. "The Battle off the Capes" prevented the crucial reinforcements from reaching Cornwallis, thus hastening his surrender.

Nearby is another monument, a large, red granite square depicting the area of the battle, overlaid with the following quotations.

"I wish it was in my power to express to Congress how much I feel myself indebted to the Comte de Grasse and his fleet.
G. Washington, Oct. 19, 1781"

"I consider myself infinitely happy to have been of some service to the United States . . . Reserve me a place in your memory."
de Grasse, Nov. 3, 1781"

These two monuments are lasting memorials of our gratitude to the French nation and their courage in commitment to our cause. If it had not been for such as de Grasse, the Marquis de Lafayette, the Comte de Rochambeau and many other gallant Frenchmen, the sand we walk on here might still be British.

Lookouts on the shore had certainly passed the word of the arrival of the French fleet, and then the British, and many must have been watching, wondering about the outcome.

Lafayette had been warily watching the British as they built their fortifications at Yorktown since August 1. A month later, there were 10 redoubts and 14 artillery positions surrounding the town to the west, and four outer redoubts and gun emplacements. In front of these redoubts, pointed stakes had been driven into the mounds of earth to obstruct attacks. On the north side of the York River at Gloucester Point, Cornwallis had built another barrier of earthworks, and by August 1, he had positioned Colonel Tarleton here. Aware of this, Lafayette had deployed the Duc de Lauzun with his cavalry nearby to keep an eye on him.

On September 24, Washington and the combined forces arrived at Williamsburg. On September 28, they marched the 16 miles to Yorktown, and the siege began. As they marched, there was a sharp contrast between the French in their resplendent uniforms and the Americans in their rags. An American soldier prophesied, " . . . that if the war is continued through the winter, the British troops will be scared at the sight of our men, for as they never fought with naked men, the novelty of it will terrify them."

The allies immediately began digging their own fortifications to the north and east, and while harassed by minor skirmishes, they kept on night and day. The fatigued troops slept on their arms all night as the workers continued. The next morning, they were astounded to find that the British had abandoned their outer line defense posts and moved behind the inner line. The Americans and French quickly moved in. On October 4, as the trenching went forward doggedly, deserters brought the encouraging word that many of the British were ill, that they were crowded together in uncomfortable quarters, and that their cavalry was very short of fodder. A Hessian had written in his journal: "We get terrible provisions now, putrid ship's meat and wormy biscuits that have spoiled on the ships. Many of the men have taken sick here with dysentery or the bloody flux, or diarrhea. Also the foul fever is spreading, partly on account of the many hardships from which we have had little rest day or night, and partly on account of the wretched food; but mostly the nitre-bearing water is the blame for it."

The "foul fever" was the smallpox, and the many deserters from the British brought it with them. Scores of blacks, with no resistance to the disease fled the town and battlefield to die in the woods. A few Americans deserted to the British, inexplicably, but possibly because of the prospect of hand-to-hand fighting over those sharp stakes. One from Pennsylvania deserted and pinpointed his former countrymen's position for British gunners. Washington then ordered that anyone deserting thereafter would be hanged immediately after the capture of Yorktown. Desertions immediately ceased.

These were minor difficulties in that fateful battle. Many more died in the fighting as the might of the British with their best commander was finally pitted against the combined forces of the allies. The troops of Washington, Lafayette, Rochambeau, von Steuben, the fresh French troops brought by de Grasse the cavalry under the Duc de Lauzun, and the Virginia militia under Thomas Nelson, Jr., later governor, brought their number close to 17,000. The British, including the Hessian mercenaries, numbered about 7,500.

Completing their own fortifications on October 9, the allied bombardment began and continued through the night. It was the most tremendous fire that the British had experienced in America. The village of Yorktown did not escape. Governor Nelson even directed fire on his own house, as he suspected that to be Cornwallis' headquarters. It is said that Cornwallis took refuge in a cave down on the shore still known as "Cornwallis' Cave."

Pushing the seige lines forward was impeded by two large redoubts, Number 10 and Number 9. The one on the left, was assigned to a brigade under Colonel Alexander Hamilton, the favorite of Washington. The attack was with unloaded guns, by bayonet. Hamilton, so small he could not get over the stakes, jumped on the back of a larger man and led the brigade. One of the many heroes of this battle, Hamilton later became the bitter enemy of Jefferson as he struggled for a strong central government and Jefferson held out for sovereignty of the states. Under heavy British fire, the other British redoubt was taken and the British fled. The pincers were closing on the beleaguered Cornwallis who had now despaired of receiving the promised reinforcements.

On the night of October 16, Cornwallis attempted to move the bulk of his well troops across the York River to Gloucester Point in small boats, but even that was unsuccessful. A sudden storm came up, and so many of the boats were swamped that he gave up the attempt.

The next morning, October 17, at 10 o'clock, a drummer boy in red appeared on a parapet of the British defenses and beat the signal for a parley. The guns gradually ceased firing, and an officer appeared in front of the lines carrying a white handkerchief. He carried a letter from Cornwallis to Washington.

> "Sir, I propose a cessation of hostilities for twenty-four hours, and that two officers may be appointed by each side to meet at Mr. Moore's house to settle terms for the surrender of the posts at York and Gloucester.
> I have the honor to be, etc.
>
> Cornwallis"

The next day, the commissioners were sent, the articles of the surrender drawn up and signed.

The following day, October 19, at 2 o'clock, the British, bedecked in new uniforms issued them by Cornwallis, marched out between the lines of the ragged Americans and the sparkling French in their cream and silver. In spite of the arrogance of the British as they looked toward the French while trying to ignore the ragged backwoodsmen of "the Rebellion," there were tears in many of their eyes as they threw down their weapons. Their band played, not a military air, but an old nursery rhyme—"The World Turned Upside Down."

"If buttercups buzzed after the bee
If boats were on land, churches on sea
If ponies rode men, and grass ate cows
And cats should be chased to holes by a mouse
If the mamas sold their babies to the gypsies
   for half a crown
Summer were Spring and t'other way round
Then all the world would be upside down."

To many, it was indeed a world turned upside-down. The finest British force to fight in this American Revolution was surrendering to George Washington!

The absence of General Cornwallis did little to mar this spectacular event on this beautiful day. Colonel Banastre Tarleton was not here either. He declined to attend, he said, because of his bad reputation among the Americans. We think that he was afraid, for the ferocious cruelty of this "terror of the colonials" was legendary, and most of his Loyalist cavalry were as cruel as he. He was allowed to surrender, instead, to the French general, the Duc de Lauzun, at Gloucester. These two men had been bitter personal enemies, and both had been lovers of Mrs. Robinson, the toast of the London stage, and also of Marie Antoinette, though not at the same time. Both stationed near Gloucester during the seige of Yorktown, they had come face to face accidentally and had rushed forward for a duel. Tarleton's horse had been knocked down by another horse, but he was saved from Lauzun's sword by one of his legionnaires. This shame was doubled by his surrender to Lauzun.

Cornwallis did not appear as he was "indisposed," and he probably was, with the malady which had affected so many of his men. He sent, instead, General Charles O'Hara, his second-in-command. Offering his sword to Washington, he was directed to General Benjamin Lincoln, as Washington refused the offer from a second-in-command. This was a graceful gesture on the part of Washington, recompense for Lincoln's surrender at Charleston under humiliating terms.

As Washington's officers watched the British and Hessians ground their weapons, he returned to his headquarters to prepare to host a dinner for General O'Hara. Other dinners followed to entertain the British officers, who were now "gentlemen in distress." Washington's dinner for O'Hara was a pleasant and sociable occasion, with the entire company at ease. The next morning, Tench Tilghman of Maryland sailed from Yorktown for Philadelphia carrying Washington's official report of the victory.

For three weeks, cannon had been rumbling or booming day and night. Now, there was silence. Enlisted men and officers roamed the battlefield and shattered Yorktown, fraternizing easily. The country people had come to see the spectacle of the surrender and the remains of the battle, to marvel at the strange tongues and beautiful uniforms of the French and Germans and to gawk at the profusion of European nobility. They searched among those of the Virginia militia, dead or alive, for those whom they knew or loved.

The farmers headed back to their farms to carry the news and to pick up the pieces of their lives after the long six years of war and hardship.

The terms of the surrender included all "artillery, Arms, Accoutrements, Military Chests and Public Stores of every Denomination" to be turned over "unimpaired" to the allies. These were welcome rewards, especially the military chests which contained over £5,000 Sterling, a blessing to the American soldiers who were short of even their meager pay. Four frigates and 39 transports were among the 82 British ships in the harbor which were surrendered, a boon to the Virginia Navy which had lost all but one of its ships, the "Liberty," in struggles against the British in the Chesapeake Bay.

Women had played a part, though minor, throughout the war. Washington encouraged wives to accompany their husbands, feeling that the men would be happier and less inclined to desert. Many did go along; cooking, washing and sewing for the troops. The legend of the tough "Molly Pitcher" in the battle of Monmouth is well-known. She helped her husband load and fire his cannon when his regular helper was shot. Another tale is of a woman who, dressing as a man, was actually in the fighting until exposed.

Sarah Osborn Benjamin's deposition when she applied at the age of 81 for a pension for two husbands is the only factual account of wives traveling with the army. An entertaining picture of her experiences is recorded in the National Archives and from *The Revolution Remembered*, edited by John C. Dann.

Sarah was working as a servant in the household of a blacksmith in Albany, New York, when she married Aaron Osborn, a soldier working between enlistments as an assistant to her employer. This was in 1780. Assured by his captain, a James Gregg, who had survived a scalping by the Indians, that she would have conveyance by wagon or horseback and urged by her husband, she went along with Osborn on his enlistment. After spending the winter at West Point, the army marched to Philadelphia under the command of General Washington.

Here, the Quaker ladies urged Sarah to stay. But her husband said, "No, he could not leave her behind."

They went on to Baltimore, thence down the bay by boat and 12 miles up the James, where they disembarked and "had a fine time catching sea lobsters which they ate." On foot with the army from Williamsburg to Yorktown, they encamped about a mile away, where she saw "a number of dead negroes lying around the encampments, whom she understood the British had driven out of the town and left to starve." Here, she busied herself in cooking, washing and mending, assisted by the other females. Carrying beef, bread and coffee into the entrenchments, on one occasion she met General Washington who asked her, "Are you not afraid of the cannonballs?" Her reply was, "No, bullets would not cheat the gallows," and, "It would not do for the men to fight and starve too."

She was a little way off when the firing stopped, but the next day was on the other side of the road from the Americans when the British officers came out of the town and delivered up their swords. She recollected that, "Their band played a melancholy air, that their drums were covered with black handkerchiefs, and their fifes with black ribbons tied around them. The British general at the head of the army (O'Hara) was a large, portly man, full face, and the tears rolled down his cheeks as he passed. It was not Cornwallis as she saw him afterwards and noticed his being a man of diminutive appearance and having cross eyes." A splendid eye-witness account.

Her husband remained in the service until discharged, and they lived at West Point and then New Windsor, New York, where she produced two children. After the second birth, her husband left her. After learning of his two unlawful marriages to other women, she herself remarried, to John Benjamin, also a veteran. He lived in Blooming Grove, New York, where she had grown up. After Benjamin died and she heard that both Osborn and his second wife had died—"she—dead drunk"—she applied for the pensions of both husbands, which she received. According to Mr. Dann, "She deserved every penny of it" and died at the over-ripe old age of 109.

Although it is said that occasionally some women in cities acted as spies, we have no record of the women of Princess Anne County as participating in any of these activities. In this county of mostly small farms, they apparently stayed home and struggled to maintain the land.

As opposed to most whites, who enlisted when the fighting was in their area, the blacks enlisted for the duration, hoping thereby to gain their freedom. Fighting side by side with the whites, they were at Valley Forge, Princeton, Trenton, Saratoga and Yorktown, and in the Southern campaign as well. We have already noted the numbers in the Virginia Navy. Free blacks were also fighting for their rights, pointing out that they were "freeborn people who had been dragged here aginst their will."

Few names survive of these blacks, slave or free, from Princess Anne County, who fought. In the Virginia Navy, there was Cuffee, probably William, serving on Captain Calvert's *Revenge;* Nimrod Perkins, serving on the *Diligence;* and Ninny was another pilot. Others in the army were Aaron Weaver, James Jackson, Demcy and Nathaniel Anderson, James Murdin, who was a spy and guide at Great Bridge, and Saul Matthews, a spy and guide at Portsmouth.

As stated earlier, for the free blacks who had fought and endured through these years, the victory meant a bonus of 100 acres of land of their own, and for this they had reason to exult. For slaves who had served three years or more, it meant their own personal freedom at last. Congress had encouraged masters to enlist their slaves for a reimbursement of $1,000 and freedom for the slave plus $50.00. "I am free!" rang out joyously among them.

On this happy occasion, few if any officers or men, black or white, looked ahead to the difficulties of a new nation which had struggled to be born and now must take and keep its right to survive.

PART FIVE
THE NEW ORDER

PART FIVE
Chapter 1
ADJUSTMENT

The victory at Yorktown, glorious as it was, was not the end, but only the beginning of the end. Over two years passed before the Treaty of Paris was ratified by the British and by our new Congress on April 15, 1783. Britain was still at war with France and had to resolve that conflict. After their disastrous defeats in the West Indies, the British people had had enough. The coercive policy of Lord North, the determined "hawk," forced him to resign, and even George III threatened to abdicate. North was succeeded by the conciliatory Lord Rockingham, and direct negotiations with the American peace commissioners were immediately opened. General Clinton, whose bungling was credited with the defeat at Yorktown, was recalled from New York, and his successor began to concentrate all British forces there, preparatory to leaving. Savannah was evacuated and, finally, Charleston, but not before the vengeful British had their last fling at raids and skirmishes.

Virginia seemed to have escaped most of those last acts of vengeance so common in other areas. In South Carolina and New York, fights were ferocious on both sides between Tories and Patriots, and even "suspected" Tories were tarred and feathered and their property damaged. The British forces captured at Yorktown were relieved of their weapons and put into prison camps in Maryland, Pennsylvania and some in Virginia, but not in this county. Some were put to work on neighboring farms. Whether it was the pretty American girls, the opportunities here or the kindness accorded them, we do not know. Perhaps it was the weather which appealed to them, and they felt as Captain John Smith had in 1612 when he wrote of Virginia: "The mildness of the air, the fertility of the soil, and situation of the rivers are so propitious to the nature and use of man, as no place is more convenient for pleasure, profit and man's sustenance under that latitude or climate. . . ." Whatever it was that lured them, many elected to stay, particularly the Hessian mercenaries who had been sent to Pennsylvania.

For the Americans, there was almost total confusion. Landon Carter, son of "King" Carter, the richest man in the Colony, had said when he heard of the Declaration of Independence: "Hurrah for independence, sedition, and confusion!" This cantankerous old man, who died before the victory at Yorktown, was right in his prediction of confusion.

Each state, jealous of the others, fought for leadership, and the leaders of each squabbled with each other. Sectionalism between the industrial North and the rural South reared its ugly head, leading in a large degree to the conflict of civil war 80 years later. The motive for the Revolution in New England was primarily economic. There, the working classes were more severely hurt by the Navigation Acts, and they had responded with the first violence against the British. In Virginia, it was political in origin, led by the upper classes whose members dominated the Conventions.

In 1777, at a meeting of the Continental Congress in Philadelphia, Richard Henry Lee had proposed a plan of confederation to be prepared and submitted to the respective states for their consideration and approbation. This plan was completed and presented to the Congress, which now had the new title of "The United States in Congress Assembled," on March 2, 1781. Most of the states had already formulated their own constitutions, but there was not yet a National Constitution.

In the three years before the articles of the peace treaty were finally ratified by Congress on May 12, 1784, the inhabitants of Princess Anne County lived in a state of suspended animation, not being sure that the war was really over. The Committee of Safety was abolished, and the courts attempted to resume normal operations. But the returning soldiers, who had endured such hardships in the fight for freedom and equality, were disappointed to find the same men as justices and other officials as before. Faced with their neglected farms, some removed to Kentucky for fresh and cheap land. Others took advantage of the sale of Loyalists' lands which had already been escheated to the state, such as those of John Saunders and George Logan. These properties were sold at bargain prices, which enabled some of the small farmers to increase their holdings and thereby move up in the social scale.

The early "test acts" of 1776–1777 had required the exiling of all

Adjustment

prominent Tories and had disenfranchised all Loyalists with the confiscation of all their estates. But in Princess Anne County, accustomed to bending laws when it was convenient, the leaders were reluctant in many cases to dispossess their former friends, and many were left unmolested. This had always been a close-knit community and that closeness continued. As one modern-day contemporary put it, "Once a friend, always a friend." The law of 1776 had banished all British merchants and those British born who had been in partnership with or acted as agents for British firms. There was an economic reason for not wishing to obey this law to the letter. Norfolk had been the center of commerce for this part of Tidewater, led by the Scottish and British mercantile establishments, and that city was beginning to rise again from the ashes. The inhabitants of Princess Anne felt they needed this Norfolk business to survive. In all, only six estates in this county were escheated to the state in 1779, amounting to less than 3,000 acres, which included some lots in Newtown and Kemp's Landing and at least two fine dwellings. So hostility, which had never been very strong, was soon forgotten as other problems seemed more important. Patrick Henry, first Governor of the State of Virginia, had instituted a Land Tax, and the records show that many of the same Scots who had owned land in this county in 1775 still owned it.

The most crucial problem for all the states at this time was money. The currency situation was chaotic, with each state issuing paper money of their own and refusing to honor that of another state. Virginia had authorized huge issues of treasury notes without adequate taxation as security, and tens of millions of these notes became worthless. Returning one dollar for every thousand caused ruin for many who in good faith had exchanged valuable property for these notes. Princess Anne County wills at this time show a marked decrease in value of estates, and most people were very poor. Having no money, they reverted to the barter system, while the state fell back on tobacco as currency.

While debate over ratification of the peace treaty was going on in Richmond, the Assembly, formerly the House of Burgesses, was busy with local matters. As a result of petitions by the leaders of Princess Anne County, the following act was passed in 1783 (The Calendar of State Papers).

> "Be it enacted by the General Assembly,
> That sixty acres of land lying at the place commonly called and known by the name of Kemp's Landing, in the county of Princess Anne, be, and the same is hereby vested in John Thoroughgood

[first spelling of the name from Thorowgood], Anthony Lawson, William Wishart, John Ackiss, Lemuel Thoroughgood, Lemuel Cornick, John Hancock, and Joel Cornick, gentlemen trustees, to be by them, or any five of them, laid out into lots of half an acre each, with convenient streets; which shall be, and the same is hereby established a town by the name of Kempsville. That as soon as the sixty acres shall be so laid off into lots and streets, the said trustees, or any five of them, shall proceed to sell the same at public auction, for the best price that can be had, the time and place of which sale shall be previously advertised for one month in the Virginia Gazette; the purchasers to hold the said lots respectively, subject to the condition of building on each of the said lots a dwelling-house twenty feet square at least, with a brick chimney, to be finished for habitation within three years from the date of sale. . . ."

Newtown had formerly been the seat of government of the county, but it had declined during the war as the population shifted eastward to Kemp's Landing, and court was already being held in George Logan's former store. Also, traffic had increased greatly from eastern North Carolina, so much so, in fact, that in October of that same year, 1783, an act was passed for cutting a navigable canal from the waters of the Elizabeth River to the waters of the North River.

"Whereas the opening of communication of the waters of Elizabeth River with those of North river, will be of great benefit and advantage, as well to the inhabitants of the interior parts of this state as those of the state of North Carolina, and it is represented to this present assembly that many persons are willing and desirous to subscribe and contribute thereto: For the encouragement therefore of so useful an undertaking."

Nine trustees were appointed to collect the subscriptions and to decide on the land to be used, after being viewed and valued by a jury for the purchase of said land, and to set and collect the fees for any vessel entering or passing through the canal.

George Washington, during his two terms as President of the United States, was an ardent advocate of better communication between all areas and states of the new republic. Virginius Dabney, in *The New Dominion*, says, "The canals, turnpikes and railroads built in Virginia in subsequent years were to a considerable degree the outgrowth of Washington's imaginative planning." And Robert McColley wrote, "If Jefferson was possessed by dreams of freedom, education and rustic tranquility, Washington was equally, if less poetically, possessed with visions of roads, canals, factories and cities, all knitted together in a richly varied, self-supporting and powerful America."

This canal would have been a boon to Norfolk, now enjoying a resurgence of its former mercantile and shipping business due to the creation, also by Washington, of the James River Company, which was designed to ship goods from the West down the James to Richmond, and thence to Norfolk. Washington's insistence on the creation of links between the Ohio River and the Virginia rivers was aimed to divert shipping from the Mississippi to the East. At this time, all land west of the Mississippi belonged to Spain, including New Orleans, but in the Treaty of 1783, Spain gave the Americans free navigation of the Mississippi, from the source to the mouth, and the right of deposit there for their goods for three years. But, in 1801, New Orleans was secretly ceded to France, and both Washington and Jefferson were concerned by the threat posed by a neighboring imperial and aggressive power.

After all these plans and arrangements, the canal was never realized. Evidently, some land was purchased near Kempsville and some preliminary work done, for a former resident of the town remembers playing in the ruins as a boy.

Abandoning this project was probably due to the lack of necessary subscribers, as the majority of the inhabitants of Princess Anne County at this time were impoverished. Yet, in 1787, the first Dismal Swamp Canal was cut through to facilitate water traffic from Elizabeth City to Norfolk. This project attracted sufficient subscribers, including Thomas Jefferson, and it greatly helped the transportation of lumber for the merchants and the Norfolk Shipyard, which once again was starting to build ships.

William Robertson, perhaps too proud to admit that he had nothing to leave, left this will in 1782.

> "To my dearly beloved wife I leave all the affection, I ever had for her.
> To the lawyers, their honesty, and wish them to avoid quibbling.
> To the doctors, I leave them their extravagant charges, and wish them a reformation.
> And as to the Clergy—I leave them their penury, hoping and wishing they may enjoy a sufficiency of it until they are more active in propagating the Christian religion."

And some of the wealthier, who had not fought but who had contributed heavily to the cause by purchasing these notes, found themselves penniless. One of the Thorowgood families, no longer able to feed and clothe their slaves, "traded" them, according to one descendant of these slaves. "Do you mean sold them?" was the question. "Oh, no," he said, "they wouldn't do that. They traded us for provisions." He went on to say that he still bears the name "Thorowgood" because they were fond of the Thorowgoods and understood their predicament, preferring to keep their name rather than taking that of the new master, as was customary.

This may have been an unusual case for two of the wealthiest leaders. Thomas Walke IV and Anthony Lawson had more slaves in 1785 than they had in 1775.

One article of the peace treaty which greatly upset Virginians was that all debts due creditors of either country by citizens of the other were validated, only then would the slaves be returned. All planters in Virginia were in debt to British merchants before the war, and Thomas Jefferson alone is said to have owed them £ 2,000,000. This resulted in a stalemate. The debts were not paid, and the slaves were not returned. Whitney Bates, writing in the *William and Mary Quarterly* on "Northern Speculators and Southern Debts," says that in 1790, Northern speculators preyed on the uninformed South, and that nearly the whole of the Virginia state debt was transferred from the hands of the original owners. Pennsylvania, New York and Maryland led the list of nonresident owners of the Virginia State securities, paying between 20 and 30 cents on the dollar. Northern speculation in the Southern states intensified a developing economic sectionalism and helps explain the dominance of Southern leadership in creating a Republican (Jefferson's Democratic-Republican) Party more responsive to their needs and interests than were the Federalists.

While it is certain that the majority of the inhabitants of Princess Anne were poor, there were exceptions. Ten new houses were built between 1779 and 1793, five of brick and five of frame, and all survive. Those of brick which have best withstood the ravages of time and renovation are: Ferry Farm, built by William Walke in 1779; the Thomas Murray house, built in 1791; Green Hill Farm, built by Lancaster Lovett in 1791; and the Jonathan Fentress house, built in 1794. There is a slight controversy over Pleasant Hall in Kempsville. Some feel that it was not built by George Logan before the war, but by Peter Singleton who owned it in 1779. There is a brick on the south outside wall with the date 1779, which might confirm this. Frame houses have not endured as well, but the Thomas Lovett house, built in 1790, and the John Forrest house, which some feel was built by Henry Woodhouse in 1785, have remained as they were. The J. A.

Fentress house, built in 1789, is just as it once was but appears in danger of collapsing at any time. The market for lumber was booming at this time, both for export and shipbuilding in Norfolk and Portsmouth, much of it coming from the Dismal Swamp, and more houses were being built of wood, unfortunately. The lumber business was so brisk that in 1787, the General Assembly passed "An act authorizing the courts in the counties of Norfolk, Princess Anne and the borough of Norfolk to appoint inspectors of lumber." Inspectors had not been necessary since the boom days of tobacco here.

In the Calendar of State Papers, vol. 3, is a list of inhabitants of Princess Anne County in 1783, stating that there were then 3,999 whites and 2,656 blacks. In spite of Dunmore's proclamation, few blacks from this county had joined him, and there had been no insurrections here or in the rest of the state as he had hoped. There had been a few solitary, unorganized fugitives who joined whichever army, British or American, seemed to offer them the most favorable prospects of freedom.

From time to time in the 18th century, slaves had been freed, usually by wills. Due partly to "The Great Awakening," manumission societies, surprisingly enough, originated in the South. Gerald W. Mullin, in *Flight and Freedom*, says that Robert "Councilor" Carter of Nomini Hall and a prominent member of the House of Burgesses, after a prolonged religious experience that took him out of the Anglican Church into the Baptist faith, then joined the American New Church, a sect based on the writings of Emanuel Swedenborg. He at once manumitted more than 500 of his slaves. Most did not go to that extreme, and no one in Princess Anne County had even 150 slaves. But the slaves freed here were usually endowed with money, land or some sort of training to support themselves.

So there was a number of free black landowners already in Princess Anne County at the time of the Revolution. Their numbers were increased by those who received their freedom by enlisting in the service with permission of owners or serving as substitutes. They received freedom and $50 at the termination of the war and bounties if their service lasted over three years. However, the number of free blacks in this county was not significantly increased, as those free blacks without land tended to go to urban areas where there were more of their own kind and better work prospects.

It is estimated that 10,000 slaves were manumitted from 1782–1790 in the state of Virginia, but it is sad that while whites at this time were easing the transition from slave to free status, they sought to further restrict those who remained in bondage. After the bloody insurrection against the French in Haiti in 1789, the slave code of Virginia was revised to stringently regulate ship captains who harboured runaways, the hiring-out procedures, and slaves who met for religious services.

As runaways became more frequent, free blacks were looked upon with suspicion as encouraging them. Practically all slaves had been taught a trade, and now they headed North to find jobs in the states which had abolished slavery; Pennsylvania in 1780; Connecticut and Rhode Island in 1784; New York in 1785; and New Jersey in 1786. In 1780, a judicial decision in Massachusetts had been construed as having abolished slavery. The blacks felt that they were protected from extradition in the industrial North. But after 1800, when the huge Gabriel Plot to destroy all whites in Richmond and possibly in the state was thwarted at the last minute, the Northern states refused to admit blacks—slave or free.

Since 1792, American ship captains had been forbidden to import slaves, and if caught, they were indicted for piracy. But both they and the British continued to smuggle them in.

In the *William and Mary Quarterly* is an item from the Princess Anne County Records which could easily be misinterpreted.

> "A copy of the Third Census, Dec. 15, 1810, to remain at the Clerk's office for the inspection of all concerned. The Report shows that there were in the County 2,681 white males, 2,624 white females, 267 free negroes, and 3,926 slaves: that 646 heads of families owned slaves and 421 did not, and that of the slave owners, nine were Negroes, and that they owned fourteen slaves."

This is not as startling as it sounds, for those 14 slaves were family members of the nine, who had bought them from their former masters.

Some members of the House of Burgesses had long since tried to find a way to get rid of this "peculiar institution" of slavery, but the opposition had not even permitted debate. The main crop of Princess Anne County was now grain, which did not require the labor necessary for tobacco, and the slaves had become a burden to many. In 1790, Eli Whitney invented the cotton gin, and the Deep South rushed to plant cotton. The device was supposed to eliminate the number of laborers, but this did not happen. Cotton was in such demand that everyone wanted to plant this profitable crop, which even superseded tobacco by 1803.

The Anglican Church, as it had existed in the colonial era, was a casualty of the Revolution. In spite of its power through the interlocking of church and state through all those years, its influence had declined steadily during the 18th century. The rising middle class regarded it as only for the aristocracy and had turned for inspiration in droves to the other Protestant sects.

The oath of allegiance to the Church, as well as to the King, had been increasingly resented, but even more resented was the tax imposed on every inhabitant for its support. Governor Jefferson proposed a statute for religious freedom in 1779, but it was defeated by the wealthy planters, mostly Anglican Church members, in the House of Burgesses. James Madison proposed the identical statute in 1785, and this time it was adopted, making Virginia the first of the states to abolish all religious restrictions. The gist of the statute was, "no man shall be compelled to frequent or support any religious worship, place, or ministry whatsoever," since "God Almighty hath created the mind free."

On Thomas Jefferson's Memorial in Washington, D.C., at his direction, is inscribed: "On the altar of God I have sworn eternal enmity against all forms of tyranny over the mind of man." Of all his many other accomplishments, this is most indicative of the character of this great man. He considered the successful sponsorship of this statute one of the three greatest accomplishments of his life. The others were "Author of the Declaration of Independence" and "Father of the University of Virginia."

In 1802, the Assembly directed the overseers of the poor, a committee which had taken over the obligations of the vestry, to sell all glebe lands, with the money realized to go to the poor. This almost wrecked the now-called Protestant Episcopal Church, but it finally recovered.

Evidently, the parish of Lynnhaven had been a bit slow in adjusting to the new laws of the Protestant Episcopal Church, for in May 1783, an act was passed by the Assembly specifically ordering them to conform.

> "I. Whereas it hath been represented to this general assembly, that the present vestry of the parish of Lynnhaven, in the county of Princess Anne, have not been elected by the freeholders and housekeepers of the said parish, and that for the last two years a vestry for the said parish has not been held, whereby the poor have been neglected and much distressed: For remedy whereof.
> II. Be it enacted, That the vestry of the said parish of Lynnhaven be, and the same is hereby dissolved.
> III. And be it further enacted, That the freeholders and housekeepers of the said parish of Lynnhaven shall, before the thirty-first of

August next, meet at some convenient time and place, to be appointed and publicly advertised by the Sheriff of the said county of Princess Anne, at least one month before such meeting, and then and there elect twelve of the most able and discreet persons, being freeholders and residing in the said parish, for vestrymen, which vestrymen, so elected, having in the court of the said county of Princess Anne, taken the oaths prescribed by law, shall to all invents and purposes be deemed and taken to be the vestry of the said parish of Lynnhaven.

IV. And be it further enacted, That the vestry to be elected by virtue of this act, shall levy and assess upon the tithable persons of the said parish of Lynnhaven, all such sums of money and quantities of tobacco as ought to have been levied and assessed by the said vestry. Provided nevertheless, That not withstanding any thing in this act contained, any suit or suits brought by or against the vestry or church wardens of the said parish, and now depending, may be prosecuted in the same manner as if this act had never been made."

In May 1785, two years later, the Reverend Mr. James Simpson was secured as a minister for the parish, and the vestry took the oath as follows.

"We, the Subscribers, being legally Chosen by the majority of the people, this day subscribe in Vestry to be conformable to the Doctrine, Discipline & Worship of the Protestant Episcopal Church."

With the sale of the Glebe lands, the last evidence of the power of the colonial religious establishment disappeared.

Unfortunately, Jefferson's dream of state-supported public schools did not succeed. His "Bill for the More General Diffusion of Knowledge" was ignored. The money which had been realized from the sale of the church lands might have gone into such a system, but instead, most of it went to private academies. Even the few town-supported schools in New England dwindled away as the private academies increased. There were a few "pauper" schools scattered throughout the state, but these were only for the poor. One of these was in Princess Anne County. The Reverend Robert Dickson, one of the few able ministers of Lynnhaven Parish, had died in 1776, after serving the parish for 25 years. He left his slaves and property, including his plantation near the parish church, to the parish, "to be sold, rented, or otherwise appropriated for the Benefit of Educating poor male orphans, and retained for the said purpose, and called by the name of Dickson's Free School." This school lasted for many years but was finally disbanded. The present Old Donation Church received its name from this generous donation, as it was so called in vestry records of 1822, "Old Donation Church."

But the leading method for educating the poor throughout the state in the 18th century was apprenticeship, which required that the apprentice be taught to read, write and cipher, as well as to learn a trade.

The private academies sprang up all over New England. In the South, among those who could afford it, children were taught at home by tutors, but there were a few of these academies in Virginia. Among them and the most notable were: Prince Edward Academy, later Hampton-Sydney; Liberty Hall Academy, later Washington College; and Norfolk Academy. Norfolk Academy was chartered in 1728 by leading citizens of the city for boys of St. Paul's Parish and it continues today as a private preparatory school.

These academies were, of course, for boys only. An academy for girls was proposed in Boston, but it was voted down as unnecessary. One voter said, "It would be a bad thing, for then wives would correct their husband's spelling." There were schools for girls, but they gave instruction only in the ladylike arts of fine needlework, music and dancing.

On the college level, there was William and Mary in Williamsburg, founded in 1693, the second to be established (Harvard was the first). It was established by the Reverend James Blair, a power in the Colony at the time, and was supported by the Anglican Church and the Crown. During the Revolution and for some time after, William and Mary suffered hard times. As the teachers had been all Anglican ministers and Loyalists who fled back to England, there remained neither teachers nor funds.

The first state university was the University of North Carolina, founded in 1789. It was followed by the University of Vermont, 1800; University of South Carolina, 1801; and the University of Virginia, 1819, conceived by Thomas Jefferson.

There were other academies, church affiliated, during the antebellum period, but their scope was narrow, and the great mass of the whites and all of the blacks were untouched by them. It was not until after the War Between the States that free public schools were established in the South under federal legislation.

If Virginia was slow to educate the masses, these private academies and the College of William and Mary produced more learned great men in the 18th century than in any other of the colonies. These men—George Washington, Thomas Jefferson, James Madison, James Monroe, George Wythe, Richard Henry Lee, George Mason and

Edmund Randolph—working with those of other states—John Adams, Benjamin Franklin, Benjamin Rush and Alexander Hamilton—created through their unselfish work a democracy which would endure, although many of them died impoverished or from overwork. It was no easy task, for this was the first democracy since ancient Greece and Rome. As James Madison commented to Jefferson in 1789: "We are in a wilderness without a single footstep to guide us. Our successors will have an easier task."

Thomas Jefferson had written the Declaration of Independence in 1776, and George Mason was the author of the Bill of Rights. Virginia and many other states had already formulated their own constitutions, and in 1787, 55 delegates from the 13 states met in Philadelphia for a National Constitutional Convention. Of these, 29 were college trained, over half were lawyers, while planters and merchants together with a few physicians and college professors made up the rest. When the convention opened, Robert Morris nominated George Washington as President, which immediately won unanimous approval.

Edmund Randolph proposed 15 resolutions known as the "Virginia Plan,": closely following the Virginia Constitution, which was quickly followed by the proposal of "The New Jersey Plan" in opposition. Connecticut offered a compromise plan, and long debates followed. Finally, on September 17, each of the 12 state delegations voted approval (Rhode Island was not represented). Randolph and Mason had refused to sign, but the majority had won, and the Constitution was to become effective when ratified by nine states. Under the leadership of Alexander Hamilton, the articles had called for a strengthened central government, and he had won the majority, as opposed to Randolph and Mason who wished more autonomy for the states.

There was a flood of propaganda in all the states, for and against, including the well-known *Federalist Papers* by Hamilton, John Jay and Madison, defending and explaining the Constitution as setting forth the importance of a strong central government. This was contrary to Jefferson's ideal of the Constitution, and the debate in the Virginia Assembly was long and heated, with Patrick Henry leading the opposition and Madison for ratification. Jefferson was Minister to France at the time, and he counted on Henry's oratory to win over the Assembly. But Madison's logic prevailed. The debate lasted for five months, with the final vote showing 89 for and 79 against. But Virginia had attached to the ratification a proposal for Mason's Bill of

Rights, along with 20 other changes. Thus, Virginia, whose leadership in the Revolution was unquestioned, was the eleventh state to ratify the Constitution.

This struggle between a strong central government and autonomy of the states was the beginning of a long and bitter feud between Jefferson and Hamilton, which continued until Hamilton was killed in a duel with Aaron Burr in 1804. It was also the beginning of the two political parties—the Federalists led by Hamilton, and the Whigs (Democratic-Republicans) led by Jefferson.

George Washington was elected the first President of the United States in 1789, and he appointed Hamilton as Secretary of the Treasury and Jefferson as Secretary of State, hoping to reconcile the two. But they continued to clash. Jefferson's main principles were: (1) a democratic agrarian order based on the individual freeholder; (2) a broad diffusion of wealth; (3) relative freedom from industrialism, urbanism and organized finance; (4) distrust of centralized government; and (5) that the people, acting through representative institutions, could be left alone to govern themselves. Hamilton's main principles were: (1) active governmental encouragement of finance, industry, commerce and shipping; (2) advocacy of a strong national government under executive leadership; (3) distrust of the people's capacity to govern; and (4) a belief that the best government was that of the elite. While the names of the two parties changed, the Federalists becoming Republicans and the Whigs Democrats, the principles of the two men as applied to the two parties remained loosely the same.

Washington was inaugurated April 30, 1790, and when Congress met, Mason's Bill of Rights became part of the Constitution. It was not long before Hamilton and Jefferson were at odds again. Hamilton in 1790 instituted a plan for all states to assume equally the public debt, which Jefferson opposed. Massachusetts had, by far, the largest debt of any of the states, and Jefferson did not wish Virginians to be taxed again, since they had already made plans to dispose of their state's debts themselves. Even Madison opposed Hamilton's plan. A compromise was finally reached in the debate over the location of the central government. Madison agreed to provide a sufficient number of Southern votes to effect Hamilton's tax plan in return for locating the National Capitol along the Potomac. When Washington gave his support to Hamilton, Jefferson resigned, returning to Monticello.

Jefferson had long since regained his popularity and power in Virginia, after the short dissatisfaction when he was governor of the state.

His political theories met with no argument in Princess Anne County, whose inhabitants had long before become fiercely jealous of their independence, preferring to settle their own problems in their own way. But a situation was shaping up over which they had no control, and they began to look to the central government to protect their exposed shoreline on the ocean and the bay.

PART FIVE
Chapter 2
THE WAR OF 1812

In 1787, Benjamin Franklin had said: "The American war is over, but this is far from being the case with the American Revolution. On the contrary, nothing but the first act is closed. It remains yet to establish and perfect our new form of government."

The phenomenal growth of Norfolk after 1790 had now once more produced a sizeable city. There were two newspapers, the *Norfolk Herald* and the *Norfolk and Portsmouth Advertiser* (preceded by the *Norfolk & Portsmouth Chronicle* of short duration) and the *Norfolk Gazette*), all of which had wide circulation in Princess Anne County. The people here were able to be well-informed about international events which concerned them, as well as the struggles of the new government.

At first, happy over the French Revolution, in 1789, they were horrified by the ensuing slaughter and the coup d'etat which resulted in Napolean's becoming the emperor with unlimited powers. The French had begun interfering with American shipping, the lifeblood of Tidewater, and by 1797, America's former allies had captured almost 3,000 American ships. The war hawks were badgering John Adams, who had succeeded Washington as President in that year, to declare war. Adams managed to sidestep their demands, preferring to strengthen national defense.

England also was making trouble. Urged by the Canadian fur traders, she had violated the Treaty of 1783 by refusing to turn over the forts along the Great Lakes on American soil until the Loyalist properties were restored and British merchants paid.

Powerless to enforce these terms on the states, Congress was looked upon with scorn by the European nations as impoverished, ineffective and fragmented as each state bickered over the constitution. As Europe waited hopefully for the downfall of the new

American ship passing the port of Dover, England, 1797. Fourteen stars on flag on stern includes one for the state of Vermont, admitted to the Union that year.

The War of 1812

government, British ships preyed on the Americans, and privateers raided in the Chesapeake at will, impressing American seamen.

The British Navy for 400 years had been raiding their own villages and towns and carrying off able-bodied men to serve in the Navy, where the pay was poor, the food wretched and discipline on shipboard severe. Their impressment is further described by Rebecca Brooks Gruver in *An American History*, Vol. 1.

> "When war resumed in 1803 (with France), the British Navy was in desperate need of sailors. Under British law, any subject of the king could be impressed into the Royal Navy in an emergency. British regulations also permitted the Navy to stop any neutral vessel on the high seas and capture from it any British subjects. Under official sanction, British naval officers began to search American merchant vessels at sea.
> "In truth, many British sailors were serving on American ships. American commerce was so active and American ships so understaffed that British sailors were offered comparatively high wages and good working conditions. They regularly deserted their own vessels and joined crews on American vessels. In 1804, for instance, twelve British men-of-war which had stopped over in Norfolk, Virginia, were detained in the port because their crews had all jumped ship.
> "When searching for English subjects among American crews, British officers were not particularly scrupulous. Swedes, Danes, and Portuguese sailors on American ships were glibly dubbed 'Englishmen' and hauled away. . . . Between 1793 and 1811, the British impressed about 10,000 native-born Americans."

A letter from Anthony Walke of Kempsville in Princess Anne County to Governor James Monroe early in 1797, from The Calendar of State Papers, details this custom and the resentment of the people of Princess Anne.

> "1797 March 28, 1797.
> There is an evil here which may be productive of considerable inconvenience if not checked in the beginning and of which my duty calls upon me to inform you. Sailors frequently desert from the English and French ships of war, and as soon as they proceed a few miles into the country the inhabitants facilitate their escape. On Thursday last the British Consul applied to me, as a Justice of Peace, to aid four officers from a ship lying in Hampton Roads who were pursuing seven deserters. In conformity to the President's proclamation of neutrality I thought myself bound to see that these men should be given up if to be found, and told a Constable that he

would be well rewarded if he would exert himself in apprehending them.

"Several citizens collected together in Kempsville and one of them, I am told, threatened to raise a party and rescue them if taken, and the rest came to one opinion, that the civil officers ought not to interfere. Some of the deserters had arrived at Great Bridge and I accompanied one officer thither, where a man undertook to arrest them and bring them to Norfolk; but some of the inhabitants there also were disposed to favor their escape. The Captain observed to me that he was now desirous of protecting our trade, but if we did not deliver up his deserters that he would take an equal number of men off of our vessels. This is indeed to be expected as the natural and inevitable consequence.

"You and the Council may perhaps judge it expedient to make public your sentiments on this subject. At least let me hear from you.

"I am your humble servant

Anthony Walke"

England and France were now at war again, and the United States, declaring itself neutral, hoped to supply both belligerents with American products. The result was that France captured American vessels headed for England and England took American ships sailing for France. British warships seized some 250 American vessels, condemning them for violating the rights of neutrals in wartime. Worse still, 1,000 redcoats were still in the Northwest, actually building a fort in Ohio territory.

Added to the general fear and confusion was the trouble with the Barbary Pirates. Like the European nations, Washington and Adams had been paying tribute to the Barbary states of Algiers, Morocco, Tripoli and Tunis to buy immunity for their commerce in the Mediterranean and along the African coast—to the tune of $10,000 a year! When the Pasha of Tripoli increased his demands and declared war on the United States, this was too much even for the peace-loving Jefferson, who had been elected President in 1801. He sent a squadron of vessels of the newly created United States Navy, loaded with marines, to get any Americans out and to negotiate with the Pasha. While this small force did not overwhelm the pirates, the Americans did manage to get their own men out along with a reduction in tribute. And the marine song now includes, ". . . to the shores of Tripoli."

The Virginia Navy had been disbanded in 1789. In 1794, Congress had authorized President Washington to provide, purchase and equip a national navy, beginning with four large frigates of 44 guns and two smaller ones of 36 guns. The four larger frigates were commissioned in 1797: the *Constitution,* the *President,* the *United States* and the *Constellation.* In 1880, Captain James Barron was in command of the *President.* Captain Barron was the son of the Commodore James Barron who had created the Virginia Navy in 1776, then becoming Commodore of the Continental Fleet.

Although Captain Barron was a part of this expedition, it was the young Lieutenant Stephen Decatur who was the real hero. In February 1804, he led a troop into the harbor of Tripoli and burned the *U.S. Philadelphia,* one of the smaller frigates which had fallen into enemy hands. He and his group made their escape with only one man wounded. This exploit earned him a promotion to captain and a sword of honour from Congress. Later, in the War of 1812, his ship, the *United States,* captured the British *HMS Macedonian.* He was appointed Commodore and later commanded in the Mediterranean against the corsairs of Tunis, Algiers and Tripoli with great success. In 1815, he was appointed a Navy commissioner.

By 1807, Captain James Barron, now Commodore Barron, was sailing the frigate *USS Chesapeake* out of Hampton Roads for a test as it was under repair, its cannon unmounted and its crew untrained. Just beyond the three-mile limit, the *USS Chesapeake* was hailed by the *HMS Leopard,* whose captain desired to come aboard to search for deserters. When Commodore Barron refused the request, the *Leopard* opened fire, killing three men and wounding 18, including Barron. The Commodore surrendered, the British removed the four alleged deserters, and the *Chesapeake* limped back to Norfolk.

The Navy Board investigated the incident and, in its infinite wisdom, suspended Commodore Barron for five years without pay. But this was the spark which ignited the flame of anti-British feeling, and President Jefferson issued a proclamation ordering British warships to leave U.S. territorial waters. This was followed by a British proclamation ordering a more vigorous prosecution of British subjects from neutral vessels. Then, Congress passed Jefferson's Embargo Act, which prohibited all U.S. vessels from leaving for foreign ports, and importation was severely limited by the provision that foreign vessels could not carry goods out of an American port. Norfolk was severely hurt by this act, as was New England. In the face of much opposition and widespread smuggling, Jefferson repealed the act in 1809, reopening trade with all nations except France and Great Britain.

Washington, in his plan for roads and canals during and after his

Presidency, had attempted to divert all shipping down the Mississippi to the East Coast, even though the arrangement with Spain, which held New Orleans and the territory now known as Louisiana, was satisfactory to the settlers of the lower east bank of the Mississippi. But, in 1801, Napolean had secretly persuaded Spain to cede all of this territory to him, projecting a revival of a French colonial empire in North America. Jefferson, alarmed, declared: "The day that France takes New Orleans . . . we must marry ourselves to the British fleet and nation."

James Monroe was sent to Paris to negotiate a sale of this land to the United States for a top price of $2,000,000. Napolean, after the costly failure to suppress the slave revolt in Haiti, agreed. But he outbargained Monroe, and the cost was $15,000,000. After opposition, the Senate approved the purchase, and Louisiana became the first state admitted from the territory.

Sectionalism was a constant worry during the administrations of John Adams of Massachusetts and Jefferson. Vermont was even negotiating with Great Britain to become a part of Canada, the feeling in New England was rampant from time to time that their states should be a separate country, and in the western part of the South, there was talk of secession. Only Virginia seemed to hold fast to the Union, possibly out of loyalty to their own leaders who, with the exception of John Adams, were in pretty firm control of the government.

In 1820, Amos Bronson Alcott, the New England author and educator, wrote from Norfolk, "hospitality is a distinguishing trait of the people, rich and poor," and, "their polished manners and agreeable conversation ingratiate the traveller."

But in these tense and hot-tempered times, the ancient practice of dueling became prevalent, although neither gracious nor polished.

In Virginia, Colonel Armistead Thomas Mason, who had served as a colonel of Virginia volunteers during the War of 1812, was killed in a duel with his brother-in-law, John Mason McCarty. Also, Commodore James Barron of Norfolk mortally wounded Commodore Stephen Decatur in a duel March 22, 1820. This duel was the result of a personal feud between these two men, jealousy within the ranks perhaps but it is believed that Decatur, while a Navy commissioner, influenced the harsh verdict that Barron received in the investigation of the *Chesapeake-Leopard* incident.

Commodore Stephen Decatur was not only the naval hero honored by Congress for his victory over the Barbary pirates, but he also had a

The War of 1812

spectacular career for which he was honored by the cities of New York, Baltimore, and Philadelphia with elaborate gifts of silver in appreciation of his service in that war. He was the author of a famous toast at a dinner given in his honor: "Our country! In her intercourse with foreign nations may she always be in the right; but our country, right or wrong."

The most famous duel of the time was that between the two titans of the political arena, Alexander Hamilton and Aaron Burr, on July 11, 1804. Burr was a man of overpowering ambition. He had been vice president under Jefferson, but he was defeated in his campaign for governor of New York State, mainly due to the efforts of Alexander Hamilton. Hamilton is reported to have said that Burr "was a dangerous man, and one who ought not to be trusted with the reins of government." When Burr demanded an explanation, Hamilton refused and was then challenged to meet Burr "on the field of honor." Hamilton was mortally wounded and died the next day. Although Aaron Burr, the dapper dandy, was far more popular than Alexander Hamilton, Hamilton's policies of a strong central government probably saved the nation from being fragmented by the sectionalism of the states.

Princess Anne County had its share of duels. Although ordinary men were more likely to use their fists to settle their differences, prominent men, as those above and the two below, used swords or pistols, which supposedly were outlawed.

> "11 Mar 1787—Princess Anne County Order Book
> Warrant for Nathaniel Newton and Charles Smith, who have already fought one duel today, and mean to fight another. Ordered to give bond for their good behavior."

War talk was heating up. The inhabitants of Princess Anne County had missed the peak of the tobacco boom and suffered through the depression of 1786, when farm products dropped disastrously. The cotton boom also missed them, as cotton did not grow well here, and the embargoes had further hurt them. The older people shuddered at the thought of a repetition of their sufferings in the Revolution, when they were occupied by the British. On this vulnerable point of land, wide open to sea attack from the beach, the bay and Hampton Roads, they felt like sitting ducks.

The younger men, as well aware of their exposed position as their elders, agreed with the young war hawks now in Congress that the

English and any other foreign nation should be swept from our continent. These war hawks, led by Henry Clay of Kentucky, were frontiersmen from Tennessee, Ohio and Indiana, and the Northern areas even wanted to take over Canada. Their excuse was that the British were supplying Tecumseh, the powerful chief of the Indian Confederacy, with weapons. The Southerners wanted to take Florida from Spain.

The men of Princess Anne were not particularly interested in Canada and no longer concerned themselves with Indians, but they were in agreement about the acquisition of Florida, which still belonged to Spain, England's current ally. It was the maritime and commercial issues which affected them.

In 1807, Virginia was preparing for defense by forming brigades of all the counties. William Nimmo, Jr. of Princess Anne was appointed agent for the counties of Accomac, Northampton, Princess Anne and Norfolk and the Borough of Norfolk. In all, 19 brigades were formed. "The Agents to give Bond and security for double the amount he has to collect in the District so appointed. The Governor to call upon the Attorney General to have proper Bond formed to be given by the Agents appointed to arrearage."

When James Madison became President in 1809, he was as conservative as Jefferson and as anxious to avoid war. He attempted to bargain with both France and England so that trade might be continued peaceably. When diplomacy failed, he went along with the war hawks. On June 1, 1812, he sent a message to Congress requesting a declaration of war on England, and on June 18, war was declared. France was not included in this declaration. As Henry Clay put it: "As to France we have no complaint . . . but of the past. Of England we have to complain in all tenses."

The United States was not really prepared for war. A war has to be financed, and the charter of the U.S. Bank, Alexander Hamilton's creation, had expired in 1811 and had not been renewed. Jefferson's policy of economy had reduced the army drastically, and Madison had continued this policy. Also, the states were divided on the war issue. New England was especially strong against it but they were outvoted, and this signaled the end of the power of the Federalist Party.

The plan was to attack Canada first while England was still fighting Napolean, and even Jefferson was confident that taking Canada would be easy. But the army was a shambles. Congress ordered it expanded to 35,000 men, but they were poorly commanded and untrained, and many state militiamen refused to serve outside their own boundaries. Detroit was captured by the British, and another defeat followed, only vindicated by the spectacular victory of Captain Oliver Hazard Perry with a small squadron against the British on Lake Erie. On September 10, 1813, he secured the Great Lakes and reported, "We have met the enemy and they are ours." This was followed by a land success. On October 5, General William Henry Harrison, with his Kentucky riflemen, routed the British and their Indian allies in the Battle of the Thames. Chief Tecumseh was killed, his confederacy fell apart, and the Americans had gained all territory west of the Niagara peninsula.

According to William Miller in *A New American History of the United States,* "Supported by naval ships on Lake Ontario, the Americans invaded York (now Toronto) and burned the Canadian Parliament House. Nothing more substantial came of this expedition and the attempt at conquest was a failure."

Recently, two American schooners have been discovered on the bottom of Lake Ontario. They are the *Scourge* and the *Hamilton,* missing merchant vessels converted to men-of-war and in that fleet. After 11 years of searching by Americans and Canadians with the help of the National Geographic Society, they have been located off the south shore of Lake Ontario, across from Toronto. Lying 290 feet down, they have been photographed with sophisticated technology and identified. One had been a Canadian merchant vessel captured by Americans, armed and renamed the *Scourge,* keeping the figurehead of Lord Nelson on the bow. The other, an American merchant ship originally named the *Diana,* had also been armed and was renamed the *Hamilton,* also keeping the figurehead of the beautiful goddess of the hunt. Both were in the United States fleet which succeeded in getting to Toronto, but these two never made it. A sudden violent storm had sent them to the bottom in minutes, only eight crewmen from each escaping. The pictures show the ships almost intact, with the bones of the drowned crew inside.

The story of this disaster is told by James Fennimore Cooper in *Ned Myers—A Life Before the Mast.* Ned Myers, a young, able seaman on the *Scourge* with a photographic memory, had told the graphic story of the storm and his escape to the famous writer in 1843, 30 years later. The dramatic account of the search and pictures of the find are in the March 1983 issue of the *National Geographic Magazine.*

Meanwhile, Norfolk had scurried to rebuild Fort Nelson and Fort

Norfolk, setting up guns and manning the forts with volunteers. Late in the summer of 1812, an armed schooner from Norfolk captured the British brig *Leonidas*, laden with a rich cargo of sugar and coffee. After this, a large British squadron entered the Capes and blockaded the ports of the Chesapeake Bay in February 1813. Up to this time, Norfolk's shipping had continued with little interruption. Now it was impossible to get through. According to *Norfolk, An Historic Southern Port,* by Wertenberger and Schlegel, "the British, in their anxiety to watch the main entrance to Norfolk, left the back door wide open. The produce of all southeast Virginia began to pour into Albemarle Sound, where it went out to foreign countries or further south to Wilmington or Charleston." Determined not to let any provisions fall into enemy hands, the government soon put a stop to this traffic by an embargo on ships crossing from the James River to the Elizabeth, and again Norfolk commerce ceased.

No history of Princess Anne County would be complete without the story of "The Pleasure House." Visitors driving along Shore Drive today are immediately convulsed with laughter when they spot the street sign, "Pleasure House Road." One block north, on Chesapeake Bay, was really the site of an historic tavern, so-named at least as far back as 1781, when it appears on a map made for Benedict Arnold when he was at Portsmouth. At that time, this land belonged to a Major Thorowgood, whose house is marked nearby. Perhaps this tavern was one of the projects of the formidable Sarah Thorowgood, widow of the first Adam Thorowgood, and the nearby house was the original Adam Thorowgood house. At any rate, the tavern survived the Revolution, as did the road leading to it.

In 1807, one Andrew Fife ran an ad in the Norfolk newspapers that he had rented The Pleasure House and would keep it "in such a manner as he presumes to hope will meet with the approbation of those who favor him with their company." Then, in 1811, Joel Cornick was the innkeeper and advertised that he "now keeps it as a Haven of Entertainment."

In 1812, General Robert Barraud Taylor was appointed to protect Hampton Roads, and he charged the local militia with patrolling the beach from Cape Henry to Norfolk. Surprised by a British scouting party while the soldiers were playing cards, the guardhouse was burned and the tavern damaged.

The Governor received a poor report concerning the state of military readiness at the Pleasure House, which said, "It is a suitable lounge for gamblers, tipsters, and those gentry of pleasure who love idleness, lack of discipline, and prefer convenience to their country's safety."

But military units continued to be stationed there as the war went on. One soldier wrote the following to his wife in Goochland. (These original letters are the property of The Princess Anne County Historical Society. They and two others, one from William George's wife, were found in the back of a drawer of a fine old Virginia-made secretary. The secretary had been purchased in Goochland County by Commander and Mrs. N. C. Evans at an auction, and they gave the letters to the Society.)

> "Pleasure House August 22nd 1813.
> which is about 12 miles below the City of Norfolk, and it is called the house of Pleasure but I should and I will give it the Name of Trouble and disagreeableness for it is a place where was a regiment of soldiers but a little time ago and they have left behind them both fleas and lice which to me are both disagreeable and camp companions for which I have no love or esteem, and it was the dirtiest house I have ever seen in my life.
> "I have to stay here about 8 days more to close on the enemy lines for they are about 4 (?) miles from where I am and then we ride the beach and watch their movements, and the duty is very hard, for I and all the men which are with me have to stand on Guard every night half the Knight which is very hard on us. There are 12 men with me and there is a seventy-four (?) a Schooner and a Tender in about 3 or 4 miles which looks very disagreeable and very daring to us, and bids defiance to us. In safety they ride on the waves and inhabit the watery globe in site of us and out of danger. "Oh God, I wish that we had a sufficiency of ships of the line and we would bid defiance as they do to us."

In his next letter, he writes, after flowery hopes for good health of all the family:

> "Dear Wife,
> May we the Americans prove victorius over the nation which has and are trying to make us slaves and may we conquer them and prove to them that it is in vain to fight against the sons of freedom and the cause of liberty and justice. I have just viewed the villainous—which are anchored in the Hampton Roads with a spyglass and you may be shure that it is a dredful site to behold from our shore and it does appear very dangerous if it was at an engagement.
> "I heard the beat of their drums this morning and they are in full

view of the place where I am at one of the outposts and can see them when they go out to water but cannot hurt them, but I hope that I shall not be on board of his Majesty's ships that are now in site.

"I have sent to you an emblem of my love by Furtton—a wring of Gold. . . . and that wring is without end and so is my love. . . . I hope that you will be a good girl and I do not doubt it. Therefore, I bid you a due and I remain your friend and ever affectionate friend and husband

Wm. George, Jr.
in the troop of hors under
Captain Bolling"

After this letter, William George became ill with the fever or smallpox and was moved to the hospital in Norfolk. At this time, he was more concerned in his letters with when he would be released or get a furlough, and gave his wife minute instructions as to sunning his clothes and getting new ones made. His wife, whose spelling, punctuation and writing were even worse than his, responded that she was spinning the wool for his new suit and apparently had produced a "dear little boy," whom William advised her to feed well with milk and peaches.

While in the hospital, he missed the landing of the British at Cape Henry, for he says in his letter dated October 1st: ". . . there is a fireing at Cape Henry where the British landed for the purpose of watering. We sent about 400 men there yesterday to attack them and there have to be a great fireing but the result is not known at present. A great part of the men on our side are rifle men who the British have more fear of then any others."

The "fireing at Cape Henry" came about when the British landed a company there, supposedly for watering. The leader accosted a patrol, demanding provisions. Fortunately, this was witnessed by Robert Ward of Princess Anne County, who quickly rounded up enough militia to drive them back to their ship, in spite of the militia running out of ammunition. Little damage resulted, but for 50 years, the stretch of beach from Cape Henry down was known as "The sea attack." Eventually, "Sea attack" was slurred into "Seatack" and is applied to another area west of the beach, the oldest enclave of free blacks in the City of Virginia Beach. Robert Ward received a certificate of valor (Virginia Historical Magazine):

> "This is to certify that Robert Ward has served the Virginia forces as a volunteer since 1 Jan. and that he has conducted himself as an obedient and willing soldier, hazarded his life on several dangerous

attempts with uncommon bravery, and been very active in Scouting and harassing the enemy and driving them to their shipping."

The embargo was finally lifted in April 1814, but not before the British had made an all-out attempt to capture Norfolk. After the blockading force was amplified by 2,650 troops from Bermuda, marines, Canadian chasseurs and French captives, they prepared to attack Norfolk. This, General Taylor had determined, they would not do. He had acquired and trained militia, sailors and volunteers, put up breastworks on the east side of the city and erected a fort on the east side of Craney Island, several miles down the river on the left side. The island was connected to the mainland by a foot-bridge, and on this side he threw up redoubts. In the river channel to the east, he had stationed 20 gunboats in a wide arc to Lamberts Point. On Craney Island, he posted 550 men.

On June 21, the entire British squadron moved across Hampton Roads and anchored off the mouth of the Nansemond River. At dawn the next morning, they began to land the redcoats and marines. Obviously, they meant to attack from the west, so the Americans moved their guns to that side of the island, and as the British approached, they gave them such a sizzling fire that they retreated. The battle was not over. Two long columns of 40–50 barges with marines and sailors moved from the west to the island, led by Admiral Warren's beautiful barge with a large brass cannon in the bow. As they came within range, Captain Emerson of the Americans shouted to his men: "Now, my brave boys, are you ready? FIRE!" Met by merciless fire, several barges were sunk, the others in confusion, and Admiral Warren's barge cut through. As it sank, the rest were ordered to retreat by the Admiral, who had promised his men that they could loot Norfolk for three days and have their "disposal" of all the prettiest women. As the invaders withdrew, the Virginians waded out into the water and brought in survivors as prisoners.

Captain John Hanchett, the illegitimate son of George III, was severely wounded and captured. And one of the heroes of this battle was William Flora, the free black from Portsmouth who had been the hero of the battle of Great Bridge.

Smarting under this defeat by a much smaller force, the British turned on the unprotected town of Hampton for revenge. A garrison of the militia had been posted at the plantation of Little England, just outside of town, and four guns had been placed at the waterfront, but this was not much of a defense. During the night, a British force of

2,500 moved in light vessels from Admiral Cockburn's fleet. One detachment was landed two miles out of town, while a squadron of 30–40 launches made directly for the mouth of the river.

Neither the battery in town nor the small garrison at Little England plantation could hold out. The garrison was forced to flee, and the small guns at the waterfront abandoned. Only the county clerk kept his head. When he fled the town, he had the county records with him.

The British occupied the town and it was a scene of saturnalia. While the British said that the worst deeds were done by the French captives who had been put into the British service, at least four women were raped by soldiers who spoke perfect English. The elderly were killed or mistreated, and the soldiers plundered the county so thoroughly that it is said that not one house was left with a knife or fork or piece of plate. It is thought that the British would have burned the town except for the rumor of an advancing American army, which some clever person probably started. The British then embarked in such a hurry that they left behind a large amount of ammunition and 3,000 pounds of beef. But they had already taken a large number of sheep and cattle and many slaves. Some slaves were stolen, but others, remembering Lord Dunmore's proclamation of freedom, seized the opportunity and went on board, complete with wives and children.

The people of Hampton were apparently led to believe that their property would be returned, and many went on board the ships to look for their belongings and their slaves. But they got nothing back. All thefts were blamed on the French, and although the visitors recognized many of their slaves, they could not do anything about that either.

Princess Anne expected to be next, but there were no more attacks of this sort, although the sporadic foraging raids continued. Finally, in August, most of the British fleet moved up the bay, leaving only enough ships to continue the blockade.

Admiral Cockburn's fleet had been joined by 4,000 British veterans of the war with France. Their aim was to raid Washington and Alexandria and then descend on Baltimore. After a victory over a smaller force at Bladensburg, Maryland, they marched unopposed on Washington. The panic-stricken American army fled with government officers, including President and Mrs. Madison, to Virginia. Under orders of General Robert Ross, the British soldiers on August 25 set fire to the Capitol, the White House, and most of the department buildings, as well as private homes and the newspaper office. The destruction would have been worse if a storm had not come up, compelling them to return to their camp. As it was, the estimate of damages was $1,500,000. The next day, they boarded their transports on the Patuxent, and the fleet proceeded up the Bay to Baltimore.

Now, with their Capitol burned and their President in flight, the situation had gone from desperate to hopeless. The Patriots of Princess Anne wondered what would happen to them once they were back in the hands of the British. Would they be safer in Kentucky or Ohio?

But Baltimore did not fall. During the British march on Washington, General Samuel Smith had prepared a formidable system of defense. When General Ross' army disembarked at North Point, 14 miles from Baltimore, they were met by 3,200 militia who fell back only after inflicting heavy loss on the British and killing General Ross. The fleet had moved up the Patapsco River to Fort McKenry, where 1,000 men were posted on the heights and a line of sunken hulks barred the harbor. The British bombardment was heavy but unsuccessful, only inspiring a witness, Francis Scott Key, to write "The Star Spangled Banner." The attempt to capture the city was given up, and after collecting the troops, the fleet left the Chesapeake Bay and sailed for Jamaica.

Word had filtered down to Virginia that the New England states had been supplying the British blockade with provisions, even during the embargo, and that a devious plan of the British was to annex them to Canada, which would be welcome to many of the Yankees. The national feeling, so carefully nurtured by Jefferson, was at a low ebb.

Finally, they heard that the British move to retake Niagara was turned back by Generals Jacob Brown and Winfield Scott in July 1814, that an American fleet under Captain Macdonough had won a decisive victory at Plattsburg in September, and that the British had retreated to Canada. But the animosity toward New England continued.

This will shows the effects of the general confusion and apprehension during the difficult years of adjustment to the new national laws and the ongoing troubles with Britain.

> "Will Book 3, 25 Jan 1812
> In the name of God, Amen, I, Thomas Cornick of the County of Princess Anne & State of Virginia, being of a sound and disposing mind & seeing mortality raging with such unabating violence sweeping all that is attacked & feeling some little indisposition myself, think it time that some arrangements were made respecting the manner which I wish my property divided.

> To my son, Joel Barlow, at age 21, I give the plantation whereon I now live, also 6 slaves & increase. The balance of slaves to be divided among my 3 children: Eliza Walke Cornick, Thomas Keeling Cornick & Mary Woodhouse Cornick.
>
> Executors: My brother Adam Cornick, my friend Lemuel Cornick & my friend Arthur Sayer Woodhouse."

Then, the wonderful news came of General Andrew Jackson's amazing victory at New Orleans January 8, 1815. Jackson had been made commander of the Mobile-New Orleans area and the U.S. Army in the Southwest. He captured and destroyed Pensacola in Spanish Florida to prevent its being used as a British base and then marched through Mobile to New Orleans. The British Admiral Cockburn had set sail from Jamaica with 8,000 men. "It took him a week to unload them, and Jackson was ready with his army composed of pirates, government forces, and the French-speaking militia. In five minutes Jackson inflicted 2,036 casualties and sustained only 21. The crippled British army retreated in haste. The Battle of New Orleans made Andrew Jackson the most popular American hero since George Washington." (*An American History*, Rebecca Brooks Gruver.)

In those days of slow communication, Jackson did not know that the peace treaty had already been signed, at Ghent on December 24, 1814. It was probably the most unsatisfactory peace treaty ever composed, as it was more of a truce than a treaty. Nothing at all was said about impressment, the issue over which the United States had gone to war. Nothing was said about neutral rights, boundaries, fisheries or compensation to the United States for shipping losses. John Quincy Adams, of the peace commission, said, "Nothing was adjusted, nothing was settled, nothing in substance but an indefinite suspension of hostilities." But the Americans were jubilant: "Not one inch of territory ceded or lost," and "not one of our rights surrendered."

While the Treaty of Ghent seemed to accomplish nothing, it really accomplished a great deal. The joy of the people that they had "licked the British twice" restored a feeling of national pride. The British were gone, the Indian Confederacy under Tecumseh was crushed, and the area east of the Mississippi was opened to rapid settlement by frontier farmers. American manufacturing, started during the embargo in New England, had made the country prosperous. Diplomats continued to negotiate with good results. Both Canada and the United States promised to demilitarize its side of the Great Lakes, banned all discriminatory duties on each other's commerce, and reopened the Newfoundland fisheries to Americans. America could now take its place with honor in the family of nations, so the American people could turn their backs on Europe and tend to domestic concerns.

In 1816, James Monroe was elected President, assuring the continuation of "the Virginia dynasty." The waning strength of the Federalists, coupled with their popular discredit during the war years, had given Monroe an overwhelming victory. His tour of the Eastern Seaboard and the West moved even the Boston paper to call the times "an era of good feelings."

PART FIVE
Chapter 3
SETTLING DOWN

While Norfolk fumed over the restrictions of her trade with the West Indies after the war, Princess Anne County quickly relaxed into the old ways. Still a close-knit, rural community with little interest in the outside world, the people here adjusted to their own social and economic changes resulting from the two wars for independence. Members of the former upper class had ceased to exist as leaders. Their places were taken by the more energetic young men of the rising middle class. Many of the great plantations were broken up as their owners sold out and moved to the city, or to Kentucky or Tennessee, and farming for subsistance was the rule. Agriculture had always been almost a "sacred calling," and industry did not concern them.

In 1810, the assistant marshals who took the census were required by law to take an account of the several manufacturing establishments within their several divisions. The one taking the census in Princess Anne County reported:

> "With few exceptions, every household employs a common weaving loom, and almost without exception, every family tans their own leather. No machines of a peculiar kind are used or belong to the county. The materials for clothing are raised and consumed by its inhabitants. The quantity is near as may be to 26 yds. for each person. The weaving with few exceptions is performed by females. There are about three female weavers to every loom."

The population of Norfolk had rapidly increased, and seeing the demand there for their produce, the Princess Anne farmers began truck farming, taking their fruits and vegetables to the City Market in small boats. Soon they were sending North their winter vegetables—such as spinach, kale and cabbage—as well as root vegetables whenever they could load them on a boat. Cattle raising dwindled at this time, as they were no longer allowed to winter them in the marshes, and hog raising became more popular and more profitable.

The number of slaves decreased as they were sold to the "cotton states" or freed. Although many of the free blacks left for the city, the number of free black land owners here was increasing, according to the Land Tax lists. There is no estimate of the total of free blacks at that time in Princess Anne County, but in Hening's *Statutes at Large*, there are estimates for the whole state of Virginia: in 1782, there were 20,000 freedmen: in 1790, there were 12,866: in 1800, 20,124: and in 1820, 30,570. Princess Anne had its share but not as many as Norfolk, where the free blacks were mostly laborers without land. Some free blacks owning land in this county listed in the Land Tax Records were William Shepherd, James Owen, Jesse Whitehurst, George Cuffy, Mary Jones, Aaron Haynes, George Lewis, George Valentine, Demce Anderson, Marshall Anderson, Isaac Anderson and William and James Dawley, who had been freed by the Methodist minister, the Reverand Mr. Dawley.

This increase was due to the number of blacks from this county who had fought in the Revolution. If free, they were given land for service of three years. If slave, they were given freedom and $50. Either way, they had back pay and with money in their pockets, they could buy land. Some whites, impoverished by the war, were only too happy to sell them fifty acres, or less.

This was not true in richer counties where the planters were reluctant to sell to them, through fear of these newly freed slaves stirring up trouble among those still in bondage. In 1814 Emanuel Fentress, a bachelor, freed his three slaves, Litty, Chloe and Daniel, in his will, and left all of his property to be divided between them. The old law that emancipation of a slave, by will or otherwise, had to be approved by the Legislature still held, and these three were denied both freedom and property. This cruelty was a far cry from the 17th century when it was a common practice to free slaves in wills, and also leave them property of some sort. Between 1637 and 1710 at least five slaves were freed in wills of different owners. The rejection of this will was a burden on the white men's conscience here, but with their pity was beginning a fear of reprisal.

The newspapers at this time show no advertisements for runaway slaves from Princess Anne County. The troublesome ones were the first to be sold to the cotton belt, and to most slaves, the threat of being "sold down the river" was usually enough to keep them in line. Clement Eaton says, in *Flight and Rebellion*, "The paramount evil of southern slavery was not that the slaves were mistreated, but they were deprived of opportunity." A law was passed in Virginia in 1819 prohibiting the teaching of Negroes. But, true to their custom of ignoring laws when they chose, the whites here usually taught the blacks anyway, the daughters of the household teaching them reading, writing and simple arithmetic, and skills were picked up by the men as they worked with their masters.

In 1811, an event occurred in Richmond, only 11 years after the Gabriel Revolt, which was unfortunately not circulated in Northern newspapers. A fire broke out in a theatre while a performance was going on. It spread rapidly and the stairs were impassable. Dr. James Drew McCaw, one of the audience, spied a large black man walking along the street below. Calling to him to help, Dr. McCaw proceeded to drop some of the ladies out of the window, one by one, into the arms of this man. He was Gilbert Hunt, a free black, and he saved many lives by his heroic assistance. Most of the audience perished in this disastrous blaze, but the city of Richmond rewarded Gilbert Hunt handsomely for his unselfish courage.

Another social disappointment was the rejection of a petition to the Legislature in 1811, signed by 235 prominent citizens of the county, to establish an academy by raising the necessary money with a lottery. This too was denied.

Only one event of international importance occurred in Princess Anne County during this time, and that was the building of the lighthouse at Cape Henry. Still standing high on a dune overlooking the entrance to the Chesapeake Bay, it is the oldest public building in the county. The foundation was laid August 8, 1791, amid much fanfare, and it was completed in 1792.

The question is, why was a lighthouse not built here before? The Boston Light was erected in 1716 by the city of Boston, where there were landmarks which could be seen for miles. Here, the two capes, Cape Henry and Cape Charles, 17 miles apart, are almost identical flat, sandy stretches. The constantly shifting shoals were always a menace to ships, even to the shallow-draft vessels of colonial times. There was a great deal of traffic going in and out during "The Golden Age," and even skilled native pilots had difficulty finding a safe channel.

In 1690, Governor Francis Nicholson had ordered the militia under Major Argall Thorowgood to patrol the beach constantly to watch for the approach of any enemy ship, mainly pirates at that time. On the approach of a friendly ship, they sometimes set a beacon, a brazier on the highest dune containing wood or coal fires. But this was hardly enough and many ships ran aground.

In 1720, Governor Spotswood had petitioned the House of Burgesses for a lighthouse at Cape Henry. An act was passed to build one, provided the Province of Maryland would contribute. Maryland declined and nothing came of the project.

In 1727, Governor Gooch tried again, but for some reason the project was defeated by vote of the House.

In 1773, William Byrd drew plans for a lighthouse here and acquired estimates for the necessary sandstone from quarries on the Potomac and Rappahannock. This time the House agreed, and the sandstone was delivered in 1775. Due to the war, nothing further was done and plans were abandoned.

By 1782, the stone had sunk into the sand, some to the depth of 40 feet, and could not be recovered. An interim measure was ordered by the Council of State of the Commonwealth to erect a pole 50 feet high topped by a white flag striped with red, and at night, a proper light was to be kept burning when there was no enemy approaching. If an enemy was detected, the fire was to be extinguished. Obviously, this was ineffectual, and it seemed a ridiculous idea in the first place.

After the war, when the national government took over construction of lighthouses, a contract was finally signed by Alexander Hamilton, Secretary of the Treasury, allocating funds. This was the first contract for the construction of a lighthouse entered into by the federal government. It included a house for the keeper and a storage shed for the fish oil to be used for the lantern. Some of the original sandstone was recovered and used for the foundation. More was sent for, and the lighthouse was finally completed. When the two acres of land had been ceded to the United States government by the state of Virginia in 1791, the deed provided that the lighthouse was to be completed within seven years and that in no way should the fishermen there be incommoded. In general, the people of the county did not care much about the lighthouse one way or another, but the fishermen complained that the light frightened the fish away!

The first lighthouse keeper was Laban Goffigan of Norfolk, and under succeeding keepers, the lighthouse continued in operation until 1896. Then, a more modern one was built close by, operated by electricity and still in use.

The old one, a truly magnificent structure, was then deeded by the government to the Association for the Preservation of Virginia Antiquities. It is currently on loan from them to the City of Virginia Beach on condition that the city maintain it. This old landmark has seen better days, but it still stands proudly near the cross, which marks the first landing of English settlers on this continent, and near the bronze figure of the Comte de Grasse, whose help insured the victory at Yorktown.

Concerned that this lighthouse was not sufficient for navigation, Congress appropriated money in 1819 for a light vessel of 70 tons to be placed off Willoughby Spit near Norfolk. The small ship was completed in 1820, but it was too light for the choppy waters off the spit and in a few months was moved to Craney Island. This lightship carried two lanterns, and at first the keepers were nearby farmers. They would row out at night to light the lanterns, returning the next morning to douse them.

Soon, more lightships were built and positioned all over the bay at the entrance to harbors and rivers. Once there were 50 in the American fleet, but they were rapidly replaced by lighthouses. It was a lonely life for the men on these small ships and often dangerous in a storm since they had no engines. Virginia's last lightship, the *Chesapeake*, was replaced in 1965. The only one now operating is the *Nantucket*, standing off the rugged coast of Massachusetts and manned by the United States Coast Guard.

But the lighthouse and the lightships came too late. After the War of 1812, Virginia was losing its influence. Thousands of the state's ablest and most adventurous citizens were leaving the lands exhausted by tobacco for the newly developed South and West. A public school system had not been established, and illiteracy was high. A French historian, Jean Gottman, attributed the "failure of Virginians to maintain their eighteenth century leadership in the nation was to a large extent due to the feeble numbers of their educated elite."

In the legislature, there was not only sectionalism between the older eastern counties and those of the west, but rivalry between the eastern cities of Richmond, Petersburg, Fredericksburg, Alexandria and Norfolk. When they finally woke up to the fact that New York was getting the largest share of the import-export business and the cotton states were shipping directly from Charleston and New Orleans, it was too late. Virginia had not grasped the significance of the new era of transportation. Halfway measures were attempted, in short railroads and canals, but they were mismanaged, costly and failures.

The other river towns had been jealous of Norfolk's prosperity through the colonial period, and they would not consent to help finance a railway from Norfolk west. Instead, Norfolk built the Dismal Swamp Canal, too narrow and too shallow. Only small ships could get through. Then, at Norfolk, the cargo had to be transferred to larger coastwise ships to go to New York, where it was transferred again to the new, larger and faster oceangoing vessels which Norfolk had neglected to build. No wonder Norfolk was bypassed. In Wertenberger's *History of Norfolk,* he says, "Norfolk never realized its potential in the years after the War of 1812. This city had reigned supreme as the top port for commerce on the east coast. Now it sank into despondency as the Erie Canal provided New York with access to and from the west, and Baltimore built the B & O Railroad with the same purpose."

Princess Anne County was sympathetic, for the people here shared with Norfolk an aversion to change and a distrust of "progress." Always rather narrow in their viewpoint, the county now withdrew even more into itself. Barter continued to be, as before, the common method of trade because it was the most practical method of doing business at that time when money was scarce and of uncertain value.

Bishop Meade, of the Protestant Episcopal Church, writing in 1830 says, "In those days this immediate section (Princess Anne County) was noted for the best society in Virginia. The families were interesting, hospitable, given to visiting and social pleasures." He goes on to condemn the drinking, horse racing and card playing, but his hosts were the remnants of the leading families of the extinct Church of England, who had always indulged in these pastimes and continued to do so. However, the majority of the people then had become Methodists or Baptists who, while they adhered more strictly to the rules of conduct laid down by their churches, were not averse to having a good time.

Bishop Meade also said, "In no part of Virginia has the destruction of all that is old been greater." If he was speaking of the old Church of England edifices, that is true. The new Protestant Episcopal Church was having a hard time keeping alive, and many of the old buildings had fallen into ruin or had been demolished.

The most important event to the people of Princess Anne County at this time was the removal of the county seat from Kempsville to the small town of Princess Anne. In response to a petition to the legislature of the state to remove the courthouse to a site nearer the geographic and population center of the county, Princess Anne was selected in 1820, and construction of a new courthouse, jail and other facilities was authorized. Construction began and on December 3, 1922 court was held for the first time in this beautiful building. Carefully preserved and still in use, it stands majestically on a small rise in the center of the town, commanding a huge modern complex of municipal buildings in the same colonial style. There is a proud and serene sense of the past here, and a calm acceptance of the changes it has seen in 161 years.

On land not used then for the building was once a tavern and a green, so important in the early days, but no more. Court is only serious business now.

Yet, through the turbulence of the two wars and the confusing creation of the new government, the essential character of the people of Princess Anne County had not changed. Few of the large middle class had immigrated to other parts. The love of the land still predominated, and other uses were found for it. It was "nice" that the country still had a Virginian as President, but they took no part in the controversies swirling in the Congress and the state legislature. At last, they had churches sympathetic to their needs, and they put their troubles during the two wars behind them. As a community, they grew closer together, and worried little about the increasing problem of slavery. Here, as one present day black put it, "We needed each other, and we helped each other." Contented with their lot in life, and indifferent to class distinctions, it was a peaceful, quiet time.

APPENDIX 1

COUNTY GOVERNMENT

A further explanatory note concerning the government of the county appears to be in order. The justices of the court, Justices of the Peace, as they were called, collectively constituted the county courts, exercising important executive and legislative powers in addition to the judicial responsibility, for more than two hundred years. Also, in the colonial period, there were three other offices with important duties and carrying influence as well as prestige.

The sheriff was very important to the administration of the law. He was appointed by the governor from a list of candidates submitted by the justices at first, and in 1661 the Assembly directed that one of the members of the court should be sheriff on a rotating one-year basis. He was the law enforcement official; pursuing fugitives, arresting offenders, caring for prisoners, and executing orders and sentences of the courts, the Assembly, and the King. He was also the finance official, collecting quit rents, poll taxes, and the parish levy fixed by the vestry for support of the church, the sick and the poor. He received a collection fee of from 4–6%. Unfortunately, there were many abuses of this power and in the 1776 Constitution tax commissioners were appointed for each precinct.

The sheriff was also in charge of the management of elections for the county's two seats in the House of Burgesses. When notified by the governor, he set the date and time for the election on a future court day, posted notices and directed ministers to announce the date and time. He presided over the election, certifying the outcome to the colonial secretary's office. This duty was also abolished in 1818 when the General Assembly created election commissioners.

The Clerk of the Court was also a prestigious office with many duties. At first appointed by the county court, by 1700 the appointment was made by the colonial secretary until the Revolution and he characteristically came from a distinguished family and had a long tenure. In a time when so many except for the elite could neither read nor write this was a natural choice, since he kept all minutes of court proceedings, filed all documents, prepared the docket, probated all wills and issued writs, summons, and processes. He was the preserver of all records, and registered deeds, wills, contracts, liens, etc., as well as registering all vital statistics. By 1670 he issued marriage licenses for which he received a fee in addition to his salary. After the Revolution, the appointment of the clerk of the court was returned to the county court and he was to hold office during his good behavior as determined by the State General Court.

The third important office was that of King's attorney at first appointed by the colonial attorney general, and in the 18th century by the governor. This office was the forerunner of the Commonwealth's Attorney, appointed by the county court in the early 19th century, but the 1851 Constitution provided that he be elected by the voters for a four year term.

Most of this information is from an article, "Virginia's Local Executive and Constitutional Officers in Historical Perspective," by Stanley A. Cook. *University of Virginia Newsletter,* September, 1981.

A list of those who held the office of Clerk of the Court for Princess Anne County follows. It bears out the conclusion that the people here were generally satisfied with their officials and saw no reason to change. George Savage probably died.

Patrick Angus	1691–1700	9 years
Christopher Cocke	1700–1716	16 years
Charles Sayer	1716–1740	24 years
Arthur Sayer	1740–1761	21 years
Robert Ballard	1761–1770	9 years
George Savage	1770–1771	1 year
E. H. Moseley, Jr.	1771–1814	43 years
William T. Nimmo	1814–1821	7 years
John J. Burroughs	1821–1869	48 years

When Princess Anne County was formed in 1691 county government for all the colonial counties had already been established.

The Burgesses, who were the elected representatives of each county to the House of Burgesses in Williamsburg whenever the governor called for an election, were two from this county, although sometimes only one attended the sessions. They were:

Appendix I 277

1691–1692. Malachy Thruston and John Richardson
1692–1693. Jacob Johnson
(no election from 1693–1695)
1695–1696. Benoni Burroughs and John Thorowgood
1691–1697. Benoni Burroughs and John Thorowgood
1698. Benoni Burroughs and John Thorowgood
1699. Benoni Burroughs and John Thorowgood
1700–1702. John Thorowgood and Edward Moseley
1702–1705. Adam Thorowgood and Edward Moseley
1705–1706. Adam Thorowgood and Edward Moseley
(no election 1705–1710)
1710–1712. Maximillian Boush and Henry Spratt
1712–1714. Maximillian Boush and Thomas Walke
1715. Maximillian Boush and Horatio Woodhouse
1718. Maximillian Boush and Horatio Woodhouse
1720–1722. Maximillian Boush and Anthony Walke
1723–1726. Maximillian Boush and Henry Spratt
1727–1734. _____ Land and Anthony Walke
1734–1740. Anthony Walke and Jacob Ellegood
1742–1747. Anthony Walke and Jacob Ellegood
1748–1749. Anthony Walke and Jacob Ellegood
(election 1749–1752)
1752–1758. Thomas Walke and William Keeling
1760. Thomas Walke and Anthony Walke, Jr.
1761. Anthony Walke and Edward Hack Moseley
1762. Anthony Walke and Edward Hack Moseley
1763. Anthony Walke and Edward Hack Moseley
1764. Anthony Walke and Edward Hack Moseley
1765. Anthony Walke and Edward Hack Moseley
1766. Robert Ballard and Edward Hack Moseley
1768. Robert Ballard and Edward Hack Moseley
1769. John Ackiss and Edward Hack Moseley
1770. John Ackiss and Edward Hack Moseley
1771. John Ackiss and Edward Hack Moseley
1772. Christopher Wright and Edward Hack Moseley, Jr.
1773. Christopher Wright and Edward Hack Moseley, Jr.
1774. Christopher Wright and Edward Hack Moseley, Jr.
1775. Christopher Wright and William Robinson

APPENDIX 2

HOUSES AND BUILDINGS BUILT BEFORE 1824 STILL STANDING

The following list is for quick reference, including those already described and others which we know little about, or which have been remodeled for other uses.

Houses—17th century

Thomas Allen House, circa 1636. Once a one-room house. A later house built around it. Privately owned.
Adam Thorowgood House, 1636–1640. Owned by the City of Norfolk. Now spelled "Thoroughgood". Open to the public. 1636 Parish Road.
John Stratton House, circa 1650. Small 2-story house behind larger 18th century "Green Hill Farm".
John Weblin House circa 1670. Much the same as when built. Privately owned.
Thomas Keeling House—1680. Fine house elegantly restored. Privately owned.

Houses—18th century

The Hermitage circa 1700. Believed built by John Thorowgood, grandson of Adam Thorowgood. Privately owned.
Carraway House—1713. Built by William Carraway. Restored, now an antique shop. Open every day except Wednesday. 317 S. Witchduck Road.
Wolf's Snare Plantation—1715. Part of original Keeling grant of 1636. Being restored by present owners.
Lynnhaven House, 1725–1730. Owned and restored by The Association for the Preservation of Virginia Antiquities. Open to the

public Wednesday through Sunday, April–Dec. 24th. Activities and tours. Wishart Road.

Francis Land House—1732. Owned by City of Virginia Beach. Hopefully soon open to public. Virginia Beach Boulevard.

Richard Murray House—1736, according to brick in chimney. Privately owned.

Upper Wolfsnare—1759. Built by Thomas Walke III. Owned by Princess Anne County Historical Society. Open to public every Wednesday April through September.

Poplar Hall—1760. Thought to have been built by Thurmer Hoggard. Beautiful house and grounds overlooking Broad Creek. Privately owned.

Jonathan Woodhouse House—1760. Date and "W W P" incised in brick on outside wall. Privately owned.

Pembroke Manor—1764. Home of John Saunders, the Loyalist in the Revolution. Built by his grandfather Jonathan Saunders. Owned by Princess Anne County Historical Society. Under restoration.

Henry T. Cornick House—1765. Built by him or one of the Woodhouse family, who owned it later. Privately owned.

John Biddle House—1765. Charming small house, much the same as when built. Privately owned.

Anthony Fentress House, circa 1765. Interesting saltbox type. rare in this area. Privately owned.

Broad Bay Manor—1770. Built by Lemuel Cornick. Beautiful. Privately owned.

Ferry Farm, 1779. Built by William Walke, son of Anthony. Privately owned.

Pleasant Hall—1779. Georgian. Beautiful woodwork in interior. Built either by Peter Singleton in that year or earlier by George Logan, with two wings east and west. Privately owned.

John Forrest House—1785. Later purchased by Henry B. Woodhouse, a general in War of 1812. His gravestone nearby. Now a business office.

J. A. Fentress House—1789. Another small saltbox, unrestored. Privately owned.

Thomas Lovett House—1790. Known as "Peter's House". On a small rise with a long driveway. Half clapboard, half brick. Privately owned.

William Nimmo House—1790. Exterior hardly changed since built. William's wife Anne gave land for Nimmo Methodist Church. Privately owned.

Green Hill Farm—1791. Built by Lancaster Lovett. Exceptional interior. Privately owned.

Thomas Murray House—1791. Son of Richard Murray. Privately owned. Restored.

Edward James House—1793. Added to and renovated, but interior much the same. Graveyard. Privately owned.

> *Reuben Lovett House*—1793. Built by Reuben Lovett or by Daniel Whitehurst. Originally frame, now bricked over. Privately owned.
> *James-Bell House*, circa 1815. Now owned by United States Government and used as residence for commanding officer Oceana Air Base. Restored. Magnificent.

Most old houses are said to have a resident ghost, and there certainly is a strong sense of the past in all of them. But in only four has a ghost actually been seen. In the Weblin House, the Biddle House, and Upper Wolfsnare "he" is in colonial dress, and in the Reuben Lovett House "he" is a veteran of the War Between the States and has a long white beard. This one has only been seen by children.

Buildings

> *Old Donation Church*—1736. The third Lynnhaven Parish Church. Burned in 1822, rebuilt 1911. Gravestones of Walkes, Saunders, and others of the 18th century. Anglican, after Revolution Episcopalian. Witchduck Road.
> *Nimmo Methodist Church*—1791. Oldest Methodist Church in continuous use in Virginia. Extensive remodeling, but gated pews and slave gallery (now choir gallery) remain. Oceana Boulevard at Princess Anne Road.
> *Old Lighthouse*—1791. Owned by Association for Preservation of Virginia Antiquities. Open to public. In continuous use until 1821, when new one was built. On army base of Fort Story at Cape Henry.
> *Old Courthouse*—1821. Center of town of Princess Anne at Princess Anne and North Landing Road. Open to public.

BIBLIOGRAPHY

Extensive reading was involved in the compiling of this volume. Listed here are the sources quoted or referred to in the preceding text. Also included are sources found most helpful in understanding life in these years.

For brevity, the following abbreviations are used to show where most of these sources may be found locally:

> R.R.—Reference Room, Bayside Library, Virginia Beach
> S.R.—Sargeant Room, Kirn Library, Norfolk

PRIMARY SOURCES

LOWER NORFOLK COUNTY RECORDS, Deed Room, Office of the Clerk of the Circuit Court, Great Bridge, Chesapeake, Va.

NORFOLK COUNTY RECORDS, Earliest at Great Bridge, later ones in Norfolk, Office of the Clerk of the Circuit Court

PRINCESS ANNE COUNTY RECORDS 1691–1963, Deed Room, Office of the Clerk of the Circuit Court, Princess Anne Va. Anything after 1963 listed under VIRGINIA BEACH.

PRINCESS ANNE COUNTY LEGISLATIVE PETITIONS 1670–1861, Virginia State Library Archives, Richmond.

PAPERS OF JOHN SAUNDERS, Public Library, Frederickton, New Brunswick, Canada, and private collections of descendants. Some copies of originals in R.R.

STATUTES AT LARGE, BEING ALL THE LAWS ENACTED BY THE HOUSE OF BURGESSES, William Waller Hening, Vo. 1 missing in R.R., all in S.R. Also SUPPLEMENT. University Press, Charlottesville.

VIRGINIA JOURNALS OF THE HOUSE OF BURGESSES, 13 vol. R.R. Virginia State Library, Richmond. R.R.

CALENDAR OF STATE PAPERS 1632–1786. R.R. Virginia State Library Archives, Richmond. R.R.

JOURNALS OF THE COUNCIL OF STATE, 3 vol. R.R. Virginia State Library, Richmond, R.R.

CAVALIERS AND PIONEERS, Abstracts of Virginia Land Patents and Grants, 1623–1732. Nell Marion Nugent. R.R. Genealogical Publishing Company, Baltimore, Md. R.R.

RECORDS OF THE VIRGINIA COMPANY OF LONDON 1619–1626. 4 vol. R.R. Library of Congress, Washington, D.C.R.R.

TRACTS AND OTHER PAPERS RELATING PRINCIPALLY TO THE ORIGIN, SETTLEMENT, AND PROGRESS OF THE COLONIES IN NORTH AMERICA. Collected and printed by Peter Force, Washington, D.C. 1836–1837. American Archives, 4th series. R.R. has some, complete series in Swem Library, Williamsburg.

Appendix II

ARCHAEOLOGICAL REPORTS

ADAM THOROWGOOD SITE. Artifacts found by Floyd Painter. Virginia Center for Archaeology, Yorktown, Virginia.

NEWTOWN. An Archaeological and Historical Survey of the Cultural Resources at Newtown, Norfolk, Va. Circa 1741. Martha McCartney 1979. Virginia Research Center for Archaeology.

UPPER WOLFSNARE. Report of archaeological findings by Dr. William Kelso, and Dr. Norman Barca at Thomas Walke house, circa 1759. Both reports at R.R. and at Virginia Archaeological Center.

EARLY NEWSPAPERS

VIRGINIA GAZETTE. Originals in Virginia Historical Society Archives, Richmond. 1737–1755. Microfilm in R.R., plus 1765 & 1766. Photostats in S.R.

NORFOLK AND PORTSMOUTH HERALD AND GENERAL ADVERTISER. Microfilm R.R. Photostats S.R.

NORFOLK WEEKLY HOURNAL & COUNTY INTELLIGENCER. S.R. film

NORFOLK GAZETTE. S.R.

UNPUBLISHED THESES

Bogger, Dr. Tommy, THE SLAVE AND THE FREE BLACK COMMUNITY IN NORFOLK 1775–1865. University of Virginia, Charlottesville.

Donavan, Ken, THE MILITARY CAREER OF JOHN SAUNDERS, 1776–1782. R.R.

Hughes, Sarah. S. ELIZABETH CITY COUNTY, VIRGINIA 1782–1810. William & Mary College, Williamsburg, Va.

Nadelholf, Jerome, THE SOMERSET CASE AND SLAVERY. Published only in the Journal of Negro History, vol. LI, Old Dominion University, Norfolk

Zimmer, Carmeline V. SELECTED LETTERS FROM THE PARKER FAMILY PAPERS. (Complete papers on film, Old Dominion University, Norfolk.

Appendix II 283

MAGAZINES AND PERIODICALS

Swem, Earl Gregg, HISTORICAL INDEX (A COMPREHENSIVE INDEX OF NAMES AND LOCALES IN THE FOLLOWING MAGAZINES) R.R. S.R. 350 Anniversary Celebration, Williamsburg. These are on file in R.R. and in bound volumes in S.R. R.R.
VIRGINIA CAVALCADE, Virginia State Library, Richmond
VIRGINIA MAGAZINE OF HISTORY AND BIOGRAPHY, County Publishing Co. Middleburg, Va.
VIRGINIA HISTORICAL MAGAZINE OF HISTORY AND BIOGRAPHY, Virginia Historical Society, Richmond
TYLER'S QUARTERLY, AN HISTORICAL AND GENEALOGICAL MAGAZINE, Whittet & Shepperson, Richmond
WILLIAM AND MARY COLLEGE QUARTERLY HISTORICAL MAGAZINE, WILLIAMSBURG, S.R.
THE CHESOPEAN, A JOURNAL OF NORTH AMERICAN ARCHAEOLOGY, Floyd Painter, ed. Norfolk

CONTEMPORARY WRITINGS, ORIGINAL PRINTS & REPRINTS

Beverley, Robert, HISTORY AND PRESENT STATE OF VIRGINIA. Dominio Books, University Press, Charlottesville, Va.
Burnaby, Rev. Andrew, A.M. TRAVELS THROUGH THE MIDDLE SETTLEMENTS IN NORTH AMERICA IN THE YEARS 1759-1760. Cornell University Press, Ithaca, N.Y.
Byrd, William, THE SECRET DIARY OF WILLIAM BYRD OF WESTOVER. Translated from the shorthand and edited by Lewis B. Wright and Marion B. Tinling, Dietz Press, Richmond
Fithian, Philip Vickers, JOURNALS AND LETTERS OF PHILIP VICKERS FITHIAN, ed. Hunter Dickinson Farish, University Press, Charlottesville, Va. R.R.
Fleet, Beverly, VIRGINIA COLONIAL ABSTRACTS, 31 vols. Lower Norfolk County 1651-1654. Dominion Books, University Press, Charlottesville. S.R.
THE FEDERALIST PAPERS, by Alexander Hamilton, James Madison & John Jay. Ed. and reprinted by Clinton Rossiter, New American Library, New York 1961

Hawke- David Freeman, CAPTAIN JOHN SMITH'S HISTORY OF VIRGINIA. Bobbs, Merrill, Indianapolis 1970. R.R.

Hamor, Ralph, A TRUE DISCOURSE ON THE PRESENT STATE OF VIRGINIA. Reprinted from London edition of 1615, with introduction by A. L. Rowse, Virginia State Library, Richmond.

Hotten, John Camden, ed. ORIGINAL LISTS OF PERSONS OF QUALITY 1600-1700. Genealogical Publishing Co., Baltimore, Md. R.R.

Jefferson, Thomas, NOTES ON THE STATE OF VIRGINIA. Library of Congress. Washington, W.W. Norton Co., New York. 1980

Jones, Hugh, THE PRESENT STATE OF VIRGINIA. Virginia Historical Society, Richmond. University of North Carolina Press, Chapel Hill 1956.

Percy, George, A DISCOURSE ON THE PLANTATION OF THE SOUTHERN COLONY OF VIRGINIA (abstracted). University of Virginia Press, Charlottesville 1967.

Sams, C. Whittle, THE CONQUEST OF VIRGINIA, THE FOREST PRIMEVAL. Reprint Co. Spartanburg, S.C. R.R.

Strachey, William, THE HISTORIE OF TRAVAILE INTO VIRGINIA BRITANNICA 1612. ed. R. H. Major, Hakluyt Society Publication VI, London 1849.

Vaughan, Alden T., AMERICAN GENESIS, CAPTAIN JOHN SMITH AND THE FOUNDING OF VIRGINIA. ed. O car Handlin, Little, Brown & Co. Boston 1975

White, John, THE NEW WORLD. The First Pictures of America, ed. Jacques LeMoyne, engraved by Theodore deBry. ed. and annoted by Stefan Lorant. Duell, Sloan & Pierce 1940.

BOOKS

Ames, Susie E. READING, WRITING AND ARITHMETIC IN VIRGINIA 1607-1699. 350th Anniversary Corp. Williamsburg 1957

Billings, Warren M. THE OLD DOMINION IN THE SEVENTEENTH CENTURY. A DOCUMENTARY HISTORY OF VIRGINIA. University of North Carolina Press, Chapel Hill 1975. R.R.

Bliss, William Root, SIDE GLIMPSES FROM THE COLONIAL MEETING HOUSES, Gale Research Co., Detroit, Mich. R.R.

Brown, Alexander Crosby, CHESAPEAKE LANDFALLS. Norfolk County Historical Society of Chesapeake, c/o Chesapeake Library Great Bridge, Va. R.R.

Brown, Robert Eldon & B. Katherine, VIRGINIA 1705-1786, DEMOCRACY OR ARISTOCRACY? Old Dominion University Library, Norfolk. Michigan State University Press, East Lansing, Mich. 1964.

Bruce, Philip Alexander, ECONOMIC HISTORY OF VIRGINIA IN THE SEVENTEENTH CENTURY. Corner House Publishing Co, Williamstown, Mass. 1968. R.R.

———, SOCIAL LIFE IN VIRGINIA IN THE SEVENTEENTH CENTURY. Corner House Publishing Co. Williamstown, Mass. R.R.

Brumbaugh, Gaius Marcus, REVOLUTIONARY WAR RECORDS. Genealogical Publishing Co., Baltimore. R.R.

Burgess, Louis Alexander, ed. VIRGINIA SOLDIERS OF 1776. Reprint Co. Spartanburg, S.C. R.R.

Cometti, Elizabeth, SOCIAL LIFE IN VIRGINIA DURING THE WAR FOR INDEPENDENCE. Virginia independence Bicentenniel Commission, Box JF, Williamsburg, 1978

Craven, Wesley Frank, RED, WHITE AND BLACK, W.W. Norton Co. New York 1971

Creecy, John Harvie, ed. VIRGINIA ANTIQUARY, Vol. 1. PRINCESS ANNE COUNTY LOOSE PAPERS 1700-1789. Dietz Press, Richmond. R.R.

Cross, Charles B., Jr. & Eleanor, FROM THE ARCHIVES. Norfolk County Historical Society of Chesapeake, c/o Chesapeake Library, Great Bridge, Va. 1974

———, MEMOIRS OF HELEN CALVERT MAXWELL. Norfolk County Historical Society of Chesapeake, etc. R.R.

Crow, Jeffery L. and Tise, Larry E., eds. THE SOUTHERN EXPERIENCE IN THE AMERICAN REVOLUTION. University of North Carolina Press, Chapel Hill, N.C. 1978

Dabney, Virginius, VIRGINIA, THE NEW DOMINION. Doubleday & Co. Garden City, N.Y. 1921. R.R.

Dann, John C. ed. THE REVOLUTION REMEMBERED, EYE WITNESS ACCOUNTS OF THE WAR FOR INDEPENDENCE. University of Chicago Press, ©1980. pp. 240-250

Earle, Alice Morse, CUSTOMS AND FASHIONS IN OLD NEW ENGLAND. Kempsville Library, Va. Beach. Singing Tree Press, Detroit.

Appendix II

Eckenrode, M.J. THE REVOLUTION IN VIRGINIA. Genealogical Publishing Co., Baltimore S.R.
———, HISTORICAL REGISTER OF VIRGINIANS IN THE REVOLUTION. 1775–1783. Genealogical Publishing Co., Baltimore. R.R.
Eigmey, Kathleen, THE BEACH, City of Virginia Beach Department of Libraries, R.R.
Fowler, William N. Jr. REBELS UNDER SAIL, THE AMERICAN NAVY DURING THE REVOLUTION. Charles Scribner's Sons, New York 1976. R.R.
Franklin, John Hope, FROM SLAVERY TO FREEDOM, A HISTORY OF NEGRO AMERICANS. 5th edition, Alfred Knopf, New York 1980.
Fridell, Guy, MIRACLE AT YORKTOWN. Colonial National Bicentenniel Commission, Yorktown.
———, WE BEGAN AT YORKTOWN. Dietz Press, Richmond, R.R.
———, THE VIRGINIA WAY. Burda GmBh, West Germany.
Genovese, Eugene, Roll Jordan Roll, Oxford University Press, New York. R.R.
Gwathmey, John R. HISTORICAL REGISTER OF VIRGINIANS IN THE REVOLUTION 1775–1783. Genealogical Publishing Co., Baltimore, R.R.
Haws, Charles, SCOTS IN THE OLD DOMINION, J. Dunlop, Edinburgh, Scotland, R.R.
Henley, Barbara and Flanagan, Susan Brown, CHARITY- ITS PAST AND ITS PEOPLE. Teagle & Little, Norfolk 1974. R.R.
Hume, Ivor Noel, MARTIN'S HUNDRED. Alfred A. Knopf, New York 1983.
James, Edward W. ed. THE LOWER NORFOLK COUNTY ANTIQUARY, 2 vol. Peter Smith New York, R.R.
Jester, Annie Lash, DOMESTIC LIFE IN VIRGINIA IN THE SEVENTEENTH CENTURY. University Press, Charlottesville. R.R.
Jordan, James and Frederick, VIRGINIA BEACH. Jordan Associates, Virginia Beach, 1974. R.R.
Kellam, Sadie Scott & V. Hope, OLD HOUSES IN PRINCESS ANNE, VIRGINIA. Printcraft Press, Portsmouth, Va. R.R.
Kyle, Louisa Venable, EASTERN SHORE CHAPEL AND THE LYNNHAVEN PARISH. Teagle & Little, Norfolk 19669. R.R.

―――, THE WITCH OF PUNGO, Four O'clock Press, R.R. Virginia Beach, 1973.
Malone, Dumas, JEFFERSON, THE VIRGINIAN, LITTLE BROWN & CO. BOSTON 1951
―――, JEFFERSON, AND THE RIGHTS OF MAN BROWN & CO. BOSTON
―――, JEFFERSON AND THE ORDEAL OF LIBERTY BROWN & CO.
―――, JEFFERSON, THE PRESIDENT, FIRST TERM BROWN & CO.
―――, JEFFERSON THE PRESIDENT, SECOND TERM BROWN & CO.
―――, JEFFERSON AND HIS TIME, THE SAGE OF MONTICELLO BOSTON
Mapp, Alf J. Jr. THE VIRGINIA EXPERIMENT. Open Court, La Salle, Ill. 1957. R.R.
Mason, Frances Norton, ed. JOHN NORTON AND SON, MERCHANTS OF LONDON AND VIRGINIA. Dietz Press, Richmond, 1967.
Mason, George Carrington, COLONIAL CHURCHES OF TIDEWATER, VIRGINIA. Willet & Shepperson, R.R.
―――, ed COLONIAL VESTRY BOOK OF LYNNHAVEN PARISH, PRINCESS ANNE COUNTY 1725–1786. P.O. 720, Newport News, Va. R.R.
Mays, David, EDMUND PENDLETON, A BIOGRAPHY. Harvard University Press, Cambridge, Mass. 1952. S.R.
McCary, Ben C. INDIANS IN SEVENTEENTH CENTURY, VIRGINIA. Jamestown Booklet #3. Virginia 350th Anniversary Celebration Corp. Williamsburg, Va. 7th printing. University Press, Charlottesville 1979
McColley, Robert, SLAVERY IN JEFFERSONIAN VIRGINIA. University of Illinois Press, Urbanna, Ill.
McIntosh, Charles Fleming, BRIEF ABSTRACTS OF LOWER NORFOLK COUNTY AND NORFOLK COUNTY WILLS, 1637–1710. Reprint 1982 by Southern Historical Press, Easley, S.C.
―――, BRIEF ABSTRACTS OF NORFOLK COUNTY WILLS 1710–1753. Reprint by Southern Historical Press, Easley, S.C.
Mencken, H. L., THE AMERICAN LANGUAGE. 2 vol. Alfred A. Knopf, New York 1919.

Miller, Katherine Byrd. A GLANCE AT THE PAST, A POTPOURRI OF COLONIAL VIRGINIA RECORDS. National Society of Colonial Dames of America in The Commonwealth of Virginia 1978. Richmond.

———, THE SIMPLE'S TRUTH. Kan Press of Miller Enterprises, 1978. Virginia Beach, Va.

Morgan, Edmund S. AMERICAN SLAVERY AMERICAN FREEDOM. W. W. Norton, Inc. New York, 1975.

Mullin, Gerald W. FLIGHT AND REBELLION, SLAVE RESISTANCE IN EIGHTEENTH CENTURY VIRGINIA. Oxford University Press, New York, 1972.

NOTABLE AMERICAN WOMEN, ed. Edward T. James. Belknap Press of Harvard University Press, Cambridge, Mass. 1971. R.R.

Quarles, Benjamin, THE NEGRO IN THE AMERICAN REVOLUTION. Univ. of North Carolina Press, Chapel Hill, 1973.

Rouse, Parke, PLANTERS AND PIONEERS, Hastings House, New York, 1968. R.R.

———, ROLL, CHESAPEAKE, ROLL, Norfolk County Historical Society of Chesapeake, c/o Chesapeake Library, Great Bridge, Va. R.R.

———, BELOW THE JAMES LIES DIXIE. Dietz Press, Richmond, R.R.

Sanchez, Saavedre, E.N. DESCRIPTIONS OF THE COUNTRY, VIRGINIA'S CARTOGRAPHERS AND THEIR MAPS 1697–1881. Virginia State Library Richmond.

Sellers, John B. THE VIRGINIA CONTINENTAL LINE. Virginia Independence Bicentenniel Commission, Box jf, Williamsburg, 1978

Sheehan, Bernard, SAVAGES AND CIVILITY, INDIANS AND ENGLISHMEN IN COLONIAL VIRGINIA, Cambridge University Press, New York.

Simmons, R.C. THE AMERICAN COLONIES FROM SETTLEMENT TO INDEPENDENCE. W. W. Norton, Inc. New York

Smith, James Morton, ed. SEVENTEENTH CENTURY AMERICA, ESSAYS IN COLONIAL HISTORY. W. W. Norton, Inc. New York 1959

Smith, Page, A NEW AGE NOW BEGINS. 2 vol. McGraw-Hill, New York 1976

———, THE SHAPING OF AMERICA. 1 vol. McGraw-Hill, New York 1980

Appendix II

———, THE NATION COMES OF AGE. 1 vol. McGraw-Hill, New York 1981

Spruill, Julia Cherry, WOMEN'S LIFE AND WORK IN THE SOUTHERN COLONIES. W.W. Norton Co. New York

Standard, Mary Newton, COLONIAL VIRGINIA, ITS PEOPLE AND CUSTOMS, Singing Tree Press, Detroit. R.R.

Stewart, Robert Armistead, THE RESEARCHER, A MAGAZINE OF HISTORY AND GENEAOLOGICAL EXCHANGE. Vol. ed. 109 E. Cary St., Richmond, S.R.

Tate- Thad W. and Ammerman, David L. THE CHESAPEAKE IN THE SEVENTEENTH CENTURY, ESSAYS ON ANGLO-AMERICAN SOCIETY AND POLITICS. W.W. Norton, Inc. New York. R.R.

Virginia Writers Project, THE NEGRO IN VIRGINIA. New York 1940 R.R.

Walker, Lester, AMERICAN SHELTER, Oceanfront Library, Virginia Beach The Overlook Press, Woodstock, N.Y.

Walter, Alice Granberry, GENEALOGICAL ABSTRACTS OF PRINCESS ANNE COUNTY. Ed. and published by the author. R.R.

———, VIRGINIA COURT RECORDS FROM DEED BOOKS 6 AND 7, AND MINUTE BOOKS 6 AND 7, 1710–1762. R.R.

Wertenberger, Thomas J. and Schlegel, Marvin, NORFOLK, HISTORIC SOUTHERN PORT. Duke University Press, Durham, N.C. S.R. & R.R.

Whichard, Rogers Dey, HISTORY OF LOWER TIDEWATER, VIRGINIA. Lewis Historical Publishers, New York R.R.

Wingo, Elizabeth B. ed. and published by the author. S.R. & R.R.

———, MARRIAGE BONDS OF PRINCESS ANNE COUNTY 1749–1829. S.R. & R.R.

REFERENCE

Morris, Richard B. ENCYCLOPEDIA OF AMERICAN HISTORY. Harper & Brothers, New York

ENCYCLOPEDIA BRITANNICA, Funk & Wagnalls, New York
  Where the location is unlisted, these books were borrowed, purchased, or secured from other libraries on loan through the Reference Room of the Virginia Beach Public Libraries.

HISTORICAL RESEARCHERS

Floyd Painter, Okey Townsend, Alice McCaw, Esther Piskorski, Curtis Fruit, and Jose Escajeda.

INDEX

ACKISS
  John, Sr. 166,173,240
  John, Jr., 178
ADAMS
  John, 248,251,256
  John Quincy, 266
  Samuel, 164,165
AITCHIESON
  William, 166,174,186,197,199
ALFORD
  William, 83
ALLEN
  Thomas, 50,56
ALLERSON
  Ann, 34
ALPORTE
  Jon., 34
AMES
  William, 88
ANDERSON
  Demce, 215,234,269
  Isaac, 215,269
  Marshall, 215,269
  Nathaniel, 215,234
ANNE
  Princess of England, 122
  Queen of England, 122,123
ANTOINETTE
  Marie, 231
ARCHER
  Capt. Gabriel, 20
ARMISTEAD
  William, 224,225
ARMSTON
  E., (see E. Gardner), 123
ARNOLD
  Benedict, 44,112,182,206,219,
    220,221,224,260
ASBURY
  Francis, 148
ASHALL
  George, 61,78
ATKINS
  Rob., 88
  Wm., 34
ATMORE
  Thomas, 34

BACKUS
  Isaac, 147
BACON
  Nathaniel (Bacon's Rebellion),
    60
BAKER
  Midshipman, 108
BALFOUR
  Col., 194
BALTIMORE
  Lord, 89,90,1102
BARGRAVE
  Capt., 22
BARNES
  Anthony, 79
  Celia, 211
  Elizabeth, 79,80
  Isaac, 211

BARRETT
  Amy, 211
  Jonathan, 211
BARRON
  Brothers, 177,205
  James, Capt., 187,205,206,211,255
    (Commodore)
  James, Jr., 206,255,256 (Commodore)
  Richard, 205,215
  Robert, 205
  Samuel, 205
BASNETT
  William, 65,97
BATTESON
  Nathaniel, 49
BATTS
  Nathaniel, 45,64
BELL
  Alexander, 78
BELLY
  James, 34
BEMROSE
  Tho., 88
BENJAMIN
  John, 233
  Sarah Osborn, 232,233
BENNETT
  Ann, 47
  Mr. Bennett, 90
BERKELEY
  Gov. Wm. (Baron de Botetourt),
    43,52,59,163
BERNARD
  Jon., 34
  Stephen, 34
BENARDS
  Jon., 34
BILBIE
  Margaret, 34
BLACKBEARD
  (Edward Teach), 106,107,108
BLAIR
  James, 113,247
BLACOCK
  Patrick, 34
BLAND
  Peregrine, 55
  Richard, 168
BOSTON
  215
BOUDEN
  Mordecay, 65
BOULTON
  Ann, 34
  Thomas, 34
BOURY
  Elinor, 215
BOUSH
  Charles Sayer, 95,96,213
  Eliza, 76(see Eliza J.S. Walke)
  Frederick, 76,142,173
  Goodrich, 213
  Mary, 76,77
  Maximillian, 103,189
  Robert Goodrich, 213
  Samuel (Col.), 95,142

291

BOUSH, cont'd.
  William, 76,77,213
  William F.W., 77
  Wilson, 213
BOYER
  Andrew, 34
  Thomas, 34
BOYER
  Andrew, 34
  Thomas, 34
BRAITHWAITE
  James, 175
BRAMLEY
  Francis, 34
BRANKER
  Nathaniel, 131
BRAY
  Plumer, 66
  Robert, 50
BREWTON
  Jon., 34
BRIDGER
  Joseph, Esq. (Col.), 84
BRIGHT
  Francis, 114
BROAD BAY MANOR, 50,138,167
BROADWAY
  Tho., 88
BROCK
  210,214
  Allan, 214
  Edwin, 112
  Elias, 214
  Henry, 214
  Jesse, 214
  John, 219
  Matthias, 214
  Mayer, 214
  Nathaniel, 214
  Thomas, 173,214
  Uriah, 214
BROOKE
  William, 65
BROOKS
  Thomas, 34
BROWN
  Gen. Jacob, 265
  Thomas, 141
BUGBY
  Peter, 88
BULLOCK
  Thomas, 41
BURR
  Aaron, 249,257
BURROUGHS (BURROUGH, BURROWES, BURRUS)
  Ann, 34
  Ben, 146
  Benoni, 103
  Christopher, 28,41,103
  Wm., 34
BURT
  (Sergeant), 103
BURWELL
  43
BUTT
  Elizabeth, 147
  Richard, 147
  Thomas, 147

BYRD
  William II, 66,102,145,271

CABOT
  John, 18
CLAVERT
  Capt. Christopher, 206
  Cornelius, 96
  George (physician), 37
  John (Capt.), 205,208
  Margaret (Walke), 208
  Sampson, 58
CAMM
  Robert, 29,52,73
CAMPBELL
  Capt. Hugh, 111
  Mungo, 96
CANNON
  Edward, 173
  William, 173
CAPPS
  Obediah, 210,214
CARRAWAY
  House, 139,167
  Ann, 140
  John, 139,140
  Carter, 43
  Robert (King), 238
  Landon, 238
  Robert, Jr., 243
CARVER
  William, 60,85
  Cary, Mr., 90
CASADY
  William, 215
CATON
  John, 216,217
CAUSON
  Thomas, 53
  Chloe, 269
CLAIBORNE
  William, 89
CLAY
  Henry, 258
CLINTON
  Gen., 218,227,237
COCKBURN
  Admiral, 182,264,266
COCKE
  Christopher, 111
COLEMAN
  Whitehead, 214
COLLIER
  Admiral Sir George, 207,209,210, 218,219
COLLINS
  Henry, 202
CONQUEST
  Richard, 59
COLUMBUS
  Christopher, 18
CONWAY
  Capt., 215
COOPER
  Edward, 56,146
  Thomas, 78
CORBIN
  Richard, 175

CORNICK (CORNIX)
  103,210
  Eliza Walke, 266
  Henry, 214
  Joel, 67,166,240,260
  Joel Barlow, 266
  Joel, Jr., 173
  John, 214
  Lemuel, 167,214,240,266
  Mary Woodhouse, 266
  Simon, 39,57
  Thomas, 265
  Thomas Keeling, 266
  William, 57,66,67,103,146
CORNWALLIS
  Lord, 182,193,194,219,221,224,
    228,230,231
COWES
  John, 34
COWLES
  William, 215
CRAMMOND
  John, 195
CREASER
  Eliza, 34
  Thomas, 34
CRIPPS, Anthony, 88
CROMWELL
  Oliver, 43
CROUTCH
  William, 71
CUFFEY
  William, 215,234
CUFFY
  George, 269
CURTISSE
  Eliza, 34
CUSHIN
  Judge, 212

DALE
  Sir Thomas (Governor), 22,23
DANGGONE
  Thomas, 41
DANIEO
  215,269
DARE
  Virginia, 19
DARTMOUTH
  Lord, 176,177,185
DAVIES
  Rev. Samuel, 147
  William, 214
DAVIS
  Hugh, 90,91
DAWLEY
  Dennis, 173,214,210
  Dennis, Rev., 269
  Gilbert, 78
  James, 269
  William, 269
DAYNES
  William, 46,47
DECATUR
  Stephen, 255,256
DECKAN
  Mary, 89
DE GRASSE
  Admiral, 225,227,228,229,272

DELAUNEE
  Francis, 105
DE LAUZUN
  Duc., 228,220,231
DE ROCHAMBEAU
  Lt. Gen., 225,229
DENNY
  George, 214
DICKSON
  Amy, 130
  Rev. Robert, 130,246
DOLL
  Benjamin, 90
DORGON
  Jno., 80
DOUD
  William, 214
DRANKE
  Sir Francis, 18
DUDLEY
  Guilford,210
DUNMORE
  Lord, 123,154,166,168,176,177,178,
    182,183,186,187,188,189,190,191,
    192,194,197,201,217,264
  Lady Dunmore, 123,166

EASTWOOD
  199
EDEN
  Gov. Charles (North Carolina), 106
    108
EDGERTON
  Arthur, 85
EDWARFD
  William, 34
EGERTON
  Charles, 46,47
EGGLESTON
  Arthur, 34
ELIZABETH
  Queen of England, 18,127
ELLEGOOD
  Jacob, 166,174,186,191,192,195,197,
    204,208
  Mary (Pallet), 197
  Mary (Saunders), 198,199,200
  William, 103,197,200
EMERSON
  Capt., 263
EMPEROR
  Col. Francis, 139
ENIES
  John, 34
EVANS
  Cdr. & Mrs N.C., 261
EVANS,
  John, 141
EWELL
  Charles, 213,214
  Mary Bennett, 180
  Capt. Thomas, 189,202,213,214
EYRES
  Mr., 55

FAIRFIELD
  77

FALLER
  William, 185
FANKLIN
  Henry, 34
FARNEHOUGH
  John, 53
FAWNE
  Wm., 34
FELGATE
  Philip, 48
FAUNTLEROY
  Capt. Moore, 88
FENTRESS
  Aaron, 129
  Anthony, 162
  Emanuel, 269
  Hezekiah, 129
  J.A., 242,243
  Jonathan, 242
  Nathan, 204
  Nehemiah, 214
  William, 214
FEREBEE
  Dr. Enoch Dozier, 138
  George Emory, 138
  Mrs., 138
FERNANDO
  94
FERRY FARM, 242
FIFE
  Andrew, 260
FLETCHER
  Wm., 34
FLORA
  William, 180,215,263
FORDYCE
  Capt., 180
FORREST
  John, 242
FOSTER
  Anne, 72
  Richard, 72
FOWLER
  Ann, 35,36
  George, 61,149
  Pembroke, 36
  Wm., 35,36
FRAFORD
  Victo, 34
FRANC
  Cornelius, 105
FRANKLIN
  Benjamin, 248,251
FRAZIER
  Peter, 111
FULCHER
  Thomas, 49,61

GABRIEL PLOT, 244,270
GAINIE
  Robt., 34
GARDNER
  E., 123 (see E. Armston)
GASKIN
  Anne, 72,73,74
  Savill (Saville Gascoyne), 72,
    73,74,75,77,109

GASTROCK
  Wm., 34
GEE
  Col., 230
GEORGE
  I, King of England, 102
  George III, King of England, 237,
    263
  William, 261,262
GESSARO
  Jno., 88
GIBBS
  Capt. John, 65
  Henry, Capt., 65
  John, Jr., 65
GIBSON
  Col.George, 211,212
GIGG
  John, 61
GILBERT
  Sir Humphrey, 18
  Thomas, 85
GISBURNE
  Jane, 79
  John, 79
GODFREY
  Capt. Matthew, 214
GOFFIGAN
  Laban, 271
GOODRICH
  John, 186
GOOKIN
  Daniel, 52,121
  John, 52,53,56,57,73
  Mary (Lawson), 52,54
  Sarah (Thorowgood), 52
GOOCH
  Gov. William, 109,147,153,155,271
  John, 72
GORDON
  Thomas, Rev., 47
GOSMORE
  Eliz., 34
GOSNOLD
  Capt. Bartholemew, 19
GOULSTON
  W. William, 65
GRAVES
  Admiral, 237
GREEN
  Gen. Nathaniel, 224
  Thomas, 61
GREEN HILL FARM, 242
GREGG
  James, 232
GRENVILLE
  Sir Richard, 18
GRIFFIN
  Judge, 212
GUITAR
  Louis, 104
GUNTER
  John, 213
GYE
  Gilbert, 34,35,36

HALSTEAD
  Matthew, 207
HARRIS
  Alexander, 38
  James, 61
  John, 34
  Capt. John, 205,206,209
HARRISON
  Benjamin, 168
  Thomas, 58
  Gen. William Henry, 259
HARTWELL
  Henry, 113
HARVIE, Sir John, 53
HAWKINS, Edy, 46
  Sir John, 87
  Katherine, 94
HAYES. Robert, 28,38,41
HAYNES
  Aaron, 269
  Erasmus, 173
  Henry, 202
  William, 202
HEARD
  Mary, 89
HEASELL
  Robert, 34
HEATH
  James, 65
HEIGHAM
  George, 44
HELLARD
  Geor.,89
CHARLES HENLEY HOUSE, 167
HENLEY
  210
  Charles, 167,184,185,204
  Charles, 214
  Frances (Williamson), 209
  James, 173,214
  John, 141
  Robert, 214
HENRY
  Patrick, 149,164,168,169,239,248
HERBERT
  Elizabeth, 182
  Henry, 34
HEYWARD
  Humphrey, 34
HILL
  Charles, 142
  Henry, 34
  John, 78
  Jon., 34
  Luke, 79,80
  Mary, 34
  Mary, Jr., 34
  Mistress, 79
HINES
  William, 34
HOBSON
  Eliz., 88
HODGE
  Robert, 74,75
  William, 74
HOGGARD
  David, 214
  Thurmer, 167

HOLLODAY
  Gilbert, 129
HOLMES
  Edward,78
HOLT
  John, 34,177
HOLTON
  Wm., 34
HOOKES
  Wm., 34
HOPKINS
  186
HORNIGOLD
  Benjamin, 106
HOSKINS
  Bartholomew, 41
HOSKINSON
  Jasper, 71
HOTTEN
  John, 78
HOUGHLIN
  John, 105
HOWE
  Col., 182,184
HOWELL
  Cob, 34,36
HUDSON
  Hendrick, 60
HUNT
  Gilbert, 270
  Rev. Robert, 21,22
HUNTER
  Jacob, 152,202,214
HURST
  Jonathan, 83
HUTCHINS,
  Col. Joseph, 178,209
HUTCHINSON
  Gov. (Mass.), 165
HUTON
  Daniel, 34

IVY
  Thomas (Ivey), 54,55,146

JACKSON
  Gen. Andrew, 266
  James, 215,234
  Thomas, 65
JAMES
  (see Lafayette, Armistead), 224,225
  James (King of England), 20,127
JAMIESON
  George, 173,202
  Neil, 186
JAY
  John, 158
JEFFERSON
  Thomas, 131,219,226,230,240,241,
    242,245,246,247-248,249,255,256,
    258
JENERIE
  Richardf, 34
JENKINS
  Johnson, 96
JOHNSON
  Anthony, 88,89,90

JOHNSON, cont'd.
  Antonia, 89
  John, 88,89
  Mary, 144,269
  Richard, 34,88,89
  William, 139,147
JONES
  Edward, 34
  Evan, 103
  John Paul, 209
  Richard, 61
  Robert, 214
JORDAN
  Capt., 90
JOUETT
  Capt. Jack, 225
JULIAN
  Sarah, 47
  William, 27,29,30,32,47

KEELING
  103
  ADAM KEELING HOUSE, 50
  Adam, 38,49,50
  Anne (Bray), 50
  Thomas, 28,29,34,41,48,49,50,82
    132
  William, 202
  William, Jr., 173,214
KELLY
  John, 61
  Samuel, 215
KEMP (or KEMPE), 109,202
  George, 67,68
  James, 142,173
  John, 131
KENDALL
  Capt. George, 20
KEY
  Elizabeth, 94
  Francis Scott, 265
KIDD
  Capt., 105
KISONTANEOCH
  King of Yansakin, 64
KNIGHT
  Tobias, 108

LaFAYETTE
  James (see Armistead, James),224
  Marquis de, 221,224,228,229
LAMB
  James, 216,217
LAMBERT
  Thomas, 46,49
LANCKFIELD
  John, 41
LAND
  133
  Francis Land House, 132,138,166
  Edward, 214
  Francis I, 36,58,132
  Francis II, 57
  Francis III, 132
  Francis V, 133
  John, 214
  Louis, 214

LAND, cont'd
  Moses, 214
  Thomas, 214
  William, 214
LANE
  Rachel, 34
  Ralph, 11,16
LAPHAM (LAPAN),
  James, 53
LARRINGTON
  Margaret, 47
LAWRENCE
  John, 114
LAWSON
  43,103,109,111
  Anthony I, 134,146,173
  Col. Anthony, 178,208,209,240,242
  two sons in Revolution, 210
  Thomas, 57,111,122,134
LAYTON
  Goody, 52
LEACH
  Thomas, 85
LEADING
  James, 33
LEAKE
  Jos., 34
LEE
  Major Gen. Charles, 186
  Richard, 53
  Richard Henry, 168,238,247
LELAND
  John, 147
  General, 192,193
LEWIS
  Gen. Andrew, 187
  George, 269
LINCOLN
  Gen. Benjamin, 206,218,231
LINEY
  Anthony, 78
LITTY
  269
LLOYD
  Cornelius, 46,47
  Elizabeth, 47
LOCK
  John, 34
LOGAN
  George, 68,166,178,200,240,242
LONG
  Ann, 34
LOVETT
  46
  Lancaster, 242
LYNNHAVEN
  House (see Gaskin, Thelball), 75

MACDONOUGH
  Capt., 265
MACKIE
  Rev. Josiah, 59,146,147
MADISON
  President James, 245,247,248,249,
    258,264
  Mrs., 264
MALBONE
  Reodolphus, 128

MANSFIELD
  Lord, 154
MARIE ANTOINETTE, 231
MARION
  Francis, 194
MARKHAM
  Capt., 183
MARSH
  Thomas, 72
MARSHALL
  Thomas, 180
MARTIN
  50
  Anne, 50
  Capt. John, 19,20,49
MASON
  103
  Anne, 71
  Col. Armistead Thomson, 256
  Francis, 27,28,29,32,48,57
  George, 247,248
  Jarvis, 28
  Lemuel, 29,32,49,50,57,60,64,71
MATTHEWS
  Capt. Thomas, 90,178,211,214
  Samuel, 90
  Saul, 234
MAURY
  Rev. James, 149
MAXWELL
  Capt. James, 206
MAYNARD
  Lt. Robert, 108
McCARTY
  John Mason, 256
McCAW
  Dr. James Drew, 270
MEE
  34
MELTON
  Thomas, 34
MICHAEL
  Capt. John, 54
MICHELL
  Roger, 34
MILLER
  Mary Hodge, 75
MIRES
  Thomas, 72
MOISE
  Jon., 34
MONROE
  President James, 253,256,257
MOORE
  Cason, 173
  Edmund, 65
  James, 202
  Thomas, 14
MORRIS
  Robert, 248
MORRISON
  Lt. Gov. Francis, 47
MORSE
  Francis, 103
MOSELEY
  109,123
  Betty (Thorowgood), 207
  Col. Edwrd, 111
  Edward Sr., 44,111,144,146,175

MOSELEY, cont'd.
  Edward Hack, Sr., 44,166,175
  Edward Hack, Jr., 123,166,175
  Mrs., 56
  Susannah (Susan), 44,56
  William, 39,43,44,45,49,131,134,
    139,210
  Major William, 206,207,210
  William, Jr., 43,44,109
MOSIER
  Thomas, 78
MURDAUGH
  John, 137,208
MURDEN
  210
  Edward, 214
  John, 214
  Peter, 214
MURDIN
  James, 215,234
MURRAY
  127
  Abraham, 214
  Alexander, 214
  David, 115,116.214
  David Muray House, 116
  Isaac, 115,116
  Isaac, Jr., 115
  Richard, 166
  Thomas, 116, 242
  Thomas Murray House, 116
NAPOLEAN (Bonaparte), 251,256,258
NASH
  Capt. Thomas, 180,182,210
NELSON
  Lord, 259
  Thomas, Jr., 221,225,229
  William, Esq., 141
NEWARKE
  Jon., 34
NEWGENT
  Christ., 34
  Elizabeth (Walke), 136
  Lemuel, 142
  Nathaniel, 33,257
  Thomas, 210
NATHANIEL NICHOLUS HOUSE, 167
NICHOLSON
  Lt. Gov. Francis, 109,111,146,155,
    270
NIMMO
  James, Sr., 103
  William, 111,172
  William, Jr., 111,210,214
NINNY
  234
NORRIS
  James, 137
NORTH
  Lord, 237
NORTON
  John, Jr., 176

OFFLEY (see Thorowgood), 33
O'HARA
  Gen. Charles, 220,231
OLD COMFORT, 46

OLIVER
  family, 74
OPENCHANDCANOUGH
  Chief, 127
OSBORN
  Sarah (see Benjamin), 232,233
  Aaron, 232
OVERSEE
  Simon, 54
OWEN
  James, 269

PAINTER
  Floyd, 4,12,16,35,82
PALLET
  Mary (Ellegood), 197
  Matthew, 166
PALMER
  Edward, 34
PARISH
  Edward, 34
PARKER
  George, 89,90
  James, 174
  Margaret (Ellegood), 197,199
  Patrick, 199
  Robert, Robert, 90
PARSONS
  Capt. William, 111
PEMBROKE MANOR, 139,189
PENDLETON
  Edmund, 168,173
PENTON
  Jon., 34
PENURE
  John, 78
PEPIN
  Matthew, 89
PERCY
  George, 3,10,11,21
PERKINS
  Nimrod, 215,234
PERRY
  Capt. Oliver Haxard, 259
PERSIE
  John, 34
PHILLIPS
  Anne, 58
  Josiah, 210,219
  Lawrence, 58
PHRIPP
  John, 136
  Mary Anne (see Walke), 136
PILMOOR
  Joseph, 148
"MOLLY PITCHER", 232
PITT
  Prime Minister William, 164
PITTS
  Edward, 34
PLEASANT HALL, 68,200,242
POCAHONTAS
  20,127,187
POLLARD
  Benjamin, 206
  Garland, 206
POOLE
  Richard, 34

PORTER
  145
  Rev. John, 59
  John, Sr., 67
  John, Jr., 139
  Peter, 78
PORY
  John, 124
POWHATAN
  Chief, 14,16,187
POWIS
  Robert, 49
PRESTON
  Capt., 165
PRINCE
  Anthony, 89
PROSSER
  Jane, 34
PURIFOY
  Lt., 71

RAINSHAW
  William, 72
RALEIGH
  Sir Walter, 18
RAMSAY
  Anne Phripp, 137
RANDOLPH
  Edmund, 175,248
  John, Sr., 175
  John, Jr., 175
  Peyton, 168,175
RANGER
  Joseph, 215
RATCLIFFE
  Capt. John, 20
REYNOLDS
  Edward, 34
  Jon., 34
RICHMOND
  Robert, 142
RICHARDSON
  John, 103
ROBERTS
  John (physician), 212
RICHARDSON
  John, 103
ROBERTSON
  William, 241
ROBINSON
  Mrs., 231
  Capt. Wm.,47,144,166,173,209
ROCKINGHAM
  Lord, 237
ROGERS
  Woodes, 106
ROLFE
  John, 20,24
ROSS
  Gen. Robert, 264,265
RUSH
  Benjamin,248
RUSSELL
  Dennis, 34
  Richard, 130,131

SALISBURY
  Plains, 167
SANDFORD
  John, 103
SAUNDERS
  John, 189,190,191,192,193,194,195,
    196,197,200,203,204
  Jonathan I, 189
  Jonathan II, 189
  Mary (Ellegood), 189
SAYER
  Charles, 202
  Francis, 49
  Thomas, 213
SCHUTZ
  Col., 193
SCOTT
  Gen. Winfield, 265
SEAWELL
  Henry, 29,30,32,38,51,52,128
SEDGEWICK
  Joseph, 34
SELBY
  Richard, 65
SELBYE
  Edward, 114
SHEPHERD
  William, 269
SHERLEY
  John, 71
  Thmas, 71
SHERWOOD
  Grace, 78,79,80,81,82,109
  James, 79,81,82
  John, 81,82
  Richard, 81,82
SHIPP
  Wm., 41,132
SIBSEY
  John, 29,30,52,70
SIDNEY
  Col. John, 45,56,139
SIMCOE
  Col., John Graves, 192,193,194,
    196,221
SIMONDS
  James, 71
SIMPSON
  Rev. James, 246
SINGLETON
  Peter, 68,173,174,209,242
SITTERING
  Fra., 89
SKIPPER
  Francis, 75
SMITH
  Charles, 257
  Rev. Charles, 157
  Dr., 220
  George, 76
  John, 84,207,214
  Capt. John, 6,10,16,19,20,22,127,
    237
  Joseph, 76
  Gen. Samuel, 265
  Thomas, 34
SMYTHE
  Charles, 111

SNAILE
  Henry, 78
SOMERSET
  Case, 154
  James, 154
SOUTHELL
  Henry, 65
SPADDEN
  Robert, 186
SPARK
  Ann, 34
SPEED
  William, 34
SPOTSWOOD
  Gov. Alexander, 81,106,108,140,
    160,163,271
  Major Alexander, 183
SPRATT
  Henry, 103
SPRING
  Robert, 34
SPROWLE
  Andrew, 177,186
SQUIRES
  Capt. Matthew, 176,177,178,184
STANFIELD
  Symond, 34
STANLY
  Mayor, 71
STATON
  Mr., 122
STEPHENS
  William, 38
STEWART
  Charles (Steuart), 154,199
STEVENSON
  Andrew, 185
STRATTON
  John, 41,50
STUDDS
  Mr. Colin, 133
SWEDENBORG
  Emanuel, 243

TANNER
  Charity, 71
  Daniel, 28,34,71,78
  John, 71
  William, 35
TARLETON
  Col. Banastre, 224,225,228,231
TAYLOE
  William, 145
TAYLOR
  Andrew, 114
  Jonathan, 56
  Gen. Robert Barraud, 260,263
TEACH
  Edward (see Blackbeard), 106
TENANT
  Capt. James, 205,213
THELABALL
  The La Ball), 75
  Francis, 75
  James, 61
THOMAS
  Capt., 215

THOMASON
  Henry, 28
THOROWGOOD
  103,133,144,241,242 (Thoroughgood)
  AdamThoroughgood House, 48,50
  Adam I, Capt. 27,29,33,34,35,36,
    37,39,41,48,49,51,53,54,57,102,
    109,260
  Adam I, house site, 35,48
  Adam II, 38,48,49,57,134
  Adam III, 57, (Major)
ANNE
  Chandler, 38,54
ARGALL
  36,57,103,104,109,270
  Elizabeth (Michael), 54
  Francis, 57
  John, 57,103,111,210,214,239
  Sir John, 38
  Lemuel, 214
  Major, 200
  Mitchell, 214
  Robert, 57
  Rose, 57
  Samuel, 221
  Sarah (Offley, Thorowgood, Gookin,
    Yeardley), 33,35,38,48,51,52,
    53,54,55,56,57,73,260
  Sarah, Jr. (Oversee), 38,53,54
  Thomas, 33
  William, 202
  William, Jr., 202
THRUSTON
  Malachi (Thurston), 47,103
  Mrs. Martha, 147
TILGHMAN
  Tench, 231
TODD
  Thomas, 41,44
TOOLEY
  James, 173
TRAVIS
  Lt., 180
  Capt. Edward, 211
TRIPP, John, 211
  Mary, 211
TROTT
  Nicholas, 56
TUCKER
  John, 114
  Mr. & Mrs. John, 116
  Mary, 114
  St. George (Judge), 144
  Thomas, 46

UNERWOOD
  Casander, 34
UPPER WOLFSNARE, 133,138

VALENTINE
  George, 78,269
  Capt. Jacob, 205,211,212
VIDAL
  John, 109
VINCENT
  Francis, 89
  Mary, 89
  Wm., 88

WADDILOW
  Nicholas, 88,89
WAKEFIELD
  Jon., 34
WALKE
  46,103,109,130,134,137,144,
  Anthony I, 96,130,134,144,152,153,
    175
  Anthony, Jr., 173,215,253
  Rev. Anthony, 77,96,135,136,144,
    200
  Rev. David, 77
  Eliza J.S. (Boush), 77
  Elizabeth (Williamson), 207,208
  Katherine, 135
  Mary Anne (Thorowgood), 136
  Margaret (Calvert), 208
  Thomas I, 57,88,133,134
  Thomas II, 111,133,135
  Thomas III, 129,133,135,138,144,
    166,205 (Built Upper Wolfsnare,
    1959)
  Thomas IV, 136,137,138,208,209,242
  William, 242
WALKER
  Thomas Reynolds, 202,210
WALLIS
  Edmund, 34
WARD
  Capt., 22
  Robert, 262
  Roger, 34
WARNER
  43
  Augustine, 34
WARREN
  Admiral, 263
WARWICK
  Earl of, 23
WAS
  William, 34
WASHINGTON
  George, 164,168,176,191,205,218,
    220,221,222,224,225,227,228,229,
    230,231,232,240,241,247,248,249,
    251,254,255,266
WATERMAN
  Solomon, 214
WATERS
  Col. Edward, 33
  Jon., 34
WATKINS
  John, 47
WATSON
  Sarah, 47
  Thomas, 47
WEAVER
  Aaron, 215,234
WEEKS
  Col. Amos, 210,219
WESLEY
  John, 147,148
WEST
  Gov. Francis, 33
  Richard, 28
WESTCOTT
  Capt. Wright, 137,205,208,209
WESTERFIELD
  Jane, 34

WESTWELL
  Robert, 34
WHEELER
  Dorothy, 34
WHITE
  John, 10,18,65
  Patrick, 66
WHITEHALL
  John, 114
WHITEHEAD
  George, 34
  John, 47
  Mary, 147
  Samuel, 214
WHITEHURST
  46,109,210
  Charles, 129
  Christopher, 202
  Jesse, 215
  John, 68,214
  Jonathan, 214
  Richard, 68
  Samuel, 214
  William, 68
WHITFIELD
  George, 147
WHITNEY
  Eli, 244
WHITTHORNE
  Ann, 34
WIGHT
  Geofry, 54
WILES
  Reuben, 214
WILKINSON
  Col. Nathaniel, 212
  Rev. William, 29
WILL
  215
WILLIAM III
  King of England, 22
WILLIAM
  96,97
WILLIAMS
  John, 89
  Roger, 147
  Moses, 214
WILLIAMSON
  Charles, 136,205,207,208,209
  Elizabeth (Walke), 207,208
  Frances (Henley), 209
  Mary, 96,97
WILLOUGHBY
  103,175
  John, 174,175
  Capt. John, 175
  Thomas, 27,32,38,39,48,50,51,58
WILSON
  James, 34
  John, 43
  William, 214
  Willis, 220
WINDHAM
  Edward, 29,34,38,41,52,55,73
WINGFIELD
  Capt. Edward Maria, 19,20
WISHART
  House (now called The Lynnhaven
  House), 74

WISHART
  Elizabeth, 147
  John, 147
  Peggy (Singleton), 206
  Lt. Thomas, 142,206
  William, 206,240
WITHERS
  Jo, 34
  Stephen, 34
WOLFSNARE PLANTATION, 166
WOODFORD
  Col. William, 180,182,184,197,
    207,209,216
WOOD
  Henry, 34
WOOLAN
  John, 158
WOODHOUSE
  103,167,210
  Arthur Sayer, 266
  Henry, 41,45,46,52,53
  Mr. Woodhouse, 73,103,146,214
  Horatio, 142,147
  John, 137,214
  Mary (Batts), 45
  Pembroke, 46
  Dr. Robert, 45
  Capt. William, 46,142,173,214
  William Woodhouse House, 45
  William D., 137
WRITT
  John, 34
WYATT
  Gov., 32
WYTHE
  George, 163,247

YEARDLEY
  Francis, 44,55,56,57,73
  Gov. Sir George, 23,144
YE DUDLIES
  (see Adam Keeling), 50

www.ingramcontent.com/pod-product-compliance
Lightning Source LLC
Chambersburg PA
CBHW020056020526
44112CB00031B/194